AGENTS & ASSETS

Witnessing the War on Drugs and on Communities

AGENTS & ASSETS

Witnessing the War on Drugs and on Communities

Los Angeles Poverty Department

QUEENS MUSEUM

AUTONOMEDIA

ISBN: 978-1-57027-291-2

This book is published on the occasion of "Do You Want the Cosmetic Version or Do You Want the Real Deal?" Los Angeles Poverty Department, 1986–2014 at the Queens Museum, New York, January 31–May 11, 2014. The exhibition was organized by Larissa Harris, curator, Queens Museum, with Adrianne Koteen, assistant curator.
"Agents and Assets" ("Agentes y Activos") was performed by LAPD and Drogadictos Anonimos in Spanish at the Queens Museum and elsewhere in New York on February 28th and March 1st and 2nd, 2014.

Performances of "Agents & Assets" (2001–ongoing) have been supported by The Nathan Cummings Foundation; the Animating Democracy Project of Americans for the Arts; the National Performance Network; and the Halo Group. The City of Los Angeles Department of Cultural Affairs and the National Endowment for the Arts have provided additional funding. Additional support has come from "Agents & Assets" presentation venues and the drug recovery programs with which LAPD has partnered in different cities.

The exhibition and publication are supported by grants from The Andy Warhol Foundation for the Visual Arts and National Endowment for the Arts. Project funding also provided by Surdna Foundation and Institute of Museum and Library Services. Additional support comes from the New York City Department of Cultural Affairs and New York State Council on the Arts with the support of Governor Andrew Cuomo and the New York State Legislature.

Los Angeles Poverty Department (LAPD)
PO Box 26190, Los Angeles, CA 90026
T: 213 4131077 www.lapovertydept.org

Queens Museum
New York City Building
Flushing Meadows, Corona Park, Queens, NY 11368
T: 718 592 9700 www.queensmuseum.org

This book was designed by and copublished with
Autonomedia
PO Box 568 Williamsburgh Station
Brooklyn, NY 11211-0568 www.autonomedia.org

Printed in the United States of America

Table of Contents

Introduction

Los Angeles Poverty Department (LAPD) is a performance group made up of people who live and work in Los Angeles' downtown Skid Row area. The 50-square-block Skid Row area has the largest concentration of homeless and very poor people in the nation. LAPD is among the groups and organizations and individuals who have worked to create community on Skid Row.

LAPD's mission is to create performance work that connects lived experience to the social forces that shape the lives and communities of people living in poverty. To accomplish our goals we have developed collaborations with arts organizations and with grassroots activist organizations. LAPD has worked to link communities by drawing attention to structural issues that affect people living in poverty.

LAPD has been a presence on LA's Skid Row since 1985, making performances in free workshops open to anyone in Skid Row and presenting them in Skid Row and beyond. Because we are a theater group, we travel light. Our main product is ephemeral. We work, conceptualize and strategize to confound categorization. If we do it right, our main product is confusion. Confusion begets insight. Insight plus strategy begets change.

From Skid Row LA, the war on drugs amounts to a cynical and callous endeavor. Drugs fill the community. Homeless users are routinely busted and convicted as dealers. There are not nearly enough treatment facilities, with resources and strategies to deal with the problem. This week I received a call from a probation officer about someone who had been participating in workshops for LAPD's most recent project, until he disappeared several weeks ago, a week before the production. She, the probation officer, asked if I knew him. I said yes, of course, and recounted his involvement in LAPD, and his absence. She ended the conversation saying, "I guess he's just down there doing what he's doing, and I'll go look for him and pick him up." He was in violation of his probation and when she picked him up, she'd be sending him before the judge, and he'd be headed back to jail. Here's all of what I've heard. He was in a rehab program in our Skid Row neighborhood. He came in late; they gave him a drug test. He tested positive for marijuana. They threw him out. He quit coming to rehearsals. He was homeless living on the street. He got back into his crack addiction. That saga unfolded in a week.

The lack of resources to deal with the problems of drug users, other than in the criminal justice system, exists throughout the country, and particularly impacts poor people and people of color. In eastern Kentucky, teens who fail a random drug test at the local high school are given the option of going into treatment rather than being kicked out of school. But there are no local residential programs for teens, and the programs that exist for adults in the area cost $5,000 a month. This is well beyond the reach of most families in the area.

In "Agents & Assets," we have chosen a highly controversial incident, a particular series of newspaper articles written by journalist Gary Webb alleging drug dealing into Los Angeles by Contra-connected Nicaraguans, done with the knowledge and silence of their CIA supporters. At the time, this set off a furor in communities in South Los Angeles and among the mainstream press, with the papers of record all denouncing the articles. At this point, allegations of CIA complicity in the drug trade are indisputably true, though it's still not of general knowledge. In fact the Gary Webb charges fit into a pattern of CIA activity that goes back nearly to the founding of the Agency after World War II.

From an LAPD point of view, the governmental choice embodied in that policy, besides being literally true, is also a metaphor for the numerous governmental choices where the well-being of citizens—average citizens, poor citizens, citizens of color, both here and abroad—are sacrificed to dubious foreign-policy objectives that have more to do with economic and political aggrandizement and over-reaction to largely imagined threats than they do with legitimate national interests, let alone national security.

In "Agents & Assets" we've been able to bring together, often for the first time, people who have been grappling for a long time with the reality of the failed war on drugs: academics, journalists, recovery specialists, probation officers, ministers and policy reformers. Most importantly we've been able to bring these people into dialogue in communities and with people who have had intimate lived insight into the ravages of drugs and the cruelty of the war on drugs.

"Agents & Assets" is a three-part performance event. First, LAPD performs the March 18, 1998 congressional hearing, which was the only public hearing associated with the intelligence committee's inquiry into CIA/Contra complicity in the advent of the crack epidemic in California. The performance is followed by a panel discussion on an issue arising from the hearing. The panel discussion opens into a community conversation, where the lived expertise of the audience is given center stage.

What does "Agents & Assets" mean? Any crime committed by people working for a federal agency has to be reported to the Justice Department, right? So during the run-up to the Contra era, President Reagan's attorney general sat down with the head of the CIA, also a Reagan appointee, and together they shrank the definition of CIA employee to include only people qualified for pensions. After this, CIA operatives and other people getting money didn't have to be reported. These were the people known as "assets." That's how you get around the law—in this case, a congressional mandate to not fund the Contras.

The project was conceived in 1999, rehearsed in the fall of 2000 and first presented in January 2001. From the initial presentation in 2001 through the most recent production in December 2005, documented here, we've been able to track the progress of reform efforts, and at the same time, the intertwining of the war on drugs with that of the war on terror. Throughout, the questions arising to us, the audience and citizens, in the course of "Agents & Assets," continue to produce a valuable witnessing of our government at present.

The project owes its existence to the belief and support of The Nathan Cummings Foundation; the Old Stories: New Lives, Animating Democracy Project of Americans for the Arts; the National Performance Network; and the Halo Group. The City of Los Angeles Department of Cultural Affairs and the National Endowment for the Arts have provided additional funding for project activities. Additional support has come from the venues where we've produced "Agents & Assets" events and the drug recovery programs we've partnered with in different cities. Henriëtte Brouwers, Charles Jackson, Melina Bielefelt and Ken Gruz of LAPD all put in enormous effort transcribing the texts. Enormous thanks to them and to everyone involved in this project.

JOHN MALPEDE
Los Angeles, CA, January, 2014

"Agents & Assets"

Text from the March 18, 1998 Hearing of the Congressional Select Committee on Intelligence

Script edited by "Agents & Assets" Performance Director John Malpede

The Chairman (Mr. Goss):

Good afternoon. The committee will come to order for today's hearing to review the report of the CIA Inspector General regarding allegations made in a 1996 newspaper series that the CIA was involved in the trafficking of crack cocaine to California during the 1980s.

Before we begin, I would like to advise members and the public today of how we intend to proceed. The House National Security Committee has graciously allowed us the use of this room this afternoon, and we appreciate it. We have been advised, however, that our lease on this space does expire at approximately 5 o'clock, and we are planning that our proceedings will end accordingly.

At the conclusion of my opening statement, I will recognize my colleagues on the committee for opening remarks, and then we will proceed to hear from other members of Congress. We will then proceed with the testimony of Mr. Frederick P. Hitz, the Inspector General (IG) of the CIA, beginning his presentation no later than 4 P.M. I thank all present today in assisting us in sticking to this schedule.

Today's hearing marks an important step in the ongoing process of inquiry the Intelligence Committee has undertaken to assess the validity of highly serious allegations presented in a three-part series of newspaper articles published in the *San Jose Mercury News* in 1996.

These articles detailed allegations that the CIA was involved with or was somehow complicit in the trafficking of crack cocaine to California during the 1980s. The articles further allege that the proceeds from those transactions were used to assist in financing the activities of the resistance movement in Nicaragua, known to most of us simply as the Contras.

This committee undertook an investigation onto these charges in the fall of 1996. During this time, two separate inspector general investigations have been conducted. The CIA IG's review, which is the subject of today's hearing, and the Department of Justice's review, which is yet to be released. I believe that the CIA IG has presented our committee with a solid body of work that will assist us in that regard, and we intend to consider his conclusions very carefully.

Of course, we are continuing to conduct our own independent inquiry into this matter as part of our proper oversight responsibilities. We are keenly aware that this entire episode has fueled suspicions some people have about the advent of the scourge of crack cocaine in the United States. Any suggestion of government complicity in that terrible outcome is one that must be seriously considered and answered.

It will be extremely difficult to come up with an absolute answer that will remove all doubt. Such is the nature of these cases. That said, I believe that the American people have a right to expect us to do a conscientious job in understanding the facts and in offering conclusions about the charges that have been made.

With that, let me again welcome our witness today, and my colleagues. I yield to Mr. Dicks for any opening remarks and the other members as well. We welcome Ms. Harmon and Mr. Gibbons who have come in since the gavel went down.

Mr. Dicks:

Mr. Chairman, I have seen Mr. Hitz's investigation characterized as the most extensive undertaken by an inspector general. The best defense against unjustifiable criticism of an investigation of this kind is to ensure that it is as exhaustive as possible.

In the two-page summary released by the CIA on January 29, 1998, the phrase "no information has been found" was used nine times. I want to be assured that no information was found because none existed, rather than the message that the information was not found because the effort to find it was not thorough enough.

There have been published criticisms, by at least one of those contacted by Mr. Hitz's staff, that the interview seemed designed to go through the motions. I want Mr. Hitz, whom I have known for a long time and have great respect for, to assure us that he is satisfied that the investigation was as thorough as necessary to uncover the facts on the matter at hand.

I understand that a number of persons, almost all of them former CIA officials, either refused to be interviewed or sought to limit the interviews. At least one of the individuals who refused to be interviewed by the inspector general showed no similar reluctance to be interviewed by the press. I consider the failure of these people to assist the inspector general in this investigation to be inexcusable.

Mr. Chairman, I look forward to the comments our congressional colleagues will have on Mr. Hitz's work. I welcome them and I welcome Mr. Hitz and his presentation.

Thank you, Mr. Chairman.

THE CHAIRMAN (MR. GOSS):

Thank you Mr. Dicks, very much. At this time, I recognize the distinguished gentleman from California, Mr. Julian Dixon.

MR. DIXON:

Thank you very much, Mr. Chairman. I join you and the Ranking Minority Member in welcoming members of Congress and Mr. Fred Hitz, Inspector General of the Central Intelligence Agency.

I have read the inspector general's report entitled "Allegations of Connections Between the CIA and the Contras in Cocaine Trafficking in the Unites States, Volume 1: 'The California Story'." I find the section of the report that chronicles the political history of Nicaragua from 1912, when the U.S. Marines occupied Nicaragua to protect U.S. economic interest, until the election of Violetta Chamarro on February 25th, 1990, to be extremely valuable and insightful, for it is important to note that the Contras never were a single military organization.

It is apparent to me that Nicaraguans of various political persuasions made financial contributions to the Contras and to the Sandinistas. Some of these contributions undoubtedly were the result of proceeds from illegal activities such as narcotics trafficking. Nevertheless, the mere fact that an organization received support from the fruits of illegal activities does not necessarily mean that the organization itself nor its causes are illegitimate.

For example, Ricky Ross acknowledges donating some of his crack proceeds to inner-city community programs. These programs provide alternative after-school activities for our youth and are worthwhile and valuable and in no way are diminished by the fact that some drug proceeds contributed to the operating capabilities.

In the high speed of the digital age of information technology, the "Dark Alliance" series quickly spread beyond the *Mercury News*' readers. The series was placed on the paper's website of the internet where, according to the *Mercury News*, it received more than 1,000 hits a week. Additionally, talk-show stations made it their leading story for weeks and network television gave considerable time to reporting the story on the evening news.

The fact that this story has resonated so powerfully outside the minority communities should not come as a surprise. The spread of crack cocaine in predominantly majority communities is well-documented and no longer remains a secret. Whether drug use occurs in majority or minority communities is not the issue. Drugs tear at the very fiber of our nation, the family structure. Caucasian, Asian, African-American and Hispanic families have been destabilized by drugs, resulting in lost generations of our youth and rising drug-related crimes.

In the aftermath of the *Mercury News* series, a number of newspapers initiated their own investigation of the allegations. The *Los Angeles Times* was one newspaper that concluded, and I quote: "The crack epidemic in Los Angeles followed no blueprint or master plan. It was not orchestrated by the Contras or the CIA or any single drug ring. Not one trafficker, even the kingpins who sold thousands of kilos and pocketed millions of dollars, ever came close to monopolizing the trade."

On Sunday, May 11th, the *San Jose Mercury News* Executive Editor, Jerry Ceppos, wrote an article entitled: "To the Readers of our Dark Alliance Series" that identified certain shortcomings in the "Dark Alliance" series. Specifically Mr. Ceppos asserted that: "In a few instances, we presented only one interpretation of complicated, sometimes conflicting, pieces of evidence. In one instance, we did not include information that contradicted a central assertion of the series. We made our best estimate and instead reported it as fact. We oversimplified the complex issue of how the crack epidemic in America grew. And through imprecise language and graphics, we created impressions that were open to misinterpretation."

Mr. Chairman, as earlier stated, although the *San Jose Mercury News* series deals with the African-American community in South Central Los Angeles, this issue impacts all Americans. The possibility that the government may have been involved in drug trafficking activities threatens the credibility of all government agencies and entities.

A government of the people and by the people must not be permitted to engage in such activities. When the allegations of government abuse come to our attention we are obligated to use whatever resources are necessary to fully and professionally investigate the charges.

Mr. Chairman, there is a lot of work to be done.

The Chairman (Mr. Goss):

Thank you, Mr. Dixon. I would like to advise the members who came in late that we are trying to start Mr. Hitz at 4 o'clock. If you will look at the clock on the wall, you will understand my admonition that the opening statements be kept within reason.

Please, Mr. Skelton.

MR. SKELTON:

Thank you Mr. Chairman. I join my colleagues in welcoming our congressional witnesses and the Inspector General of the Central Intelligence Agency, Mr. Fred Hitz.

As the ranking Democratic member on the National Security Committee, I am well aware of the commitment that our nation's defense establishment has made to combating the importation of drugs into our country. An allegation that an agency of the federal government has been involved in trafficking cocaine into the United States while other federal agencies, including the Defense Department, are dedicating personnel and resources to fighting a war against drugs, Mr. Chairman, is horrendous.

The position of inspector ieneral is often a lonely one. Frequently, inspectors general are criticized by the public when their reports do not verify alleged misconduct and their objectivity is then called into question. Within an agency, the inspector general is sometimes viewed as the villain who is out to harm the image and reputation of the agency.

Mr. Hitz, you have weathered all types of criticism and have always maintained a professional attitude. I wish you all the best in whatever the future holds for you and thank you for your service.

Mr. Chairman, thank you.

THE CHAIRMAN (MR. GOSS):

Thank you, Mr. Skelton. Ms. Harmon of California.

MS. HARMON:

Thank you, Mr. Chairman. I would like to point out to the audience that a majority of the committee members are here, and I think that that speaks to the importance that we give to this issue.

Mr. Chairman, I just want to say that at the root of all of this is one word: trust. A democratic society simply cannot function if the people believe that government agencies and officials participated in or condone illegal activities. Restoring trust will not be easy, but it is nonetheless an essential exercise for this committee.

Speaking as one member, we cannot shirk that responsibility nor do I feel we will. I thank you, and I yield back.

THE CHAIRMAN (MR. GOSS):

Thank You Ms. Harmon. Ms. Pelosi.

MS. PELOSI:

I want to commend you and our ranking members for having this public hearing. I still have questions, and I look forward to the inspector general's presentation.

This is an issue of great concern in San Francisco, which I represent in the Congress. Since the advent of the crack epidemic in the early '80s, there has been a suspicion in our community that the African-American community was a target, particularly women in the African-American community were a target, of a campaign to provide crack to them. The suspicions were that this would lead to undermining the African-American community by undermining the family. It is a terrible, terrible thought.

Around the same time the Contra debate was raging in the Congress of the United States. The Congress was trying to determine if the profits from weapons sold to Iran were diverted to the Contras in order to circumvent the congressional ban on funding the Contra movement.

Therefore, when this story hit, there had long been a climate that made it a credible story.

I do not think that the so-called retraction of the *San Jose*

Mercury News was that weighty. It was a few instances: we did this; we didn't include an assertion that contradicted; we were in error about the money and oversimplified. That is not exactly a major retraction. So I have, and more importantly, my constituents still have some serious questions about this. We have particular interest in the Frogman case. During the prosecution of this case, the U.S. attorney for the Northern District of California agreed to return approximately $36,000 in cash seized from one defendant in this prosecution, after two exiled Contra supporters wrote letters filed with the court that the money was for the "reinstatement of Democracy in Nicaragua."

I look forward to hearing from the inspector general concerning his findings that there is no information that the CIA had any connection with the defendants in the Frogman case and that there is no indication that the Contras benefited from the drug trafficking of the Frogman case. I also anticipate questions as to whether officials of the CIA hampered in any way the investigations of the prosecution in this matter.

Once again, Mr. Chairman, thank you for allowing us to present these questions in the open.

THE CHAIRMAN (MR. GOSS):

Thank You Ms. Pelosi. Mr. Skaggs.

MR. SKAGGS:

I will be very brief. I join in thanking the chairman for calling these hearings. And I want to make a special point of recognizing the public service of Fred Hitz to the country and to the Central Intelligence Agency.

I have known him for some time, independent of his current position. What I have to say… I pick up on Ms Harmon's comment about trust. This committee, authorized to look into the workings of the intelligence community, ultimately must rely on trusting ourselves in sorting out fact from fiction from innuendo. The key individual in establishing and nurturing a sense of trustworthiness is the inspector general.

I believe that Mr. Hitz's conduct in office and his execution of his responsibilities have been absolutely key during my service on the committee to establishing the kind of trustworthiness in both directions that enables us to do our work for the American people.

And Fred, I just want to say thank you very much and God speed.

THE CHAIRMAN (MR. GOSS):

Thank you, Mr. Skaggs. Mr. Gibbons?

MR. GIBBONS:

Thank you, Mr. Chairman. And I join my colleagues in commending you for having this hearing today, and for bringing it before the public.

Agencies that provide valuable intelligence for anti-drug, economic or military information must, themselves, be untainted by illegal acts or even the innuendo of an illegality.

The importance of this hearing today will hopefully clear the air on these issues, rebuild confidence between the citizens of this country and our intelligence agencies, and finally in an equally important matter, rebuild our confidence in the intelligence that we receive from these agencies. The men and women in our intelligence-gathering agencies deserve no less than our complete confidence in their work to promote a better America.

Thank you, Mr. Chairman.

The Chairman (Mr. Goss):

Thank you, Mr. Gibbons.

Opening statements are completed. At this time we welcome colleagues who are not on the committee. It had been my intention to call members in the order of seniority, the senior member whom we were to hear from has deferred to Juanita Millender-McDonald, since you have been out front on this matter and have held hearings in your district.

We welcome you and your commentary on the report.

Ms. Millender-McDonald:

Thank you, Mr. Chairman and members of the committee. Before I begin my testimony, please allow me a moment to express my appreciation to you. Mr. Chairman and committee members, I commend this chairman for fulfilling his commitment to hold this hearing. Like the chairman, I too was deeply disturbed by the allegations.

As many of you are aware, I convened two town hall meetings in the fall of 1996 in response to the widespread feelings of anxiety, public outrage and concern throughout my district in the wake of the news accounts.

The first Town Hall meeting, at the Compton Community College on October 19, 1996, was attended by hundreds of residents from my drug-ravaged community. I sought to find out how the local community responded to the widespread harm caused by the scourge of substance abuse, regardless of the source or cause, and allowed them to seek answers to these allegations.

Then, on November 15, Director of Central Intelligence John Deutch made an unprecedented visit to Alain Locke High School in the Watts section of my district to directly address the concerns raised by my constituents and me, during a second public town hall meeting.

I am here today to articulate some of the concerns my constituents and I have about this report and the ongoing controversy.

Did CIA personnel or assets have any involvement in supplying or assisting drug traffickers in South Central Los Angeles and/or elsewhere?

The report answers this question in the negative. However, what are we to make of the questions raised by defense attorney Harold Braun, a panelist at the October 19th town meeting, who maintains that a suspect in the custody of the Los Angeles County Deputy Sheriffs was allowed to make a long distance telephone call to Virginia after asserting he worked for the CIA? What evidence do we have in this report that this allegation was pursued, given the report does not mention investigation of telephone logs?

Did the CIA aggressively pursue its role, including the charge to, quote: "collect, produce and disseminate intelligence on foreign aspects of narcotics prohibition and trafficking," when it received information about possible Contra involvement in drug trafficking?

The information in this report suggests that the CIA turned a blind eye, at best, to information that suggested drug trafficking by Contra operatives. This report responds to specific allegations. But it remains unclear to me what the CIA actually did to investigate whether any Contras were engaged in drug trafficking.

And the ultimate question is: can the CIA investigate itself?

We are being asked to trust career employees of the agency to sort out and report the truth in the name of national security. Indeed, news reports, which followed leaks regarding the content of this report last December, suggest that some CIA personnel were either not seriously interviewed or not questioned at all. As a result, the public remains skeptical.

I hope the Select Committee will give the content, methodologies and findings of this report the scrutiny they deserve. And that committee members will make themselves available to my constituents to respond to questions that this report generates. I believe this is critical to restoration of the public trust necessary to allow intelligence-gathering activities to coexist with democracy.

Thank you, Mr. Chairman and members.

The Chairman (Mr. Goss):

Thank you very much, Ms. Millender-McDonald. That was a very fine statement. You have raised some specific questions for the committee to take under consideration. And we shall.

One of the reasons we felt it was important to have this hearing at this time is because Mr. Hitz is on to greater glories with new employment. We wanted to make sure we had the opportunity for him to explain his report, and that is why we decided to do this today.

At this time, then, I would call Ms. Maxine Waters from California's 35th District. And we are pleased to have you before us today, Maxine.

Ms. Waters:

Thank you very much, Mr. Chairman and Members. I would like to thank you for holding this hearing. Certainly it is not expected of the Intelligence Committee.

Mr. Chairman and members of the committee, I am here today to testify about the failure of the Central Intelligence Agency to conduct a serious and thorough investigation. Unfortunately, my fear that the CIA would be unable to investigate itself had been confirmed with this report. The inspector general's report lacks credibility. It is fraught with contradictions and illogical conclusions. In a September 3, 1996 memo, then-CIA Director John Deutch laid out the framework for this investigation. Director Deutch's memo stated: "I have no reason to believe that there is any substance to the allegations published in the *Mercury News*." Despite this premature conclusion, a serious substantial and credible investigation and interview process would have proven him wrong. If the CIA director's premature conclusion meant to direct the final outcome, he has succeeded. This report's sweeping denial of the CIA's knowledge of drug trafficking related to the Contras defies the evidence as to what the CIA should have known.

Many skeptics believe that the CIA could never produce a credible or truthful review of wrongdoing by its own agency. These skeptics could point to this Sunday's *Los Angeles Times* to confirm their fears. The *Times* reported in another case, that after 37 years, the CIA finally admitted publicly the most profound deception imaginable to an American family. Thomas Pete Ray and his top secret squadron of National Guard bombers were shot down during a CIA bombing mission in the Bay of Pigs debacle. For 37 years the CIA denied that Mr. Ray and his squadron even existed, much less were shot down by Cuban troops in 1961. Only this month, faced with a document obtained by a Freedom of Information Act request, did the CIA finally admit the truth, 37 years later.

After reading the "Dark Alliance" series, I interviewed Gary Webb, writer of the series—and, by the way, Mr. Chairman and Members, Mr. Gary Webb is here today. He is sitting right here. I invited him to come to my district in South Central Los Angeles to respond to questions from local residents. My community encouraged my efforts to delve deep into these allegations.

A major problem with the report, Mr. Chairman and members, is that the report cleverly refers to agents. But we should be talking about agents and/or assets.

I am going to say to you today in no uncertain terms, Mr. Adolpho Calero was a CIA asset. Many of the funds for aid were funneled through him. Mr. Enrique Bermudez was a CIA asset; Mr. Francisco Aviles, a Contra official in Costa Rica in the Frogman case; Mr. Ivan Gomez, CIA agent, who accepted drug money from Mr. Meneses; Mr. Dagoberto Nunez, who ran a shrimp company for Oliver North in Costa Rica; Mr. Edmundo Meneses, American-trained Nicaraguan General and Norwin Meneses' brother; and Mr. Sebastian Gonzalez, Contra leader in Costa Rica and drug partner of Meneses.

I assert here today that these are all CIA assets. I challenge this committee to ask the inspector general and others in the CIA, to document for you whether or not my allegations are true. They should give sworn testimony regarding their knowledge about the people I've cited as being assets of the CIA. Today, I am asking this committee to obtain the written responses from the CIA that either categorically confirms or denies they are or were CIA assets or agents.

Another major problem with the investigation underlying the report was the CIA's lack of subpoena power. This meant that some of the most important CIA officials were never interviewed. Three former senior CIA managers would only respond in writing. Six other key CIA personnel refused to be interviewed. The CIA agents included Duane Claridge, Joseph Fernandez and Claire George. All of these senior CIA officials had major responsibilities for the CIA's Contra operation. There can be no thorough investigation without sworn testimony from each of these individuals. They should be subpoenaed.

Duane Claridge was the CIA officer who helped create the Contras at a time when the Meneses ring first began dealing cocaine for the FDN; the "Frente Democratico Nacional," the political arm of the Contras.

Duane Claridge's name also appeared in Oliver North's notebooks as for making quid pro quo deals with known drug kingpin Manuel Noriega.

Claridge summed up how serious he thought this investigation was when he told reporters in December 1997 that the CIA "sent me questions that were bullshit, and I wrote back they were a bunch of bullshit."

Allegations of drug trafficking and connections between the Contras and the CIA are not new. The Senate Subcommittee on Terrorism, Narcotics and International Operations, chaired by Senator John Kerry, conducted a two-year investigation into allegations of Contra involvement in drugs and arms-trafficking.

The CIA inspector general's report summarizes some of the Kerry commission's devastating findings. Drug traffickers provided support to the Contras and used the supply network of the Contras. Contras knowingly received both financial and material assistance from the drug traffickers. The FDN/Contra group moved Contra funds through a narcotics drug trafficking and money laundering operation. U.S. State Department funds authorized by Congress for humanitarian assistance was paid to drug traffickers. In some cases, these drug traffickers received the State Department's funds after having been indicted by Federal law enforcement agencies on drug charges. In each case, one or another U.S. government agency had information regarding these matters.

Not included in the CIA IG report are other key findings of the Kerry committee. Despite widespread trafficking through the war zones of northern Costa Rica, the Kerry committee was unable to find a single case which was made on the basis of a tip or a report by an official of a U.S. intelligence agency. This, despite direct testimony that drug trafficking on the southern front was reported to CIA officials.

How can this report include these incriminating findings by elected officials, including Senators Kerry, Brock, and Moynihan, and others, while summarily dismissing any CIA knowledge of or involvement in Contra drug trafficking into the U.S.? This is an outrageous contradiction.

Moreover, the report is littered with damaging admissions. This report admits Norwin Meneses was one of the biggest drug dealers in America and that he supplied Danilo Blandon. Blandon, in turn, was the source who supplied Ricky Ross.

Meneses dealt drugs in the United States for over ten years, starting back in 1974. He dealt drugs without interference, without any intervention. He had assets and businesses in San Francisco. Congresswoman Pelosi referred to the Frogman case. When they tracked down some of Meneses' people, they tracked them to the very house that was connected with the Frogman case, where many of those same people were involved.

Meneses was well known by the CIA, the DEA and DIA, and everybody in the United States as a drug dealer who was supplying Danilo Blandon, who was supplying Ricky Ross. How he stayed in the United States all those years selling drugs that ended up helping to support the Contras, and nobody, but nobody, knew it, is absolutely amazing. The CIA and DEA records are full of knowledge about Meneses' drug dealing operation. This knowledge was substantiated in this report, even this report! The CIA knew of his drug trafficking by 1984 and the DEA had known of his trafficking activities as early as 1974.

There are many other key facts that were confirmed by this report. On pages 76–77, drug dealer Norwin Meneses admitted giving money to the California chapter of the FDN/Contras and that he was involved in the 1988 attempt to obtain "material support, medical and general supplies" for the Contra movement.

I have maintained that it does not matter how much money, it does not matter whether it was, as Eden Pastora testified, only a few thousand dollars and a couple of trucks, or as Meneses himself claimed, that he contributed $40,000 plus in medical supplies and other things.

I am outraged by this, as a public elected official. All of us must be concerned that our government could have in any way been involved in drug trafficking. Drug trafficking. That is a very, very serious offense against the people of this nation. We cannot afford to have our government, I do not care under what pretense, involved in drug trafficking.

Pages 70–71 of the report document a connection between CIA asset and Contra military leader Enrique Bermudez, Meneses and Blandon. Blandon and Meneses traveled to Bolivia in 1982 to make a drug deal and stopped en route in Honduras. While in Honduras Bermudez asked Blandon and Meneses to help raise money and supplies for the FDN. He let the drug traffickers know that their support would be welcome because, I quote and everybody quotes, even your report quotes, that he said: "The ends justify the means."

Blandon then describes how he and Meneses were escorted to the airport by armed Contras after the meeting with Bermudez. Blandon left the meeting, he left this meeting, with $100,000 in a bag to buy drugs. The profits from the sale of these drugs were to be used to buy supplies and fund the Contras. Blandon tells of how he ran into trouble at the airport in Honduras when he was caught with the $100,000. But guess what? Just like in the Frogman case, when they caught them with the dope and the money, they returned the $36,000 having been told that it was Contra money. This man with $100,000 in drug money to buy more drugs for more supplies, was assisted by the Contras at the airport. Even though he had been stopped and they had taken $100,000 out of his briefcase, with the intervention of the Contras, they gave it back to him, and he went along his merry way. Where did the $100,000 come from?

THE CHAIRMAN (MR. GOSS):

Can I ask the gentlewoman to conclude her remarks? We have been overgenerous. We are taking away time for the presentation.

MS. WATERS:

Where did the $100,000 come from? Did they give it back to Blandon for the Contra CIA connection?

Well, Mr. Chairman and members, I am going to close by saying this: this report does not do the job, Mr. Chairman.

Why do I do all this? Because I want to find some CIA operatives, assets or agents and somehow convict them? That is not going to happen. And that is not what I am trying to do. I do it because, as public policy makers, we cannot continue to put our heads in the sand. It is a shame what happened with the Kerry report. The idea that members of the United States Senate could have presented us with so much documentation, and then ten years later we have the investigation by the *San Jose Mercury* and we find more information about drug trafficking? And either the CIA absolutely knowing, or turning its head, and we still cannot come up with public policy, at the same time we are spending millions of dollars talking about a war on drugs?

Give me a break, Mr. Chairman and members. We can do better than this. I will not go away. I cannot go away. My community has been devastated, as have many communities across this nation. People are outraged and concerned about the fact that this drug problem won't go away and by the idea that the government could be involved.

I challenge this committee to create public policy that will get our government out of ever being involved in drug trafficking in any way.

I thank you.

THE CHAIRMAN (MR. GOSS):

At this time I would like to swear in Mr. Hitz. Mr. Hitz, may I ask you to raise your right hand? [Witness sworn].

THE CHAIRMAN (MR. GOSS):

I would advise members that Mr. Hitz went out of his way to accommodate our schedule. I believe he had been without sleep for at least a couple of days in order to travel back here, and we are obliged for that consideration. I yield the floor to you.

MR. HITZ:

Thank you, Mr. Chairman. I assure the committee that I am happy to be here today and hopefully I will be able to answer your questions irrespective of distance traveled. I feel a little bit as if we have had dessert first. It has been a very serious and thorough discussion by the two Congresspersons about their views of my report, and so I am happy to have the occasion now to summarize it for you.

At the request of then-Director of Central Intelligence John Deutch, on September 3, 1996, I initiated an inquiry into the allegations that stemmed from a three-part series called "Dark Alliance." I promised Congress and the American people to have my office "conduct as thorough a review as possible of all available information and report what we find candidly and completely."

I am pleased to come before this committee today and say that we have done just that.

Our report represents an exhaustive array of facts. We reviewed an estimated 250,000 pages of documents and conducted over 365 interviews of persons on four continents. We reviewed reporting from other intelligence community agencies, including the NSA and DIA. We reviewed available congressional records including information compiled by the Kerry committee and spoke with individuals associated with the joint Iran-Contra investigating committee.

Our 17-person team worked some eighteen months to identify, and let me underscore:

Number one: any information in CIA's possession relating to Danilo Blandon, Norwin Meneses or Ricky Ross.

Number two: any information in CIA's possession relating to possible drug-trafficking activities by the Contras in California and elsewhere in the United States and what action, if any, CIA may have taken upon receiving that information.

And third: any contacts between CIA and law-enforcement authorities regarding that information.

Now, let me turn to the findings. I want to make clear that we found absolutely no evidence to indicate that CIA as an organization or its employees were involved in any conspiracy to bring drugs into the United States.

The first half of the report discusses CIA knowledge of the activities of Ross, Blandon and Meneses. Ross, Blandon and Meneses are convicted drug dealers. Our investigation found no information to indicate that any past or present employee of CIA or anyone else acting on behalf of CIA had any dealings with Ross, Blandon or Meneses or had any knowledge of their drug trafficking activities.

Ross was a drug dealer who, by his own admission, says his sole motivation was to derive personal financial gain from the illegal trafficking of drugs. During the 1980s, Ross was a major cocaine and crack trafficker who says he made millions in the drug trade. His activities helped to foster the crack epidemic that erupted in South Central Los Angeles. However, Ross told us that he never sold drugs for the Contras or donated any money to the Contras. The CIA never had any relationship with Ross.

Blandon and Meneses also trafficked in drugs to derive personal financial gain. While CIA had no relationship with Blandon and Meneses, our investigation did find that they were affiliated with California Contra support organizations, and each made financial contributions to those groups. Blandon and Meneses each claim to have provided between $3,000 and $40,000 worth of support to the Contras.

Blandon says he met Contra leader Enrique Bermudez on four occasions from 1981 to 1983. Blandon states that one meeting occurred in Honduras in 1982 while he and Meneses were traveling to Bolivia to conduct a drug deal. Blandon says that Bermudez told them that the Contras were having trouble raising funds and asked that he and Meneses help, stating that: "the end justifies the means."

Blandon adds that it is his belief Bermudez did not know that he and Meneses were engaged in drug trafficking, but was aware of Meneses' alleged Nicaraguan organized crime connections. Unfortunately, we could not obtain information from Bermudez since he was murdered in Managua in 1991.

No information has been found to indicate that CIA hindered or otherwise intervened in the investigation, arrest, prosecution, conviction or sentencing of Ross, Blandon or Meneses.

The second half of our report, "The Northern California Story," pertains to a case in San Francisco often referred to as the Frogman case. The case got its name when law enforcement authorities in San Francisco arrested several swimmers who had come ashore from a Colombian freighter on January 17, 1983. The swimmers had with them some 430 pounds of cocaine. In all, some 12 arrests were made on January 17 and more followed soon thereafter, including the arrests of two Nicaraguans; Julio Zavala and Carlos Cabezas.

Unlike the events relating to Ross, Blandon and Meneses, this was a case where the CIA became involved because it mistakenly thought it had an interest to protect.

The CIA first learned of the Frogman case in late July, 1984, about a year and a half after Zavala's arrest. At the time, the CIA was informed that two representatives of the United States Attorney's office in San Francisco, which was prosecuting Zavala, planned to attend depositions in Costa Rica from two members of Contra organizations who had provided Zavala with letters that claimed that the $36,000 the authorities had seized from Zavala at the time of his arrest belonged to the Contras. CIA officials mistakenly identified one of the Contra members as a former CIA asset. There was concern that the depositions might expose a Contra support group in which the CIA had an operational interest.

No information was found to indicate that the two Contra officials who wrote the letters supporting Zavala were involved in drug trafficking. Moreover, the principal author of the letters reportedly was later expelled from the Contra group when the leadership learned he had written the letter in support of Zavala's claim.

An attorney from the CIA's Office of General Counsel met with the responsible prosecutor and possibly other representatives from the U.S. attorney's office.

Accounts differ as to why the money was returned to Zavala.

The assistant U.S. attorney who prosecuted Zavala, Joseph Russoniello, and others involved in the prosecution, state that the decision to return the money to Zavala was not based on any CIA representations, but only their own judgment as to whether it was worth the time and expense to go to Costa Rica for the depositions.

However, we found a CIA cable that was written soon after the CIA attorney had met with the responsible prosecutor. The cable indicated the money was returned to Zavala at CIA's request. Unfortunately, the CIA attorney cannot recall the facts of the case or the meeting in question.

In summary, I would emphasize that whatever impact the CIA attorney may have ultimately had on the decision of the U.S. Attorney's Office to return the money to Zavala, we have found no evidence to indicate the return of the money weakened the prosecution's case against Zavala. Zavala was convicted and sent to prison.

As I said earlier, we have found no evidence in the course of this lengthy investigation of any conspiracy by CIA or its employees to bring drugs into the United States. However, during the Contra era, CIA worked with a variety of people to support the Contra program. These included CIA assets, pilots who ferried supplies to the Contras, as well as Contra officials and others.

Let me be frank about what we are finding. There are instances where CIA did not in an expeditious or consistent fashion cut off relationships with individuals supporting the Contra program who were alleged to have engaged in drug-trafficking activity or take action to resolve the allegations. I want to underscore the fact that we are talking about allegations here.

In closing, Mr. Chairman, I would urge the American public to read the report, which is available on the internet at www.odci.gov/cia.

Thank you Mr. Chairman. I am pleased to answer your questions.

THE CHAIRMAN (MR. GOSS):

Mr. Hitz, thank you very much.

As I said at the beginning, colleagues, we have the room until 5:00. Apparently we have been able to negotiate an extension of the lease until 5:15, and if Mr. Hitz could agree to stay until that time, I would be thankful.

MR. HITZ:

I can.

THE CHAIRMAN (MR. GOSS):

I would like to start by asking, were there any warnings that CIA officers should stay clear of individuals trafficking drugs and in fact should report them accordingly?

MR. HITZ:

As you know, Mr. Chairman, at least from calendar year 1986 there was a prohibition in force against dollars, CIA money, going to individuals or groups found to be involved in drug dealing. For the most part that tone is contained in the cables, but you have to recognize that the nature of the allegations varied. In some cases, it was sort of wild-hair rumors that were circulating while some of the allegations were more deeply rooted.

THE CHAIRMAN (MR. GOSS):

With regard to the individuals who declined to be interviewed by your office, did they give you any reason for their unwillingness to participate in this? I presume you do not have the power of subpoena. Is that correct?

MR. HITZ:

No, we do not have the power for subpoena of individuals.

I talked to a number of the individuals, there were only a handful, that refused to talk to us. The attitude I encountered was that having gone through the Iran-Contra investigation, that era, several felt that they had been through enough. They did not believe there was any substance in the *Mercury News* accusations, and they just chose not to participate.

THE CHAIRMAN (MR. GOSS):

Finally for me, Mr. Hitz, did you interview Gary Webb?

MR. HITZ:

No, we did not.

THE CHAIRMAN (MR. GOSS):

Sandra Smith?

MR. HITZ:

I am sorry, Mr. Chairman, who was that? Sandra Smith?

THE CHAIRMAN (MR. GOSS):

Sandra Smith is the DEA agent in the first of the "Dark Alliance" stories, the alleged source of the beginning of this.

Mr. Hitz:

No, I did not.

The Chairman (Mr. Goss):

Thank you, sir. Mr. Lewis.

Mr. Lewis:

Thank you, Mr. Chairman and colleagues. I want to compliment both my colleagues from Los Angeles, Ms. Millender-McDonald and Maxine Waters, for their efforts.

Mr. Hitz, I too appreciate your making the effort to come and be with us today and want to express my appreciation for your long service to the country.

What were the CIA's legal and regulatory responsibilities from 1979 to 1996 regarding the reporting of potential crimes and the maintenance of relationships with persons suspected of involvement in drug trafficking?

Mr. Hitz:

Well, it was a movable feast, so to speak. The requirements kept changing. From 1976 to 1982, it was an issue that was not really addressed. From 1982 to 1995, in an agreement hammered out between Attorney General Smith and the Reagan administration, there was no requirement to report on allegations of drug trafficking with respect to non-employees of the intelligence agencies. And during the period, that did not include agents of the CIA, did not include assets.

That has been changed. The agreement in 1995, superseding the 1982–95 period, specifically lists narcotics crimes as reportable, irrespective of whether or not the agency acquires information that they are being carried on by non-employees, namely assets.

Mr. Lewis:

Thank you very much, Mr. Hitz.

Mr. Chairman, I yield back the balance of my time.

The Chairman (Mr. Goss):

Mr. Dixon.

Mr. Dixon:

Thank you very much, Mr. Chairman.

Mr. Hitz, I join those who are sorry to see you leave. I understand you are off to Princeton University.

Regarding the Frogman case, you say that the CIA became involved mistakenly. As I recall, your report indicates that the attorney from CIA traveled to northern California and had a conversation with the prosecutor. I believe your testimony today reflects that you could find no written material by the attorney who, in fact, had that engagement with the prosecutor?

Mr. Hitz:

What we did find, of course, and I believe you are familiar with this, Mr. Dixon, is the write-up that was made by the Office of General Counsel commenting on that particular exchange, that intervention with the assistant U.S. attorney. The individual whom we think was involved in the actual negotiations, in fact, doesn't have a recollection of it.

Mr. Dixon:

The write-up was not made by the person who was involved?

Mr. Hitz:

Well, we don't know that.

Mr. Dixon:

You don't know who it was made by? Is that right?

Mr. Hitz:

Correct. He has no recollection of it.

Mr. Dixon:

Now, you come to the conclusion that they interceded because of a mistake. And I believe the report indicates it is a mistaken identity of someone that the CIA did have a relationship with.

Mr. Hitz:

That's correct, Mr. Dixon. We did not, the CIA did not get involved in the Frogman case until several years after the arrest took place. It came as a consequence of a cable, a State Department cable from Costa Rica saying that a private attorney and attorneys from the United States attorney's office in San Francisco were about to come to Costa Rica to take the deposition of two signatories to a letter which had been directed to the U.S. attorney's office, seeking to reclaim the $36,000 that had been confiscated on Zavala's arrest.

The letter came from what appeared to be Contra support groups, and one of the signatories, the agency mistakenly identified as an asset.

It was a Hispanic name that was remarkably close to the name of an agent that had worked for us. In any event it was, as you suggest, a case of mistaken identity.

Not having been able to locate the lawyer who was actually involved in this, and therefore not being able to speak to his or her mindset, it appears what they were trying to do was to protect the identity of the Contra support group's connection and in that way keep it from being revealed.

Mr. Dixon:

Did your investigation make an independent evaluation that this was a mistake or is this something that the CIA told you?

Mr. Hitz:

The CIA did not tell us, and in point of fact, we were the ones that discovered that the identity of the agent was mistaken.

The Chairman (Mr. Goss):

Mr. Gibbons.

Mr. Gibbons:

Thank you very much Mr. Chairman. Mr. Hitz, let me ask a broad general question. Did your office uncover any information which would have indicated that there was any authorized or unauthorized U.S. government activity which would have facilitated narcotics trafficking in the United States or oversees?

Mr. Hitz:

No, we did not. We did not encounter any information that would suggest that there was authorized... and the unauthorized, of course, is the trigger there. Obviously, if it was unauthorized in the purest sense there wouldn't be any record of it. We were using the written record so we could ask intelligent questions.

We found no evidence of a scheme to promote the Contra effort by selling drugs by CIA employees.

Mr. Gibbons:

Thank you, Mr. Hitz. Thank you, Mr. Chairman. I'll yield back the rest of my time.

The Chairman (Mr. Goss):

Thank you Mr. Gibbons. Ms. Pelosi.

Ms. Pelosi:

Thank you, Mr. Chairman. Again, I want to compliment you for having this open hearing, but I would request that we have another opportunity to question the inspector general, because he will not be available long enough today for us to ask even a substantial part of our questions.

The Chairman (Mr. Goss):

I concur with your observation. I have several questions myself, and I know others will.

Ms. Pelosi:

In your judgment, was the contact between the CIA and the U.S. attorney's office in this case, the Frogman case, appropriate?

Mr. Hitz:

There appears to have been a difference in interpretation of the propriety of the contact by the individual attorney who engaged in it.

He stated in his write-up that he felt he was getting into an area that could cause embarrassment to the president's covert action activity in the Contra matter and drugs.

MS. PELOSI:

My concern is whether the U.S. attorney's office would perhaps not proceed in a matter for the reason you just said; to not jeopardize activities of the CIA.

MR. HITZ:

Well, my experience with the U.S. attorneys' offices has been, Ms. Pelosi, that if the U.S. attorney felt that he or she had a case in this matter, no intervention from the CIA would have warded them off.

They would have gone for it and appropriately so.

MS. PELOSI:

Mr. Chairman, I know that we won't have much more time. So I'm not going to ask any more questions but I would like to make a couple of observations.

As I listen to what you say, Mr. Hitz, I appreciate you establishing your limitations: you don't have the power of subpoena, the guidelines weren't clear, certain things were not reportable at the time. For example whether an asset that we were engaged with was involved in drug trafficking. And that leads me to conclude that we may have unwittingly, and I use that word generously, we may have been subsidizing assets who engaged in drug trafficking.

I'm glad that the law has changed, that now at least, it is reportable. But I, for the life of me, cannot figure out why, as you say in your statement, that the CIA did not know whether these people were involved in drug trafficking. At least they should know, whether it is reportable or not, we at least should know. We are CIA. Shouldn't we know? Doesn't the pen say "knowledge is our business"? Or something like that?

MR. HITZ:

We are pretty categorical on the issue of Blandon and Meneses and their lack of relationship with the CIA. Ricky Ross as well.

MS. PELOSI:

I think that in our investigation we should talk to the people you couldn't subpoena. We could figure out why it wasn't worth $36,000 to go to Costa Rica for a deposition, and we can find out whether the CIA mistakenly identified somebody or not.

This is not to say that within the limitations that you have in the inspector general's office that you haven't made a good effort, but I'm afraid it keeps open some questions that I would hope that it would close. But, nevertheless, thank you.

THE CHAIRMAN (MR. GOSS):

Mr. Bishop. Good afternoon.

MR. BISHOP:

Good afternoon and thank you very much Mr. Chairman. Let me apologize for my delinquency in getting here. I had a two-hour mechanical delay with my flight and I didn't want to rush that. But I am delighted to be here.

I've read the report and I have a few observations to make. The first of which is that I want to join my colleagues in commending you, Mr. Hitz, as you retire from the CIA. I want to take this opportunity to join them in thanking you for service to the agency and to our country.

I would also like to make the observation that allegations of CIA involvement in the introduction and distribution of crack cocaine is very, very serious, and it really created a firestorm. In minority communities it immediately generated comparisons to the Tuskegee syphilis study where African-Americans were injected with syphilis germs and were left untreated for the purpose of study. The introduction of drugs, or the allegation of the introduction of crack cocaine into our community, is equally bad and reprehensible and we certainly feel it appropriate that this committee and the agency and all interested parties really get to the bottom of it. And I commend you for your effort.

I do want to ask you a couple of questions. Were the current employees cooperative in providing information and did any government agency official or state agency or individual attempt to influence your investigation in any way?

MR. HITZ:

No, we had good cooperation and nobody tried to push us around.

MR. DICKS:

Would the gentleman yield on that point for a second? What about this fellow, the CIA attorney who could not recall the facts of the case or the meeting in question? That doesn't sound to me like full cooperation.

MR. HITZ:

Again, Mr. Dicks, it is regrettable, we would like to have gotten his... if he was the person who authored the document, and he's the person that made the intervention with the U.S. attorney's office... it would have been helpful had he remembered, but we had a pretty good written record and in point of fact, that's what we were stuck with.

MR. DICKS:

Thank you for yielding.

MR. BISHOP:

You are welcome. Would you just tell me what were the CIA's legal and regulatory responsibilities from '79 to '96 regarding reporting of potential crimes and the maintenance of relationships with persons that were suspected in involvement of drug trafficking?

MR. HITZ:

I think just before you arrived, I spoke to the rather odd history there. In point of fact, the period of '82 to '95 was one in which there was no official requirement to report on allegations of drug trafficking with respect to non-employees of the agency, and they were defined to include agents, assets, non-staff employees. That was the agreement that was struck between then Attorney General Smith and the agency. That has since been changed, since '95.

MR. BISHOP:

I appreciate the chair's indication that we will continue this at the committee's pleasure at a later time, and with that, I will ease my questioning and thank you very much, Mr. Hitz.

MR. HITZ:

Thank you, Mr. Bishop.

THE CHAIRMAN (MR. GOSS):

Mr. Bishop, thank you.

We are beyond the appointed hour, and I know that we have added even longer to the length of your already long day, Mr. Hitz, but we are thankful. As you can tell there is a great deal of interest. There, indeed, will be several follow-up questions coming along on this subject as we proceed with our investigation in the select committee.

I would like to point out to committee members, I have promised to go forward. And we are. Members, I recognize that there is a lot of concern about the seven individuals who declined to comment. We have been in contact with all seven of them and we have varying degrees of response. I offer that as a token of the resolve we have to proceed forward on this.

I would like to ask one final question Mr. Hitz, if I could. I have read this report very closely. It focuses a spotlight, as you say, on a specific series of allegations. The report, I think, is very clear in what it says. It is signed by you?

MR. HITZ:

Yes.

THE CHAIRMAN (MR. GOSS):

Did you sign this report without reservation, and do you stand behind this report and what it says?

MR. HITZ:

I did and I do.

THE CHAIRMAN (MR. GOSS):

I thank you, very much. This meeting is concluded.

Public Conversation

Los Angeles, 2001

"My name is Alexander. And I'm not that educated and I'm not that smart, but I'm not dumb and I'm not stupid. [Laughter]

I live on Skid Row and—and I got a question.

When I walk into the community that I live at, right around the corner from the police station is a known dope spot, right? That's two blocks from here. They have people over there selling dope on a nonstop basis—a known drug spot. I mean, you can walk over there now, and they'll try to sell you crack. And they smoke crack, it's like a drug-selling immune zone. [Laughter]

They got another spot on Fifth Street, Fifth and Gladys or Fifth and one of them streets... Towne. It's another spot—like a drug-immune zone. You just come there and set up shop, start selling crack. You sell out all the crack you want, and the police come right up and down Towne Street all the time—and nobody, nobody does nothing!

How can that go on year after year—a known dope spot—and nobody does nothing?"—Alexander Anderson

Los Angeles, January, 2001

LAPD began work on "Agents & Assets" in the summer of 2000 and first presented it in January of 2001. I'd heard Gary Webb discussing his "Dark Alliance" articles on the radio with broadcaster David Barsamian and then wrote Maxine Waters' office and obtained the congressional report that contained the hearing transcript that I later edited to become the text of "Agents & Assets." This was in 1999. Shortly after his election in 1996, President Clinton signed the "welfare reform" bill, which inevitably appears in quotes, not just here, because of the cynical doublespeak that it embodies. In my mind and for many others, Clinton's signing of that bill marked an abandonment of 50 years of Democratic social policy. It was an abdication of government responsibility to its citizens. Instead, it embraced the government role as coercive and punitive. When I heard Gary Webb on the radio, I didn't know, as I do now, of the long history of linkage between covert CIA operations and drug trafficking. What I did know, as I read the March 18, 1998 hearing transcript, was that the feigned concern of the congressional inquiry, was a powerful metaphor for countless other instances of government disregard for large segments of the population, in particular people of color and poor people. It was metaphor. It was real. It was the result of business as usual—another day in the life of a pattern of abuse—governmental abuse. In "Agents & Assets" the people who are on-the-ground experts on the effects of these policies of neglect, disregard and collateral damage, play the government officials who have ignored them. In so doing, the ignored, testify to the dereliction of the government. They identify the truly irresponsible, scandalously irresponsible among us.

The 2001 Los Angeles performances took place at Fourth and Main, in a former hearing room of the Regional Transit Authority, which for several years was the home of one of our producing partners, Side Street Projects. Side Street had been given the use of the space, which was otherwise empty, while the building's owner Tom Gilmore awaited the real estate boom. Located at the intersection of Skid Row with the leading edge of downtown gentrification, it was a perfect space for convening an audience. Old Stories: New Lives was our other producing partner for these performances and Old Stories: New Lives has continued to work with LAPD in subsequent "Agents & Assets" productions and residencies. The encouragement and ideational support of Old Stories: New Lives' Peter Sellars, Diane Malecki, Julia Carnahan and Kevin Higa have been pivotal in the realization of "Agents & Assets." For several years prior to "Agents & Assets," we'd been conducting performance workshops with the women of the Safe Harbor Recovery Program in Skid Row and women from that program performed significant roles as cast members in the production.

As we worked on the production in the fall of 2000, a treatment alternative to incarceration initiative for people arrested for drug possession was working its way onto the November ballot. In November it passed, receiving the approval of over 60 percent of the voters. Our January 11th, post-performance panel included Dave Fratello, who drafted the reform initiative (Ballot Proposition 36) and managed the campaign that led to its passage. The other panelist that night was Eric Newby, who as deputy probation officer in the sentenced-offender drug court was, at that time, the only probation officer in Los Angeles County working directly with treatment programs. The sentenced-offender program, unlike Proposition 36, required jail time, but allows for the early release of people convicted on charges of drug use, to treatment programs. — **JOHN MALPEDE**

TOPIC:
TREATMENT VERSUS INCARCERATION AND THE PASSAGE OF PROPOSITION 36
Saturday, January 11, 2001

TIMELINE:
JUNE, 2000 — Project Colombia Authorized by Congress
NOVEMBER, 2000 — California Voters Pass Proposition 36, Treatment Alternative to Incarceration
DECEMBER, 2000 — US Presidential Election Decided By 5–4 Vote of Supreme Court

PANELISTS:
DAVE FRATELLO: Campaign Manager of Proposition 36
ERIC NEWBY: Deputy Probation Officer, LA County Sentenced Offender Drug Court
JOHN MALPEDE: Moderator

John Malpede:

When I first started working in Skid Row, in 1985, there were very few resources in place for people for treatment or adequate housing, to sort of come out the other end of the drug tunnel. That really has changed. SRO Housing and Skid Row Housing Trust have transformed over 40 former flophouses into safe, attractive, affordable temporary and permanent housing. There are some good recovery programs and a very active 12-step culture. Still, in this neighborhood, as you walk or drive through the streets you see cardboard box after cardboard box, block after block. At the same time there is a huge population of people living in this neighborhood who are doing a million things. There are people who have transformed their lives and are doing incredible things. Actually the people in the cast of this show—like Alexander, Robert, Rick—are responsible for starting arts organizations in this neighborhood as well as activist organizations involved in quality of life issues here. In a way, that's the invisible population of Skid Row right now. These are people who are really functioning as powerful citizens, for the betterment of this neighborhood. So, at least for me personally, it seems that while a lot of horrible pessimistic things have happened on the big scale, there have been some really amazing openings that have happened. One of them is that it seems okay now to talk about drug treatment and to really question the whole "war on drugs" that has been presented as the way of dealing with the real drug problem. And specifically now, with the overwhelming passage of Proposition 36, there really is a lot of opportunity in the state of California to develop humane treatment opportunities for people to deal with the drug problems. So, tonight we have two people who really know tons about this.

We have Dave Fratello, the campaign manager of Prop. 36, and Eric Newby, a deputy probation officer working in the sentenced offender drug court. In that capacity, he works as a go-between interfacing with the courts and the treatment programs. So they are both going to share their perspectives on what the prospect is now that Prop. 36 is about to go into effect. So I'm going to turn it over to Dave.

DAVE FRATELLO:

Thank you. I have to say first of all just in appreciation of the cast and the performance here today, I really enjoyed it. But I have to tell you one of my personal reactions. I grew up in LA, in Long Beach and I lived for six years in Washington D.C. And you all had me transported right back to the congressional hearing setting. I want to talk a little bit about what Prop. 36 is, how it came about and why it passed and what that means to the future. Because most of us come from California you may not be familiar with other things that happened through the same ballot initiative process that are also related to the drug war. So I want to talk about them first.

One issue is medical marijuana, which Richard [acknowledges audience member] is very familiar with. California did pass the first medical marijuana initiative in 1996 and then I've been involved with a group that has been advocating that in several states since. This year Colorado and Nevada became the eighth and ninth states to legalize medical marijuana by ballot initiative. It's an amazing amount of progress in a very short amount of time. And that is against the argument that we cannot open the door to marijuana for patients because that's going to say it's okay and then the kids are going to smoke marijuana all the time, dumping it on the parents. It's going to be a disaster.

There is a saying that everything that you do in trying to reform the drug war, scale it back and do something different, is a slippery slope. What we have been trying to do is to show that you can make sensible changes in this orthodoxy of the drug war without the whole thing falling apart like a house of cards. And that is interesting in a lot of ways. If you can prove that, if you can give politicians the backbone, many of them really have good instincts but they cannot behave the way they want to behave because they want to be reelected. You can give them the backbone by showing them that the public is already ahead of them. They can go ahead of their colleagues. They might even get rewarded, not punished, for taking the lead on humane drug policies. We can open this whole thing up and it's not just going to be what's on the ballot this year or what's on the ballot next year; we can really change the dialog. Medical marijuana is one opening to doing that.

One other issue that was on the ballot this year was the reform of the asset forfeiture laws. I won't lecture you on the intricate legalities of that, but many are familiar with this. If you are accused of a crime, your property can be seized and if you are not proved innocent the government keeps your property. And the cops keep the money. So this is a pretty ugly piece of injustice that has been crying out for reform. There has been very little progress in this area, but this past year Utah and Oregon, by nearly 70 percent of the votes in both states, passed laws that required the government to prove that somebody actually committed a crime. In fact, in Oregon you must be convicted of a crime before your property can be taken. That's a constitutional amendment. So that's another example of an issue where this made progress. We are trying to roll back a system that has become abusive. And one of the ways to do it is to just isolate the issues and to present them to the public and say: "Here is what is going on. What do you think?"

Another issue where the public was already way ahead of the policy was drug treatment instead of jail and that is Proposition 36. And I assume that some of you are already familiar with this issue and I'll just try to walk you through what Prop. 36 really does, because we are now reaching the state of implementation and this is going to be very interesting. The initiative says, first of all, that it's for first and second time drug possession offenses, as long as there is not another crime, as long as there is no dealing, you don't do a theft at the same time. It's a pure possession case. First and second offense: you will get treatment. And treatment is a conditional probation. So you do need to go to treatment and complete it, but there is no other option. The judge cannot throw you in jail because he does not like the way you look or the way you behave. You get a chance for treatment. And the initiative puts a lot of money into the treatment system: $120 million per year in additional funds. We do spend a good amount of money in California, about $80 million in state money now, but we are adding another $120 million to cover the costs of new people coming into the system.

There are two more populations that the initiative effects. These are people on probation right now. If you had a drug possession case six months ago and you got two years of probation and you violate your probation, well, any number of things may happen to you now. Depending on what county you are in, one judge might throw you right in jail, and this begins for many kids a cycle that never stops. But these people will also be entitled to treatment under Prop. 36. We are trying to break that cycle before it starts.

The last group is parolees. People who have been in prison

and get out of prison, and while they are out test positive for drug use. Today we put 30,000 of those people back into our state prisons for an average term of six months. You know: "Why didn't you get the message when you were in prison? You need to go back." That's the attitude our society has. As long as these people have not got a serious prior strike—and it does not have to be a drug offense—if they are on parole, as long as they are not a violent offender, the positive drug test results in treatment. A lot of people will tell you that we need to have a lot more treatment in the prisons. That is probably a good thing. But where the best progress has been shown in experimental treatment up until now has been in transitional services, providing for people between prison and living in the community with no supervision. And this essentially forces an intervention. Somebody comes out of prison and demonstrates that they haven't got it together yet. They went back into their community and celebrated that they were out of prison, and before you know it they are slated to go right back. This is an intervention and the initiative pays for treatment for these people to keep them out and to try to establish a normal life in the community, drug free and crime free. At least give them a chance.

When you take all these populations together: "Is this revolutionary?" I think it is. We're going to be reaching 36,000 people who otherwise would have seen the inside of a cell for a drug violation. Instead, they are going to be in treatment programs. And that's the minimum. We think that that's going to have a tremendously positive effect. It's gonna save money, it's gonna change lives. We are going to give people a chance instead of cracking down. That's what we have accomplished here. That's what we are going to work out in the next couple of months, in the next couple of years.

ERIC NEWBY:

My name is Eric Newby. I am a probation officer in the County of Los Angeles. First, I would like to say the presentation was excellent. I grew up in Compton, California. I have been with the probation department approximately 12 years. In narcotics seven of those 12 years. I think it was my calling because I have several family members that were victims of drug use, my father and a couple of my sisters. Personally I think that Prop. 36 is going to be very effective. I think I should start off by saying that when this initiative began, a lot of judges, probation officers, law enforcement were strongly opposed. They said, "Oh my God!" They viewed the situation as a decriminalization, rather than viewing it as defendants receiving treatment. Now they are getting a little more educated. Since the passage of the proposition, the energy is going more towards strategy. "How is this going to effect our operation?" I'm speaking specifically about probation now. "How is it going to effect the probation department?" Prior to Prop. 36 we probably had about 9,000 narcotics cases that we deal with.

Now beginning July 1, 2001 that's probably going to double. So that's 18,000 cases to deal with. There is going to be no custody time, okay? These people are going to be ordered probation and drug treatment. So in turn that means more deputies are going to have to be hired, anywhere from 120 to 200. Probation tries to keep a ratio from one deputy to 100 defendants. That number is quite high. LA County is large. So for that to happen, and for these defendants to receive effective treatment rather than shuffling them, dealing with them on a non-personnel basis, that has to occur. The probation department is going to receive the funding from the government.

My experience with this is from dealing with it on a day-to-day basis. In my job, I spend time in court. It's called the sentenced-offender drug court. The judge in that court's name is Michael Tynan. Some of you may know the "Night Stalker Case." He was the judge in that famous case. His court is specifically a drug court, The sentenced-offender drug court is a program specifically designed for lifetime addicts, if you will, individuals that have been using drugs all their lives. It is a post sentence, meaning that individuals who have literally earned prison, the judge suspends their sentence, and gives them the opportunity to complete an 18-month drug-treatment program. This was all new to me: this type of program. Because in the process of this program these individuals violate, say that they test dirty or positive for a particular drug: cocaine, heroin, methamphetamine, they are afforded the opportunity to continue their treatment. This lends a lot of credence to Prop. 36. Because in the past when I was working on a regular narcotics case load, not this program, the immediate probation officer's attitude was: "Hey, this guy tested positive, we've got to report it to the court, get him back in court, we're requesting custody time." They weren't recommending that they attend some NA meetings, go to some residential treatment program. That wasn't the attitude. Now, the attitude is more treatment, treatment, treatment. Prop. 36 is forcing treatment, treatment, treatment. Probation's attitude now in the narcotics department is towards a philosophy of treatment for clients, service to clients. This is the focus now. Rather than, "Toss them in jail." Prop. 36 is forcing that. The judges, as I said before, highly opposed this. Sheriffs deputies who are dealing with the guys in custody all the time, totally opposed it. Police officers, parole officers, probation officers, they all opposed it. But Prop. 36 won. You are decriminalizing drug use, drug possession! We are not saying drug sales. These people are dealt with differently.

I want to talk a little more about the sentenced-offender drug court program. There is a ninety-day custody phase up front, which is a little in opposition with Prop. 36, which totally opposes custody time. It is highly effective though. Once a defendant is formally admitted into the sentenced-offender drug court program, you cannot have any violent offenses or any drug sales, the first 90 days is spent in custody. Right now the males are housed in the Bauchet Street Custody Center in East LA. The females in the program are housed at the Twin Towers. During those ninety days they are receiving acupuncture, they are required to go to individual and group counseling sessions. It's highly intensive. I would say 12 to 14 hours of their day is in drug treatment. All their time is accounted for. After those 90 days they are either released to a residential facility or an outpatient treatment center. However, while they are in the out-patient phase, they are living in a sober-living home, which is basically a transitional type of living. Once they reach that point they are required to attend meetings, the same type of things that was going on while in custody, but without the supervision. The sentenced-offender drug court program wanted to avoid—because these are your lifetime addicts, as I said before—trusting these people released out into the community, without first building up their confidence.

Most of the people that I deal with are people that have reached rock bottom; they have reached a point where they want to change their lives around. So, that 90-day custody period is really giving them solid foundation to stand on, the confidence to function in society while being sober. A lot of them have been using drugs for 20, 15 years. It's very uncomfortable for them to operate sober. So once they reach this point, it's still very intensive for them. Ultimately they are weaned back into society. They are able to eventually live with family members. Start a job and start earning a living. After the 18 months, graduations have been held. There have been two so far, and the next one is coming up on the 24th of January. I think it would be very interesting for you guys to attend this graduation. It's in department 113 of the criminal court building. If any of you are available, that is department 113 on the 11th floor of the criminal court building. There is going to be a graduation ceremony. Some of the speeches that graduates present are heartfelt, tearjerking. They will definitely touch you—the stories indicating where they come from and where they are at today. Some of the people have been through the worst of the worst. I listen to the stories every day. I deal with them on a daily basis. They come to me for advice. They come to me for direction. I'm not viewed as the enemy. Most people think of parole or probation officers as: "Oh, my God, this guy is going to violate me, he's going to put me back in jail." I'm primarily their liaison between the court and the drug-treatment provider.

With Prop. 36 it will be very difficult for the judge to give a defendant these conditions to comply by, or say: "attend drug treatment." How is he going to know that this individual is doing that? It is the probation officer's job, who is an officer of the court, to relay that information to the judge. So if I am not working very closely with the treatment provider and the court, I really don't know what's going on. So what is going to happen with all those additional staff that I mentioned to you: their job is going to be similar to mine. Right now, I am the only individual in LA County who has a job such as I described to you, okay? All the other deputies, pretty much, they work at their desks. They do a lot of data entry and they do a lot of violation reports. The defendants report to them at the office. Sometimes deputies will go out and do phone checks, job checks and things of that sort. Prop. 36 is definitely a good thing because it is going to thrust many more probation officers into a more personal interaction with the clients.

DAVE FRATELLO:

Because of the interaction that you've got, because you are the only person with this job, another statistic popped into my mind. One of the groups that opposed Prop. 36 with another couple of $100,000, was the prison guards union. And I happen to know their growth. In 1980 we had 8,000 prison guards in California. Since then we have built 21 new prisons and we have now 29,000 prison guards in California. Skewed priorities I think.

"AGENTS & ASSETS" CAST MEMBER IBRAHIM SABA:

Well, they can change their jobs to his. I think.

"AGENTS & ASSETS" CAST MEMBER WILLIAM WIGGINS:

Prop. 36—I don't know much about it. But from what I hear, is that it is opening up a door for the person that has been caught. Am I correct? He has been caught with the possession of drugs. But do you realize that it is closing the door for those people who have not been caught who want the same treatment? Do you know that a lot of programs are being closed down today because you guys are offering money to pay them to let the criminal in and not people such as myself who want the treatment but cannot afford it?

DAVE FRATELLO:

One aspect of this initiative that is important is that the money in this initiative: the appropriated $120,000,000 is required, constitutionally, to be above and beyond the current spending.

WILLIAM WIGGINS:

I'm not debating the program because I appreciate it. I know a whole lot of people that are in the criminal system that need it.

DAVE FRATELLO:

Given all the options that we could do, developing treatment on demand would be ideal. There is a lot of talk about this. And I have actually seen political leaders in the context of this campaign say: "we cannot go out there and advocate for more money for drug treatment. Everybody will think we are soft on drugs." Well, this initiative shows that this is what the public wants. There is some concern that I understand and appreciate that this is going to be choosing one type of population over another. The people cannot just walk up to a program. As it happens right now over the whole state, half of the people in these programs are voluntaries, they are not court referrals. That ought to persist. Plus, I think we are giving politicians a backbone to put more into the system for people who are not court referrals.

AUDIENCE MEMBER:

My question is threefold; what are the guidelines for treatment? I have been hearing a lot about going into various treatment programs. They could get into a program that might not have good treatment. So are there any guidelines to Prop. 36? Does it have to be an inpatient program or can it be outpatient?

What is the treatment modality that would be required, and how long is the program, in-patient or out-patient? And what kind of professional status would be required?

Dave Fratello:

If I summarize your question, it is: "What do you mean by treatment?" That covers all your questions. And I'll try to go through all of them if I can remember. First of all, the initiative taps into current laws and current practices as far as kinds of programs. It doesn't create special guidelines. It says that the programs have to be licensed and certified by the state. And that's an existing process.

Actually I can tell one about the people I'm dealing with in Sacramento, one that the state agency is now much more concerned with. Because they realize that the spotlight is on them now. The public just voted for treatment and if they weren't regulating as tightly as they are, they certainly are going to do it now. It's not my field. I cannot give you the blow-by-blow of what is required. I'm telling you though we are tapping into the existing system. Each county is in charge of creating the programs that they want, of funding the programs that they want in the community. So this is very much a localized decision; program by program by program.

The other issues of the qualifications of the counseling would fall under that as well. I do know that there are staffers who are counselors at programs, and then there are the people who actually have a counseling degree. There is a whole specialty social-work, health-care equivalent. It is a three-year program. You have to have at least a number of those certified professionals in a program to be licensed. So that goes back to the first issue. The initiative allows treatment to be up to 12 months of court-required time. And then there is also a probation of six months after care. And you can certainly speak to this, Eric. You may be outside of the formal treatment environment, but it is still a continuation of treatment and supervision. So it is a total of 18 months that can be required.

I guess the final issue is: one program is not the same for every single offender. One of the first things that is gonna have to happen for people coming into the system is a formal assessment. Is this a kid who was going to a party and got busted for smoking his first joint or is this a guy who is a hard core case, who has been using everything for years? So there is a range in between. This is something that the court system, especially the drug court has began to specialize in. This assessment: "Am I in the right system, am I in the right mix, to keep the person in the program?" And this system is going to grow. And the same thing is going to happen as in the probation office that is sort of the intermediary between the court and the treatment provider. The assessment teams are going to be growing as well and we try to match that up with the programs that are available.

ERIC NEWBY:

Just to add to what Dave was saying, one client may initially require some outpatient meetings. If they are not amenable to those meetings, they may be required to go to a residential facility. If that's not working, if they are determined "unamenable to treatment," they'll try a sober living facility. Different types of options.

I was speaking with Judge Tynan today and he was saying that where they are at right now is that they are going to be forced to be creative in dealing with their clients. Because they cannot just say, "We are going to give you 90 days in custody,

30 days in custody. When you come back, you'd better act right. This time. You use again, we're going to slam you back in jail." That is not an option any more. They are going to have to get really creative and exhaust a lot of the treatment options.

DAVE FRATELLO:

I just want to insert here that a person does face consequences when they repeatedly screw up. The term "unamenable to treatment" is actually a legally defined term in the initiative. If you reach a state where you violate it—you are not showing up at your program, or you have not taken it seriously, or whatever number of violations that you have compiled—the judge will determine you "unamenable to treatment" and that is the stamp that says you go to jail. You can be sentenced on that finding by the court, as you would today, which is one to three years. You can get some serious time.

"AGENTS & ASSETS" CAST MEMBER ROBERT CHAMBERS:

I think the proposition is a needed change because what they have had has not been working. What the current court system has been creating is just more misery, and more trouble and problems for people. They treat the drug addicts with the AA program, which was developed in the 1930s. And this is a whole new situation today; we have got crack cocaine, we got heroin, we got a whole lot of different drugs on the streets.

What I wanted to ask: is there going to be any funding for any new type of research for new drugs? I'm not talking about the old programs, but eventually I guess you are going to get to a point where you have to get some type of experimental programs. Are there any moneys coming forth for that?

Dave Fratello:

There is a lot of experimentation going on right now in the treatment community. And this is decentralized, what I mean by that is, each county can take the pot of money that they get from this proposition, and do whatever they want as long as it's drug treatment. And it's going to encourage new programs to come in, specifically on new drugs. There are researchers who believe that they have found drugs that can be given by prescription that will more quickly knock out the cravings, in the same way that the nicotine patch works for smokers. It's an interesting field. Nothing is ever going to be a silver bullet. A person can stop taking it and go right back to doing whatever they were doing, having treatment is hard.

Audience Question:

I want to go back to the prison guards and what many refer to as a prison-industrial complex. Do you see Prop. 36 as an effective remediation for the prison-industrial complex? And do you expect or anticipate any resistance from those who have a different agenda?

Dave Fratello:

We already have had some resistance. For anybody who does not know this already they are the biggest lobbyists next to the gambling Indians, $4.5 million in just one collection cycle. Do I see this effecting it? Yes. Is it going to drive a stake through the prison-industrial complex? Not yet. The projected impact of this on the prison system is one of the ways that you'll see an effect. Let's say an analyst looked at the people coming into the system and going back out of it and how many people it reached.

I mentioned 36,000 people a year which is their estimate of how many people were effected by this. And a lot of people are parolees who are in this endless cycle. If you get caught within the prison cycle you don't go anywhere. And this is 30,000-plus people a year that are in the prison system, that's six prisons filled with people that are failed parolees. If you take these people out, the legislative analyst says that you can have this huge reduction in parole case loads, you have fewer people are coming in. You have fewer people coming in through the back door. You are going to have fewer criminals. Right now the state is under the assumption that we need two new prisons to open their doors by 2003. One of those Gray Davis paid for with cash out of the budget, instead of out of the prison bond immediately after he was elected. So there is one more hanging in the balance. The second one now may not be put on line at all. And the constructors say, "Okay, maybe we have enough prisons for a while. We'll see how the influx of inmates continues." Three strikes is still there. But there are even district attorneys who are not fully enforcing three strikes, which is a good thing, as opposed to not fully enforcing Prop. 36, which I would consider is a bad thing. The actors in the system who have the most influence are the prosecutors and not the prison guards. The discretion that the DA has to charge someone can effect whether they qualify for Prop. 36, or not. So if they don't like a person they can pile on charges and the non-drug charges can make you ineligible for Prop. 36. You have to be convicted on these things, so it cannot be really without base. But there is a certain share, where a certain number of people who should qualify aren't going to because of a decision made by a prosecutor. Whether they are tied up with the prison guards specifically I don't know, but they all certainly got in the middle of the war on crime.

Los Angeles, Saturday, January 13, 2001

PANELISTS:

SANDRA ALVAREZ: Head of the Colombia Human Rights Program at Global Exchange

ALFRED MCCOY: University of Wisconsin, author of *The Politics of Heroin: CIA Complicity in the Global Drug Trade*

JOHN MALPEDE: Director, LA Poverty Department

PETER SELLARS: Moderator; Theater, Opera and Festival Director

JOHN MALPEDE:

The hearing of March 18, 1998 took place on the occasion of the release of CIA Inspector General Fred Hitz's investigation, Volume 1, "The California Story." It is the transcript of that open hearing by the House Intelligence Committee that I edited, and is the text of LAPD's "Agents & Assets." Volume 2, which was released six months later, and which documents extensive Contra drug-trafficking done with CIA knowledge and involvement of agency assets, was never given a public hearing.

PETER SELLARS:

I'd like to begin by thanking the performers in the previous episode. I, myself, would like to say how pleased I am to acknowledge my gratitude to the committee, for they have served their country. [*Laughter*] I understand they are all on to better things. Congratulations.

In fact, welcome back to the second part of this LAPD intervention. We're very, very pleased and actually honored to have two extraordinary guests. Alfred McCoy is really the leading scholar of drug wars. His book, 20 years ago, was pioneering in detailing CIA involvement particularly in Vietnam and Asia with drugs, not only dealing, but in cultivation, distribution and so on. And that book launched a firestorm and somehow failed to destroy a distinguished academic career. The book has come back in an expanded edition. It's really extraordinary to have with us someone whose research has begun to change the course of history.

And now, thank God, this issue has come up as a hot-button issue, finally. You know, I think it's one of those amazing things 50 years from now, people will ask: "What were people thinking?," that we were able to move in this period as if nothing was happening. And in any case, Alfred has been on this issue for quite a long time. I will ask him to share with us where this excerpt of testimony leaves off, and what is missing from this picture. It was directed quite beautifully by John Malpede to ask more questions than it answered. Then I also want to welcome Sandra Alvarez, with the Colombia Human Rights Division of Global Exchange, who has again been doing very courageous work involving personal testimony and engagement in the field of the question of the United States' new intervention in Colombia, the new escalation which, you know, in many ways is comparable to early Viet Nam days, a major, major, major initiative that has huge consequences, for this country and world politics and economics and the military reality. Now, that the Cold War Menace has been displaced by the Rogue Nation Theory.

First of all, Alfred, I'm wondering if you would speak about what's missing from this picture, what this committee failed to conclude from the evidence that was before them in this report and also in Hitz's report Volume 2.

ALFRED MCCOY:

Thanks, Peter. The way the transcript was delicately but judiciously edited really highlights what Hitz was trying to do. Inspector General Fred Hitz, the way he asked his questions, and in many ways the play is a dramatization from my perspective about questions: not so much about answers, but the way questions were asked, the way questions weren't answered. And so all of Hitz's questions were really focused on California. The report is just titled: "The California Story," and he's really trying to limit the inquiry to what happened just in the United States, indeed what happened with these three characters: Ricky Ross, Danilo Blandon and Norwin Meneses. On the other hand, the other members of the committee, particularly the character playing Juanita Millender-McDonald, is asking about what the United States did in the United States and then there's a comma, a very large comma, a slight pause "or elsewhere." And that "or elsewhere" is what the CIA was doing beyond California, beyond these three people, outside the United States. And all of the denials that the CIA made which were reported, and indeed the committee itself, this committee that we saw, really made statements about what happened in the United States, the relationship between the CIA, or the non-relationship between the CIA and these three drug dealers in California.

And indeed, later on the committee, whose dramatization we saw, wound up repudiating this series by the *San Jose Mercury News* arguing that there was no basis that the CIA was somehow involved in protecting these three California drug dealers. But if you look at paragraph 913 of Part 2 of the inspector general's report, paragraph 913, you find a very different story. In that report, Hitz, despite all his public denials of any impropriety of any description, actually went and did his job. And what he did was he examined the nature of CIA relationships with drug dealers in the Caribbean. And in that section, and then the paragraphs that followed—about 100 paragraphs—there's an incredibly detailed analysis, very well documented, with direct quotes from interviews with CIA agents, quotations from classified cables that were held in CIA headquarters, and what they described is the following: the CIA, for tactical reasons, formed a working relationship with Alan Hyde and the so-called "Bay Island Syndicate." The Bay Islands are a group of islands off the coast of Honduras, and they were strategically located for the CIA to ship arms down to the Caribbean from the United States and then ship them into Honduras and Nicaragua to provide them to the Contras.

So it happened to be that the kingpin—the smuggling kingpin of these islands—was a well-known criminal named Alan Hyde. In 1983, '84, and '85, the U.S. Drug Enforcement Administration and the U.S. Coast Guard developed detailed indications that Alan Hyde, who had 35 ships on the high seas, was a major smuggler of cocaine from Colombia, across the Caribbean to the United States. They made these reports to the CIA. So the CIA had intelligence indicating that Alan Hyde was a major-league drug smuggler into the United States. Nonetheless, in 1987 the CIA decided to form an alliance with Alan Hyde and for three critical years during the Contra War, 1987–1989, the CIA maintained this alliance with Alan Hyde. They used his warehouses and facilities in the Bay Islands to ship arms from the United States into Central America to support the Contras. Now, during that period as well, the CIA protected Alan Hyde from investigation by the Honduran authorities. And then there's one very interesting statement in the report, in 1992 in which the CIA states that they are going to block an investigation of criminal activity by Alan Hyde because this would prove embarrassing to the CIA and provide revelations about the Contra operation. In effect, what this report provides is incredibly detailed evidence ranging from field operatives in direct quotations and direct documentation, from field operatives of the CIA, all the way to the deputy director of the Central Intelligence Agency stating the CIA knowingly allied with a major drug smuggler, a major figure in the bulk shipment, not just $3,000, or $36,000 or $40,000, a major shipment, a man with 35 ships on the High Seas who's moving bulk shipments of cocaine from Colombia through the Caribbean to the United States. We knowingly allied with him and we knowingly protected him from an investigation during a critical period of the crack epidemic.

Now, what's significant about this, is first of all, it's right there on the website that Mr. Hitz very generously gave us. And I don't know if it's still there, but it was there, and I've downloaded it like all the other people that were interested in this case, and I read it and I didn't quit at paragraph, you know, one through ten. I went all the way through like anybody could have done, and there it was, in incredible detail. And I wrote an article about this. And I also looked at the press at the time. The *Los Angeles Times, The Washington Post, The New York Times,* all of the major media ignored this. They simply didn't report it. This was never reported; it never reached public consciousness. This congressional committee that we've seen did not investigate those allegations. They did not probe that.

Now, this is not an isolated incidence. What I've tried to do in my own work is show that through the entire period of the Cold War, from 1948 to 1990, particularly in Asia, the CIA mounted three covert operations, which involved serious long-term alliances with major drug lords. In the 1950s they allied with Nationalist Chinese in northeastern Burma, in the 1960s and '70s they allied with the Hmong hill tribe in northern Laos, in the 1980s they were allied with mujahideen in Afghanistan. In each case—Burma in the 1950s, Laos in the 1960s and Afghanistan in the 1980s—the CIA knowingly allied with powerful war lords who were simultaneously drug lords. The CIA during the previous alliance made no attempt whatsoever to, in any way, slow their involvement in drug activity. And third, as a consequence of the alliance of the CIA, each of these drug lords gained access to logistics, arms and political protection-above all, political protection. The kind you saw with Alan Hyde, the protection from investigation or prosecution. They gained, in effect, immunity, which allowed them to transform themselves from locally significant drug lords into globally significant drug lords. And this is a consistent pattern throughout the period of the cold war, a pattern that is contained within the Hitz report, but seemed to be too complicated for the American media or the American public to grasp.

PETER SELLARS:

The *Los Angeles Times, The New York Times,* and the *San Francisco Chronicle* all ran giant "kill stories," pleased to report that the *San Jose Mercury News* was entirely without any basis. Would you comment on how those "kill stories" see the light of day?

ALFRED McCOY:

The three "kill stories," they were all equally bad, but, they were all bad for different reasons. *The New York Times* "kill story" was bizarre, bizarre. What it said, essentially, was that African-Americans were subject to racial hysteria. That was their "kill story." That rumors of genocidal plots, of dark conspiracies against African-Americans as a group, have long been a part of African-American history and this is just the latest. That was *The New York Times* spin on the theme. That was a front-page story that went over to a full page. This wasn't just a throw-away remark, it was a detailed, long examination.

The Washington Post came out within six weeks of the initial *Mercury News* story. The *Mercury News* story came out late in August 1996. *The Washington Post* story was October. It was very dismissive and said that the story had no foundation, no basis, whatsoever. The *Los Angeles Times* story was, I think, the most troubling in a certain sense. It was a three-part series. It was massive. It started on the front page and spilled over not just to one page on the inside but several pages on the inside, and it made some valid points. I think that it established in certain areas that the *Mercury News* had been a little quick and a little sloppy in its reporting. But the *L.A. Times* was equally sloppy in their extended rebuttal. So I felt, overall, the rebuttal by the three major newspapers was badly done. But it did establish, I think, if you read them carefully, that the *Mercury News* story had problems. And I think we have to admit that.

My own feeling was that the *Mercury News* story made a lot of mistakes. My most important disagreement with it is that it focused on what, I think, even if accurate, is a relatively minor aspect of one particular CIA operation. By focusing on the CIA's supposed relationship with three drug dealers in California, it, in effect, ignored everything that was going on in Central America, and the much larger history of CIA operations in the both the Indian coca zone and the Asian opium zone, vast swaths of the globe with a history reaching back 40 years. So I think the story made some mistakes. I think, it more importantly overburdened the significance of this alliance, but in doing so, it provided a very useful service.

JOHN MALPEDE:

But could any story with that kind of content have withstood that kind of scrutiny by the national media? In other words, could the perfect story withstand the scrutiny of the national media?

ALFRED MCCOY:

The perfect story would withstand the scrutiny of the national media, but then it would be very quickly buried and forgotten. Okay, this is presumptuous, but let me tell you my own story. I did exactly the same thing that Gary Webb did, and I tried to do it in the mountains of Laos and Burma, in 1971. I went over to Southeast Asia and I marched around the mountains and I went to Hmong villages that were growing opium and I went to farmers and I asked them how much opium they were growing. I did a kind of agricultural extension survey of product, and the product happened to be opium. And I said: "Now how do you market your product?" Just like a sort of California Agricultural Extension Agent. I was going field to field. And they would say: "Well, we take it over to that landing pad, and these helicopters that say Air America—which is a CIA subsidiary—fly in, and officers in the CIA secret army get off and we sell them our opium." I went to every farmer in the village, I wrote this down and I had well-documented evidence that: 1), the Hmong, who were in the CIA secret army, were growing opium; 2), that the commander of that army and the commander-in-chief of the Laotian army were operating heroin labs; and 3), that they were shipping that heroin south to Viet Nam where at that point 34 percent—that is to say, a little more than one-third of all the U.S. Army soldiers serving in South Viet Nam—were heroin addicts.

So the consequences of this CIA complicity in the drug trade were very direct and immediate and I brought this story out. And it was on page one of *The New York Times,* basically because the director of covert operations at the CIA tried to suppress the book that I wrote. He personally went to the publisher and tried to suppress the book, which was extraordinary in itself. It came out in the media. I testified in front of Congress, in a committee rather like the one in the performance. My results were generally regarded as valid. And then there was the CIA inspector general, a predecessor to Fred Hitz. The office held by that incomparable figure conducted an examination of my charges. And I've only been able to read fragments of it in a later 1975 congressional hearing—the famous Church committee hearings on CIA assassinations.

Now, what happened in that report was that in the front part of the report, in the visible part of the report, the summary, it is stated that allegations about Air America, the CIA's airline carrying drugs in Southeast Asia were inaccurate. There was no basis for that. But, then in Volume 4 and 5 of that report, buried way back, in a comparable position to say, paragraph 913 [*Laughter*]—okay?—buried way back in that report were excerpts written by the CIA inspector general in 1971, who—after 20 interviews in the CIA headquarters and over 100 interviews in Southeast Asia—basically corroborated my charges that the CIA had been allied with drug lords and had done nothing to block their involvement in the traffic, and that they were fully cognizant of the nature of these alliances. They knew they were allied with drug lords and they knew these men were trafficking in drugs that were going to our troops. So, even if the information comes out as it did in my case, and even if there is a follow-up investigation, long after the klieg lights have turned off and the media have gone home, in those long, bureaucratic investigations, the CIA slowly grinds it down, manipulates, pressures, cuts deals and so it's discredited and forgotten.

PETER SELLARS:

Could we come right up to date, and Sandra, would you please give us a window into what is under way in Colombia at the moment—a very small bit of which has been reported in North America.

SANDRA ALVAREZ:

Sure. In Colombia, one has to know that there are actually two wars being fought there. Most people hear about the drug war and the U.S. involvement in the drug war in Colombia, but the reality is there has been civil war for many decades with roots going back the last 100 years. And so the introduction of the drug market has exacerbated the situation, but it is not the cause of the war in Colombia. The cause of the war in Colombia has economic and social roots, mainly because of things very typical to Latin America: the concentration of land ownership, inaccessibility to the political system and corruption. Colombia has long been called one of the most stable democracies in Central America. But that is really a farce, because if you don't belong to the two major parties, you have no room in politics in Colombia. In fact, it is not possible to develop a new party that is in opposition to Liberals or Conservatives, which is what a demobilized portion of the FARQ, a guerrilla group in Colombia, tried in 1985. Within five years about 4,000 members of that political party were killed. This party was wiped out. This is the government that we are supposedly supporting with drug aid.

Last June, Congress passed legislation supporting a large plan called "Plan Colombia" with $1.3 billion. Most of this is military aid, in the form of helicopters, training of elite narcotics units, advisors, fumigation equipment, etc. Since the USSR broke up and the guerrilla groups in Colombia lost support from the Soviets, they then have become more autonomous because of the inflow of narcotics money. They tax production in Colombia. As far as I know, they aren't traffickers. They tax production and protect the *campesinos* who have no other alternative but to grow coca, and this money has made them more independent. This money has also come into the political parties. You may have heard, about four years ago President Samper was accused have having accepted drug money in his political campaign for the presidency.

After the cold war, the U.S. has had to find different reasons to intervene in other countries. In Colombia, and in Latin America, in Mexico and other countries, the reason is the war on drugs. In this way, the large corporations that are very connected to our politicians are also able to use foreign policy to achieve their own goals. For instance, Occidental Petroleum has been trying for about eight years to drill on land of the U'wa, an indigenous group in northeastern Colombia. And they have lobbied the Colombian government and the U.S. government to support this effort. They testified at hearings in support of the aid package to Colombia, as did helicopter companies and Monsanto, who makes the chemical for fumigation. But, to date, the policy that the U.S. has been following, fumigation, has not been successful. Although they can give you number after number of how many areas have been eradicated by fumigation. The area cultivated in the last 10 years has multiplied by three, if I'm not mistaken.

This plays into the civil war, because the aid package that was been passed is focusing on the southern part of Colombia where the FARQ, the largest guerrilla group, has control of the territory. They say that they're going into the south because 60 percent of the drug crops are grown there, which makes sense, except that they don't say that the other 40 percent, 45 percent, or 50 percent is grown in the north, which is also where the processing labs for cocaine are found and which is also where the paramilitaries are in control. Paramilitaries are death squads that have been organized by landowners and narco-traffickers and even the military. The military are working very much in conjunction with the paramilitaries; the paramilitaries do the dirty work of the military. The north is where the paramilitaries have their stronghold and this is where Carlos Castano is. Keep his name in mind, because 20 years from now we'll probably be having another talk about U.S. involvement with Carlos Castano.

The way that the things are going, we're gonna be having hearings on the CIA, the DEA, about everybody's involvement with the paramilitaries in Colombia, because Carlos Castano comes from a family of large landowners that are known to be narco-traffickers. The U.S. agencies worked with him in the early '90s, in order to take out Pablo Escobar, who also was a notorious member of the Medellin cartel, until he was killed in December '93. To reward him for helping U.S. agencies, he came over with his family and had a day at Disney World. Another paramilitary leader was invited to go to the World Cup in '94. *The Philadelphia Inquirer*—in, I think, the end of October, November sometime—came out with a five-part series about the U.S.'s involvement with Pablo Escobar. They even had a series on the web called "Killing Pablo.com" with some of this information.

But the problem in Colombia is, even if this drug policy that has been a complete failure were to be successful, and were to eradicate coca in Colombia, it will pop up in other places. Peru and Bolivia used to be the main producers of coca. When they cracked down on Bolivia, it moved to Colombia.

Now we see paramilitary folks and other large landowners buying property in Ecuador. The Ecuadorian government is extremely worried about Plan Colombia. It was supposed to be an international plan to help Colombia, to stop drug trafficking, to strengthen the economy and the democracy in Colombia.

But for some reason the U.S. has become completely isolated, and this is because the U.S. has changed Plan Colombia and made it a tool for their own anti-drug policy. The aid package passed last June is a two-year part of an intervention that, as Barry McCaffery has said, will last at least six years.

We're going to be hearing a lot more about Colombia in the coming months, because in this legislation they included human rights conditions, which is why lot of people actually voted for it. But they also included a waiver, so the president can waive human rights conditions in national-security interests, which President Clinton did in August, and which he will do very shortly before he leaves office on January 20th. We'll just have to keep our eyes on that because it's the next big story.

PETER SELLARS:

We're kept in a media bubble, which rarely has us connect what we're buying or doing here, to where it came from, who made it and how did it get here. Coffee, sugar are very basic things which obviously are supporting the dictatorship of choice and which are in your body every day of your life, if you are an American citizen. And so the question of "pick your poison" and the question of understanding the amount of that poison that is circulating in some other part of the world, and dealing with the fact that it's a total ecology, is going to also be one of the next steps.

So, these performances are devoted to the ongoing catastrophe of the drug war after 25 years, a war that has not produced the announced results of any reduction of drug use in the United States. In fact, drug use is higher than it has ever been, after a 25-year war. So you would have to say well, something must be a failure in this drug war and yet, something else must be succeeding or else it wouldn't continue. And so the failure of the drug war is quite evident, the interesting question is then what is succeeding and for whom, and therefore why is it continuing?

Before we move into that, I'm wondering if Alfred would comment on this policy of eradication? I mean, one of the great things that the United States likes to do from time to time, is just announce something will be eradicated. And so we have zero tolerance, the idea that you can will it out of existence, and that a sufficient amount of force, violence and intolerance will solve the problem. Would you speak about eradication as a strategy and its history and its results?

ALFRED MCCOY:

Sure. In terms of recent history, the drug rar is actually now almost 30 years old. And we're in the fourth of a continuous succession of drug wars that began under President Richard Nixon in 1972–73. And I'd like to make two points about the drug war. The drug war has not succeeded, as you just said. But what I'd like to argue is that beyond its failure, the drug war has also compounded the problem. The drug war has not only failed, but it has made the problem worse.

Let me explain how that's happened. Back in 1972, the White House estimated, at the time they launched the drug war, that there were 1,000 tons of illicit opium produced in the world. Today, after 30 years and four drug wars, there are over 6,500 tons of illicit opium produced in the world. That's six-and-a-half times more than there were 30 years ago when the drug war started. And I would argue that to a considerable extent the increase in that production is a direct result of the drug war itself.

I'll give you two examples of how that works. Let's begin with the first drug war back in 1973. In 1973 President Richard Nixon declared war on the French Connection. (He went to the movies, and it was in the movies; there was a film with that same name.) The French Connection operated very simply. Turkey had a thing called the Turkish Marketing Organization. They produced legal opium for medical morphine. But the farmers in the Anatolian plateau produced above their legal quota, and they sold that to traffickers who then shipped it down through Lebanon to Marseilles, where it was manufactured into heroin and came into the United States and supplied about 80 percent of America's heroin supply. So President Richard Nixon pressured our NATO ally, Turkey—a mixture of carrot and stick, pressure and also a reward of $30 million—to wipe out opium. And since the Turkish government had a list of every single opium farmer (because they were all registered farmers in the Turkish Marketing Organization), in the space of two years, they completely wiped out opium production in Turkey.

It was 100 percent total victory in this first drug war. And that should have been history. Heroin should have disappeared from the United States. Well, it didn't work out that way. Why? Because, although Turkey provided 80 percent of our heroin supply, it only provided seven percent of the opium produced in an Asian opium zone that stretched for 5,000 miles from Turkey in the west to Thailand in the east. The metaphor that works—it's an awful metaphor, but I think it does the job—is the extended balloon. If you can imagine a great giant water-filled balloon astride the Eurasian land mass, if you press down on the Turkey end of the balloon, guess what? It pops up at the Thailand end.

Now, how did this happen in the world of economics? The global demand for heroin and opium was constant. Supply in one area went down; world price therefore went up. And farmers in the 93 percent of the Asian opium zone not affected by the drug war thus had a market incentive to increase their crop. Price was up, so they planted more. That meant, that at the end of the drug war, at the end of the drug war in Turkey, what happened? Heroin from Southwest Asia—which was no longer being consumed locally, because the G.I.'s had gone home—followed the G.I.'s home, and quickly filled the void.

Let me give you another, more recent example, in the 1980s. It was the subject of our play today. During the 1980s, the United States decided—actually we began this in the 1970s, having won the drug war in Turkey—we decided to fight it in Thailand. So as soon as that South Asian heroin began flooding into the United

States, Richard Nixon sent a team of 30 from the U.S. Drug Enforcement Administration with a war chest, a limitless war chest of funds, to Bangkok to cut the connection between Bangkok and America—to get that Southeast Asian heroin out of the United States. And they succeeded brilliantly. They put out bonus rewards. If you were a dealer in downtown Bangkok and you sold to a hapless American traveler, you could make money two ways: sell them the heroin and then dial this number, and turn them in. You get a bonus, a reward. So everybody that went to Thailand from the United States got their heroin real fast and got arrested real fast. And that cut the connection.

So what happened? The drug dealers in Thailand had two choices: they could either quit, or they could find a new market. So they began shipping to Europe. At that point, western Europe was largely heroin-free. By the end of the 1970s, within five years of the end of the Nixon drug war, western Europe had more heroin addicts than the United States. And they still do. Then the Europeans and the international community became interested in a global effort to eliminate opium production inside Thailand. And we all got together—the European community, the Canadians, the Americans and the U.N.—and we all worked together inside Thailand. And during the 1980s, we reduced Thailand's opium production from 140 tons to around 20–25 tons; from 140, down to 20 tons. Virtually eliminated. Great. Terrific. Another victory in the drug war.

Now that victory had two consequences. Inside Burma, there was a very powerful drug lord named Khun Sa, whom nobody here's probably ever heard of. At one point, by the end of the 1980s, he controlled half of the world's heroin supply. He's the lord of all drug lords, the most powerful drug lord that has ever existed. And between 1982–90, as opium production was dropping inside Thailand, this provided a stimulus inside Burma for increasing production. So production inside Burma went from 500 tons in 1982 to 2,500 tons by 1990. It went up 500 percent. Burma had a tremendous surplus of heroin. They began shipping this surplus to the United States. You've heard of "heroin chic"? You've heard of all the rock bands with heroin problems, the whole white youth culture that adopted heroin in the 1990s? Why? Because Khun Sa flooded the United States with Burmese heroin. The average purity of bags on the street went from six percent heroin to 60 percent, which meant you no longer had to shoot it—you could snort it or smoke it.

So heroin's demographics changed completely. Inside Thailand, what happened? Well, the local users that used to smoke opium couldn't get any more, because it had dropped from 140 tons down to 20 tons. So the only thing they could buy was heroin coming across the border from Burmese labs. Right? And what do they do? They used to share the pipe; now they shared the needle. Thailand today has one of the highest rates of HIV infection in the world, by far the highest HIV in Asia. And it all started with needle-sharing, as a direct result of this drug war.

So what's the upshot of thirty years of the drug war? More opium being produced in the opium zone from Turkey to Thailand, and more coca being produced in the Andes coca zone that runs from Colombia down to Bolivia. Moreover, more markets. Markets now in Russia, China, Western Europe, South Africa, the United States. That meant that there's an ever-more-complex cat's cradle of supply routes; that meant that snipping the French Connection, which we could do very easily with the War on Drugs thirty years ago, no longer was possible. It is beyond human control. The drug market is a vast global commodity that represents, according to the United Nations, eight percent of world trade. The traffic in illicit drugs, according to the United Nations, is now larger than the world trade in textiles. And if you think about that, what are the basic human needs? Food, shelter and clothing. The global trade in illicit drugs is now bigger than the global trade in textiles. I don't think that the White House would declare a war on textiles and expect to win. How can we declare war on illicit drugs and expect to win? We're using a crude, coercive mechanism to defeat a vast, dynamic, elusive, global commodity. [*Applause*]

PETER SELLARS:

Can we turn now from these large questions of statistics? How does that become personal? How are we dealing with it extremely close to home? In fact, nobody is a statistic. In fact, lives are on the line and have to be discussed as lives, have to be felt as lives, have to be understood as lives and not as percentages. John?

JOHN MALPEDE:

These last two nights we've had absolutely eloquent testimony from the cast after the presentation, and they have spoken to this, as have other members of the audience. The reason we decided to do this play is that we live in "the greatest democracy in the world." We know that—we're told that every day—and most people accept that as fact. So in presenting the House of Representatives hearing as a play, we didn't feel any need to tweak it in any way, other than to shorten the time of what goes on in the Congress of the greatest democracy in the world. And what's puzzling, and of great concern, is the extent to which citizens of this country are uncared for and uncared about. This fact surrounds us every single day, in this Skid Row neighborhood of course, but throughout the whole damned country. We're the only advanced country in the world without universal health-care, we have no functioning public transportation system. We don't even have clean, drinkable water in places like Appalachia. So there's a huge lot of brainwashed, hypnotized people in this country, and that allows for basic human needs not to be met, and for one-on-one caring for people not to exist.

Last night, Alexander, who played Mr. Lewis in the cast, brought this up really forcefully, by saying that no one cares for anyone from this neighborhood. Well, this is a socially contrived neighborhood. Up until recently, it was the place you went to when you didn't have anywhere else to go. It was a holding container, where you don't have to be Dick Tracy to find people shooting drugs, smoking crack, shooting heroin. Anytime, day or night, you can just walk down the street; there it is. So then how come the police can't figure this out? And the answer is: they don't care. They don't care about individuals living in this place.

The hidden truth is, the even-more-hidden truth about this neighborhood is—that over the last 15 years or so, there have been forces in the neighborhood working to create, to re-knit, the fabric of society within this neighborhood, and to establish connections between people. And to do it that so it's not just about beans and blankets, and it's not about charity; it's about creating conditions where people can actually live dignified lives, connected to one another, without a huge amount of money. Which is something that happens in a lot of places in the world, but in this country it's actually harder to do that than in most places in the world.

Many of the people in this cast are in the forefront of re-knitting that fabric, and they themselves have started arts and advocacy groups within the neighborhood, that at this time are really transforming this neighborhood. So these people are real agents of change in this neighborhood, but they are sort of invisible, because what we hear about is that there are people living in cardboard boxes.

That's what's seen as what this neighborhood is about. No one knows about the people who are living in modest but decent accommodations, which have been created by non-profits like SRO housing. And the drug recovery programs that do exist in this neighborhood, that have created the situation where people can actually take their transformed lives and continue to change the community.

People in the cast like Robert Chambers, who played Mr. Dixon, and Alexander, these people have been responsible for starting the Homeless Writer's Coalition, for example, which has been in the neighborhood for a long time and is really active in the neighborhood. Alexander also started—I think with some other people—Artists in Recovery. Tony Parker, with the dreads, is one of the active people in the Musician's Alliance in downtown. Musicians who live here teach others in the neighborhood to make music and they perform music. Mr. Hitz—when he's not being Mr. Hitz—is very active in LA CAN, the Community Action Network, which is an activist group that's been dealing with, among other things, the private security forces that have been hired by businesses in the neighborhood, and how they sometimes go beyond the law in enforcing private-property rights to the detriment of the people living here.

CAN is also looking at what's happening with gentrification in this neighborhood, the very elastic definition of affordable housing that's suddenly gone from housing for people who were previously homeless, to "affordable housing" for people who can afford \$1200, \$1300, \$1400–\$2,000 a month.

So this is really the untold story that's happening right here. People who are involved in these efforts are re-knitting a fabric that the drug war and other aspects of the larger, uncaring society have ripped asunder. People have come here, and they're re-creating community right here. And that's really what's going on right here. And that's the important thing here. [*Applause*]

PETER SELLARS:

I'd love to move into one topic that seems to be important in all of this. Constantly, the drug war and drugs in general is presented to the public in a completely legalistic framework of moral/immoral, legal/illegal, as if those are the only questions going on in anybody's life… or, indeed, that we all agree on those questions. This has been the topic that could not be discussed, except by the police officer visiting your junior high school class, and no one else was allowed to talk about this. And I think that something really is changing now. We're all grateful that Steven Soderbergh's movie "Traffic" is the third-biggest grossing film in America right now, which means that suddenly there's room for other viewpoints. The media has begun to open the space in the last week, and I think it's because of the Hollywood movie. And you can feel, obviously, with Proposition 36, an enormous breakthrough here in California. No one quite knows what it means. But it's at least a huge step from where we were and it's forcing a lot of official hypocrisy to have to re-examine itself and be re-examined.

At the same time, what I'm really missing in all of this, and one of the reasons why I think it's important that artists and cultural activists participate in this discussion, is the idea of "drug culture." Because it is a culture; it's actually many cultures. And yes, the paradigm has to move to a public-health paradigm and it's, of course, a health issue, a really important mental-health issue, and a physical-wellness issue. But it's a culture, and every society since the beginning of the planet has used hallucinogens in one form or another. So it's not going to be something that's just suddenly going to stop because we say so. There's obviously a much deeper human need and a much deeper set of human responses.

Some cultures have created ways in which it is regulated internally in the culture, among families, among people and in certain societies it's part of a wisdom and knowledge quest and process, which is understood and really regulated very profoundly by tradition, by what's handed down, by people taking care of each other, by understanding what this brings into your life. And what we understand so little of is the human mind, and being human, and what all is going on inside of us. And one of the things we understand the least about is all kinds of human needs, all kinds of human consciousness. What is there? And why have certain societies understood the importance of intoxicants used in certain ways and hallucinogens?

Anyway, I just wanted to talk about drug culture a bit, and the culture of it. It's a need in lots of ways, and sure it's a fad; but other, deeper, things are at work. And could we begin to recognize some of those, and where it comes from, and why people are reaching for it? And could we begin to look at that, and begin to get into a place that is way beyond anything you can make laws about? A place that is about just being with other human beings who are really needy in one way or another, are really searching in some really deep way, and are reaching towards what they perceive is available and helpful in a difficult situation?

John Malpede:

Robert, why don't you introduce yourself?

Robert Chambers:

I'm Robert Chambers, President of the Homeless Writers Coalition and part of the LAPD today. Most of the people in my community are kind of forced into that culture and the expansion of the culture now is the problem. We're talking about drugs as an epidemic, but we haven't ever taken the resources to attack the problem as a real epidemic. I guess that's because of the profit that's involved. But what they turned loose is... you know, they opened Pandora's box. Originally, it came to South Central, to the ghetto, but now you see the suburbanites taking on the gangster culture. It's not drug culture *per se* as it was in the '60s; it's a gangster culture now. They're wearing penitentiary clothing. They're doing drive-bys in suburbia.

So, we do have an epidemic. We have a real problem. We really need to research the systemic values of where this is coming from. Can we reverse it? I don't know whether we can, at this point in time. It's so predominant. Here at Skid Row, I lose about four or five people—acquaintances that I know—to overdoses of heroin and cocaine every year. All these people I know and I've lived with and I've been down here for about 15 years.

So, to us and to the Coalition—we've always talked about it until we're hoarse, and we try to get people to listen— there are things happening here and people trying to reach out like the LAPD and even the bigger social service organizations like SRO Housing, are trying to do something. But it's nowhere near what's needed to handle the problem systemically. [*Applause*]

"AGENTS & ASSETS" CAST MEMBER ALEXANDER ANDERSON: My name is Alexander, and I'm one of the founders of the Homeless Writers Coalition and I've been down here a long time and I recently founded another organization entitled "AIR." That stands for "Artists In Recovery." And, I'd like to say something about the topic that the gentleman with the beads [Peter Sellars] was talking about—about the drug culture, right? I'm a recovering drug addict. I've got five-and-a-half years off of drugs and alcohol. [*Applause*]

But I noticed that America is a drug culture. When I was born, drugs were already here. When I started growing up, it was something that you just do, just automatic. You start hanging out with the homeys, and they start drinking, and somebody pops up with a joint, and then somebody's got some red devils. "Oh damn, what's that?" "Right?" "Oh, okay, cool." High is cool. Right? I didn't know that high was "bad." It's like... America is like a major drug culture. Because they got coffee, that's a drug; cigarettes, that's a drug; alcohol, that's a drug. Right? And they sell all those, all these drugs, and get people strung out and their lives all discombooberated. [*Laughter*]

And then, they've got hard-core drugs: heroin and PCP and cocaine. And people get entangled in these hard drugs. I was one of those people. I never thought or dreamt that my life would get all entangled in cocaine and PCP. I thought it was like weed. You know, you can just smoke a joint and put it down, and then you be high and go to the library and walk around, kick it, and philosophize, talk about stuff that don't even exist. You know? [*Laughter*]

But when I got with the cocaine, even with PCP—before cocaine actually got to the black community, it was PCP. Everybody smoking sherman sticks and angel dust, and you know, getting stuck to cars and can't get off of the car, and thinking they can fly and running down the street butt-naked, and all that type of stuff, right? [*Laughter*]

It was before cocaine flooded the market, flooded the black community. I don't know about no other community but the black community, because that's the only community I lived in, right? I went to the other community, but I didn't live there, you know what I'm saying? I went there and stole shit. [*Laughter*]

I've always been industrious, right? I had a carpet business. I go buy me a $10 stick of sherman, I could sit back in my chair and smoke the sherman stick, then zonk out, hallucinate. Then I come to and I still got a pocketful of money. I could go over there and start shampooing carpet, administering carpet and the rest.

But when crack came, you had to keep running back-and-forth, back-and-forth, back-and-forth. That was a whole new thing, a whole new situation. So now that I see all this and I realize, all this happened to me, I sit back and I look and I say: "Damn. Where did my dreams and my ambitions go? Where did my hopes go?" So now the people trying to get off of drugs, and the people still on drugs, their hopes and their dreams have been cracked. That's why, I think, they call it crack. Cause all of their hopes, and their dreams, and their ambitions, just cracked up. Then they forgot about them.

So now we're trying to recover, we're trying to recover from drugs. So the people that provided the drugs to us, they should try to recover, too, right? Yeah, cause, we can't get the drugs if they don't put them in the community, right? So now that we're trying to recover off the drugs, I think that it's good what the people, what the courts are trying to do with this Proposition 36. Instead of trying to send people to jail, send them to the drug program. Because they're not bad people, they just got caught up with some bad things. But you got bad people selling drugs. Those are bad people that sell drugs to the good people that just got caught up.

I'm talking about using for five, 10, 15, 20 years, right? I mean, you're like a professional addict, right? You got a career going. I'm a career drug addict. Damn. You're in pretty deep. All your money, everything, gone. So, now, you got to regroup. You have to try to get back to first.

It's like this. Here's a good analogy: say you got two cucumbers right over there. If you dip one of those cucumbers in a gang of chemicals for a long period of time, it's going to change the chemical makeup. It's going to become a pickle. So, these people have changed, right? They're not the same no more. They're thinking that they're normal, but they're not. Because once you've become a pickle, you can't go back to a cucumber, right? [*Laughter*]

And they don't want to see, like, that's part of the problem with the rehabilitation, with helping these people that's been victimized by the drug culture. Because I think they're victims; I been victimized, right?

Because I'd like to thank John, who's my dear friend, I just met him putting this show together, and all the other people that's on the cast of LAPD—that showed me love, right? Because I didn't know a thing about acting. They gave me a chance. This is my first time ever in acting. They coached me and they nursed me and they helped me. They showed me love. So I want to thank them, because they helped me bring part of my cracked dream back to reality. [*Applause*]

So I think that they're doing a great job, But I have to also realize myself that I'm not a cucumber no more. See? I'm one of those pickle people, right? Yeah. So we have to try to look at like the recovery of the people that's been victimized by these drugs. Those are the people that we really have to try to help: the innocent people. So being a drug culture, we have to realize that—I think, myself, personally—that the government is like the enemy of the people. Some kinda way, cause how, like the young lady said the other day, how can the police spot a itty-bitty marijuana plant on the top of her roof, and you got boat-loads of cocaine coming in and they can't see that? So something is not right with that picture. So it's like the powers that be are sabotaging the American people. You know, and that creates a drug culture. This is a drug culture, right?

Now, me, myself, I don't… I don't drink alcohol. I don't smoke weed. I don't smoke cocaine. I don't smoke PCP. And my life is better. But it's a struggle everyday to try to maintain that, and to not get caught up in another drug culture, running back and forth to the recovery program. You know, I mean that's a culture to itself. "I can't make it without a drug program. I got to run to the drug program. The drug program. The drug program." And that's just another form the government cooked up to make money off of people.

So it's an ongoing struggle, and a battle, to try to figure out all this stuff going on. Because drugs is not going to never go nowhere. Cigarettes ain't going nowhere. Alcohol ain't going nowhere. Cocaine ain't going nowhere. None of that stuff ain't going nowhere.

So, to me, it's like, we the people—not the government—have to get together and build forces amongst ourselves to fight against the enemy—who is the government. And let them know that we're not taking this no more. We're not going for this.

Because you're destroying our lives, our personal lives.

See, because this is my personal life at stake. I don't know about nobody else. All that other stuff you was talking about—drugs over here and switching drugs and making heroin chic and turning expensive cocaine into itty-bitty little rocks that you could afford—that's affecting me and you and everybody. The people being affected by it are the American people. By this drug culture that the government, that the society then hooked up, all for the sake of money.

See, so the situation's so big and I'm a talkaholic, so I can talk all the time. I just wanted to say that, right? You know what I'm saying?

PETER SELLARS:

Alexander, it's great you're just warming up. I can feel that you're just getting warm, Alexander. While you're going, because you're coming into it now, since you're there, right there, please: "Artists In Recovery" is a pretty major thing to call your project. That's really powerful, and just the way you're using the word "recovery"—I'd just like you to link it to the word "artist," and just like you to say what that organization's about, because to me, one of the most interesting things is the word "recovery." It implies you could be a cucumber again. You know? Right? I mean, it's not only about "recovering" something, but actually more what life is actually about, which is that every single day our lives are being transformed. We are being changed every day, whether we want to or not, or whether we notice it or not; and then sometimes that transformation can be really, really powerful.

And so I just was wondering if you'd talk a little bit about that, that part of recovery. Cause you know, you're okay, you're not a cucumber, but you're not a pickle the whole rest of your life either. That's an interesting thing, you know? Like, what is that step? And to me one of the interesting reasons artists are getting involved in a real way is because a social program can only do so much. An official program by the government can only do so much. In fact there's so much more that makes a person's life. And there are all these other factors that our society has made invisible. But actually, in most societies, they are the most important part of most people's lives.

ALEXANDER ANDERSON:

Okay. "Artists In Recovery" is an organization that I founded because I see a need, because I'm an artist and I'm in recovery and the only thing that the recovery facilities have for artists or for anybody that's trying to get into recovery or get sober, is to go to meetings, and parties. That's it. That ain't no kind of cultural event. And culture is a part of the human makeup. You need culture, right? People who are like normies, they go to plays, they go to operas, they go to movies, they go skating, they go do all kinds of stuff, culture-type events, right?

But the people that get all discombooberated on drugs, their minds, and their lives be so tore apart, just ripped apart, right? When they go to recovery, they're willing to believe anything anybody tell them. Whatever you tell them in the drug program they gobble it up like Pac-Man. And they believe it. Cause everything else, they just been annihilated as a person, just like an H-Bomb just dropped on your spirit. And you go there for help, cause they tell you, you got to go to these meetings, and the only else as far as culture is concerned is a party every now and then.

And then I seen the need, because there's a lot of people that's trying to get their lives together that are artists. And for artists you need to—you need to practice your craft, whatever your craft is. Like, I'm a poet. I write poems. And I do artwork, abstract art. So if I'm not manifesting that, then I feel a void in my life. Even though I'm clean and sober, I'm not fulfilling my heart's desire. I'm not fulfilling what I feel like God put me on the planet to do. So I say, well, damn, we need to get some kind of poetry reading going on around here or get some kind of art going for therapy for the recovering people. You know what I'm saying? Because art is therapy.

So we came up with this organization "Artists In Recovery" as a vehicle for the people that's in recovery to express their creativity. To get them back to their dreams and their hopes and their ambitions. Because before you got hooked up on drugs you got spun out, you might have been a guitar player or a writer, an actor. Then you got on the drugs and all of a sudden you just sit around in Bay Station Zero; that's like a big old house where everybody's smoking dope. That's all you doing, smoking dope, pushing your pipe and looking on the ground and doing all this way-out, bizarre stuff. And then the next day, art and poetry and music just vanished. You're so far gone, now you're walking around the street in the rain trying to push a basket, trying to find a $2 hit; and here you was a prolific artist, a painter or something, right?

So I believe that when people are getting off of drugs and alcohol, or any kind of drug dependency or any kind of addiction, they need to find out what they loved and liked to do in the form of art. Cause everybody has some kind of something they liked to do. And anything you take to the highest level that it can go to, is an art form.

So everything in life is an art. Conversating is an art. Listening is an Art. Yeah, see? So people need to get back to that, to fill that void inside of them. And where the "recovery" part comes into that, a lot of times people think just because you're sober, that you're recovering. You're not. You're just sober, right? You could get sober in an accident. Just, you know, wake up and you're sober. It doesn't take any great mystery to do that. It doesn't take any effort to do that.

But recovery is abstinence plus change. The trick is not getting sober, the trick is staying sober. So, you got to let people know that there's something wrong with your mind, because how come this stuff has tore you up back yesterday. Now, two days later you think, "Well, a nickel hit won't be that bad." Something ain't right with your thinking. So it's not getting sober, it's staying sober.

So recovery is abstinence plus change, right? I have to change my old behavior. I can't be doing the same things I been doing while I'm sober. So that's recovery, right. Alright, so, that's what AIR is trying to stress to the people, to the artists is that: "Look. You got to stop trying to run, control and dictate and dominate other people's lives. You gotta stop being a problem." Cause people using drugs is a problem. They're problematic people. I got $5, I'm gonna go buy a $5 hit. Now, what am I gonna eat? I start a problem for myself. So, naturally I'm gonna start a problem with you. So I gotta stop being a problem.

Once I stop being a problem and I stop telling lies and gossip and slander and all this kind of stuff, then I'm on my way to recovery. Cause anything that's worth having takes a lot of work. And if you really want to get off of drugs, stay off of drugs, you gotta put in a conscious amount of work. Cause yeah, it took a lot of work to get loaded. Believe me, cause when you run out of money, you gotta come up with all kinds of ingenious ideas on how you're gonna get some more money, get some more dough. It's a lot of work, see?

So that's the concept about AIR. Not only do we want you to be sober, we want you to recover, too. So that's the whole concept: to get off the drugs and alcohol and to change my behavior while I'm off the drugs and alcohol. [*Applause*]

PETER SELLARS:

Hey. Thank you, Alexander. Wow!

ALEXANDER ANDERSON:

Hey, I am outta breath.

TIMOTHY BROTS:

My name is Timothy Brots and I'm a professor and playwright from Orange County. And the last time I was down here in LA was in August for the Democratic Convention. I got attacked by the cops down in the subway station, so I wanted to say it's good to be here with a different "LAPD." [*Laughter*]

So my question is for Professor McCoy: how serious do you think the U.S. government is with actually stopping the flow of drugs from Colombia? It seems like if they were really serious, they wouldn't be sending money to fund a group like the military and paramilitary who are just as involved as anybody in Colombia. It seems to me it has more to do with justifying military spending and supporting helicopter companies that need to sell helicopters and maybe even helping Al Gore's favorite oil company. So how serious do you think it is?

And I was struck with the comparison you made with their Nixon Administration and their success in Turkey. It seems like they may have been more serious. Do you think that is the case?

ALFRED McCOY:

That's a difficult question that I can't answer definitively. I can't say yes or no. I can put forth an opinion. First of all, the prohibition of drugs has been official government policy, really, throughout the 20th century. The Prohibition Unit of the Treasury Department was established in 1920, and that was for alcohol and there was a drugs unit of the Treasury Department. And in 1932 we got rid of the Prohibition Unit for alcohol and kept the drug part. Initially, from 1920 through the 1950s, we kept it as a domestic solution.

And what was distinctive about the Nixon era, was that he took this idea of extirpating or eliminating drugs domestically and then combined it with foreign policy, using a military metaphor, to create the "drug war." The drug war is, in effect, the combining of diplomacy, intelligence and military operations abroad to eliminate the supply, and the smuggling of narcotics into the United States. And then the metaphor has under subsequent administrations been elaborated and applied to the domestic situation.

So that we've had a kind of militarization of narcotics policy and a militarization of law enforcement over drugs in the country. Now it's fairly embedded in our foreign policy and our domestic law enforcement policy and our domestic social policy. It's so deeply embedded that it's simply a choice for each administration: yes or no, whether or not they're going to do it.

The Clinton administration faced that choice; initially they wavered. They thought about undoing the drug war and going back to what was traditional Democratic policy, instead of having a military metaphor of a drug war, they had a curing or treatment metaphor of treating and dealing with the drug problem domestically. So it's right there. It's well-established as a U.S. foreign policy.

If George W. Bush signs on to it, he will embrace a policy that reaches back 30 years. He will fight the fifth American drug war. Now, the way that war is fought, yes there is a cynical, bureaucratic element to it, indeed. And internationally that involves helicopter companies; it involves major U.S. government agencies seeking a new mission after the cold war. For example, the Central Intelligence Agency was created in 1948 to fight the cold war as a kind of counter to the Soviet intelligence agency, the KGB. Well, the cold war is over. And the CIA has survived. Its bureaucratic logic is gone. It needs new missions. The defense department again fought and won the cold war.

We should be shrinking our military far more rapidly than we are. So the defense department is eager for new missions to justify its bureaucratic existence. So it's a mixture, I suppose, at an executive level, of a policy that's continued for supposedly idealistic reasons that really survives I think through these rather cynical bureaucratic maneuvers.

PETER SELLARS:

Sandra, would you also comment on that?

SANDRA ALVAREZ:

Mainstream politicians that devise these programs are thinking about all those bad people that are doing drugs. They are making a moral argument that everyone's bad, and in the same way in Colombia and other countries, that the people that grow the drugs are also considered evil.

I think we have to be careful when we talk about the war on drugs, because, for example, there were members of the

Black Caucus that wanted to send aid to Colombia, because they didn't want the drugs to come into their communities. But that means they weren't thinking about who were the victims of the drug war in Colombia. Why are their *campesinos* addicted to growing coca? We are supporting their death and the destruction of the ecosystem in Colombia. And so when we're talking about the success of eradicating opium in Turkey, I'm very curious to know what were the consequences of that success? How many people had to die in Turkey in order to wipe out all of those drugs? I think it's really, really important to keep that in mind, because one of the problems is that we tend to think only of our own country or think only of ourselves here.

But the drug war is affecting the people of Colombia, too. In Colombia, there are two million displaced people inside the country that no longer have a place to live or work or make money or anything like that. And of those displaced people, about 70 percent are Afro-Colombian. People don't even realize that from a quarter to a third of the population of Colombia are of African ancestry. And so there are a lot of racial elements to this drug war, not only in the United States, but also in Colombia.

So when we talk about making changes, I think we really need to broaden our minds and think beyond our own borders. We also need to think beyond our own communities, because if we're living in a suburb, then we might be thinking about cocaine or we might be parents thinking about their kids doing ecstasy in a club. But we all need to be thinking about what are all the different types of drugs that are affecting all of our people.

And so we have to broaden the struggle, to cut across all of these lines to think of all the people that are being affected. And I just want to remind us that it's people in Colombia, it's people in Turkey and Thailand, people in the United States and that's where we need to make our connections and our allies and our coalitions, because the government is not listening to us. It's almost like the government is an enemy of the people. So then we have to go beyond our government. And when we're talk about the movie "Traffic," bringing information about the drug war on the mainstream, then we should notice who else has been doing this?

There have been people working on drug policy for a long time. Al McCoy's been writing on the drug war for a really long time. Just last fall, there was a conference, Students For Sensible Drug Policy, which was just unbelievable in Washington, D.C. There are numerous organizations and mobilizations around drug policy that have manifested in Proposition 36, etc., etc. So I see a lot of hope, but I think we just have to remember to think creatively and connect ourselves with other people. Sorry to digress. What was the original question?

PETER SELLARS:

Well, about the U.S.' motives in this Colombia adventure. Is that serious? Does the United States really think it's going to, or are there other motives?

SANDRA ALVAREZ:

There are many motives for the U.S. going into Colombia, and in continuing the drug war, because it supports a lot of agencies in the United States, etc., but also the other benefits of going into Colombia and controlling Colombia, including oil. Ever since the Persian Gulf, the United States has turned more attention to the northern region of South America. Venezuela has large deposits of oil. Colombia has huge deposits of oil, specifically in the south, where the aid package from the

United States is being focused. Also, Colombia is a very strategic region. It has coasts on both the Atlantic and Pacific oceans. And it's the fifth country in the world in terms of potential for hydroelectric power. So there are many mega-projects, infrastructure projects that are being built in Colombia and that are being planned for areas that have been traditionally populated by indigenous peoples, Afro-Colombians and *campesinos,* who are all being displaced by paramilitaries. Paramilitaries that are supported by the military, and that are going to be supported with this "drug aid," supposedly in the name of drugs, but really in the name of economics.

So we're going to see even more displacement than what we've been seeing. Last fall, I saw an article saying that there's 1,000 people a day leaving Colombia. A lot of them are coming here, and people like Diane Feinstein are really worried about Colombian refugees coming into California. They don't want them here. So oil, mega-infrastructure projects, other natural resources like gold and uranium —and water is really important.

And also there are proposed transportation and communications infrastructure projects they're trying to build in Colombia. They're trying to build a major road from Venezuela to the western coast of Colombia in order to help trade and product get from South America to Asia. They're also trying to build another canal, similar to the Panama Canal. They've been working on it for a while, but they're not sure if it's going be a dry canal or a wet canal joining two rivers. It's just below the Panama Canal. It's an area that is mostly indigenous and Afro-Colombian, and it's also been a major area of contention because there's a lot of drugs and arms traffic through that area. That's in the northern part of Colombia, which the U.S. is not focusing on, because their allies, the paramilitaries, are there right now.

Also, because of the situation in countries surrounding Columbia, like in Venezuela with the leftist President, and Ecuador with the indigenous uprisings, and in Peru there's instability, the U.S. has a lot of reasons to want to go into Colombia and control that area. The defense ministers of South America have met and are very concerned with the aid package that the U.S. has just passed, because it is going to destabilize the equilibrium that has been set with the different militaries of the region. Brazil is very concerned with that, because of all the resources in the Amazon that the U.S. has clear interest in. So there are many reasons besides drugs to get into Colombia.

PETER SELLARS:

Somebody coming to the mike?

AUDIENCE MEMBER:

I just have a comment, since I think a lot of us have experience in both issues of poverty and violence. One of my concerns is that there's been sort of a lack of connection to the gun trade that is attached with the drug trade. And these wars, as Professor McCoy has pointed out, have been going on essentially since Viet Nam.

But, what I would really like to do is to thank the LAPD for hosting this event and bringing us together, and for raising these concerns about addiction to violence and to drugs and consumerism. And that really the antidote is community and art and culture.

And I think one of my concerns also has been the culture we are exporting to other countries, because that culture is now manifesting itself in El Salvador and Nicaragua and Colombia. And, I'm really appreciative that we have this forum to discuss these issues. But in addition there's this culture that can also be built of community and care and concern and information. [*Applause*]

AUDIENCE MEMBER:

Hi. My name is Eric, and I also appreciate the forum that you've given us, and the broad context for the problem, and I just want to comment on the play itself, and then possibly on what Peter asked about. I hadn't thought about our human need for transcendence, and that's one element of the drug experience.

Having said that, what struck me about the hearing was that the hearing was supposed to get at truth, so we can have truth, and what they did was to create a contrived truth. And that contrived truth kind of lends itself to—people call it a corporate culture—but a culture kind of based on a "use any means to gain whatever your particular end is and then scrub or erase the rest." And we don't get at the truth, because we have this other kind of corporate truth that's eclipsing our living truth of who we are and what we want to be.

And so this was gratifying, to see in a way that we could kind of, just get anchored with it. And also to realize that the solution is human culture that takes more into consideration.

Alexander has a remarkable imagination and we are complex beings with imagination that we long to express. For all the international machinations, it feels like that the drug war is a war on ourselves and it's almost… it's something that big. We're not acknowledging a whole aspect of ourselves and it becomes an ax that we're axing ourselves with. That's my thought. [*Applause*]

PETER SELLARS:

Yes.

Audience Member:

A few years ago I heard on the radio a show about coca leaves and the history of its use, particularly in the Andes, and they talked about the farmers and working at high altitude and how the coca leaves made that possible, where it would almost be impossible. And they talked about how many chemical elements there are in the coca leaves, and what they do and that they aren't all negative to the body. So it seemed to me symbolic of what our culture does: to take one element out of context, refine it up and use it as means of profit.

If you look at the history of salt, also salt was always either from mines or came from the sea. It came with minerals. It was inconsistent in the amount of salt, but there were other things that came with it. And the industry came along: "Well, we need consistent product." So they boil it and now it's NaCl and now lots of people have illnesses exacerbated by salt. There seems to be some obsession in our culture to take things out of context, and it seems to me that that may be the clue as to what we need to bring it back.

I think what Alexander was talking about—working with art, not just meetings—is a way for a recovering person, a context. It seems to me, although I don't have a solution, that putting technology in the context of the planet earth, putting people in the context of the earth, is something that needs to be a big part of any solution. [*Applause*]

John Malpede:

I just wanted to say that I think that art is a really important thing for a full life, etc., but I want to make it clear that it's not in any sense a substitute for a recovery program, or what goes on in 12-step programs. There's a huge profundity in that, and art is no substitute for that.

RICK MANTLEY:

This is my second stint with LAPD. I became involved with LAPD before I became involved with the Los Angeles Community Action Network or the Homeless Writers Coalition. I just happened to be at the right place at the right time. And, you know, this is the only cultural organization that allows a person untutored, practically ignorant about the acting profession or how to act, and you can walk in off the street and as long as you're willing to commit yourself, they'll take you in. They don't demand you be a professional, they just demand that you have a commitment. So, I'm very grateful for that.

PETER SELLARS:

Well, I think that we probably have to wind things up. Could I ask for just one last, parting comment from each person here?

SANDRA ALVAREZ:

I just want to say I have learned a lot in these last two days from being here, and I want to thank you John and Julia for organizing this. I got a lot more from everyone here than I think I gave out, so I came out winning. So I hope to continue to see everybody and I'm in it for the long haul. And it's a very personal thing, as I hope it is for everyone here. I look forward to working with all of you to make this better.

ALFRED MCCOY:

I think as we've learned in the discussions in the last few days, the debate over the drug war is over. Drugs is another issue. As all the comments have indicated on multiple levels, at a deep philosophical, spiritual level, drugs is a complex issue. It has to do with the structure of the human brain, one of the last frontiers of our knowledge. So we don't understand drugs.

But with the drug war, I think we finally come collectively to an understanding. So beyond Barry McCaffrey, who is now retired, there is probably nobody left in the United States that is really willing to stand up and defend this policy. The debate at an intellectual, philosophical level over the drug war is over. Nobody defends it. The question is, then, how do we get rid of it?

And I think that's why the initiative in California is so fundamentally important, because I think that this can be the unraveling. One of the geniuses of the federal system is that we do in fact have 51 governments in this country, and when the second largest government in the United States ends the punitive, the key part of the drug war, incarceration for personal use, then the rest of it will unravel very, very quickly. When California decides to end mandatory incarceration for personal use of drugs, the drug war will be over. The other 50 governments will soon follow. [*Applause*]

JOHN MALPEDE:

Well, I'm very glad to hear such a hopeful prognosis. And actually David Fratello, who was here the other night, cited other such instances, like in Oregon, they made a Constitutional Amendment, so that it's no longer legal, they can't seize your property just because you were suspected of committing a drug crime. But actually, in a less optimistic vien, I was going to pick up on what Sandra said earlier describing Colombia: "Two Parties. No Room."

Public Conversation

Detroit, 2002

"If our society's policy isn't based on how do you deal with someone you care about who's taking drugs, then our drug policy is how to deal with people you don't care about—and probably about how to deal with people you hate, you demonize, you're willing to shoot, you're willing to put in jail and everything else. And that's why we have the drug policy that looks like the one we do, right? And that's a serious problem." —Audience Comment

Detroit, October 2002

When we first did "Agents & Assets" in LA in 2001, during the weekend of the performance events, we were so energized by those that I said to Julia Carnahan, who had worked closely with me to produce those events, that we should continue the project. This impulse coalesced in the idea of traveling

"Agents & Assets" to other cities and states, specifically to cities where drug-reform initiatives were projected to be on the ballot, the thought being that the production would contribute to the public discourse around drug policy.

From 1989–1994, LAPD had done a series of residencies billed as "LAPD Inspects America," where we would go to another city and work with a variety of arts and social service organizations—each set-up being different— and make an improvised show from scratch in three to six weeks with a combined cast of LAPDers and homeless people from that city. The resulting show would be a snapshot of homelessness and the issues surrounding homelessness that were first and foremost in the lives of homeless people in that city. We pulled many rabbits out from many hats as we conducted residencies in Miami; Philadelphia; San Francisco; San Diego; Chicago; Minneapolis; London; Amsterdam; Helena, Montana and more.

We decided to travel "Agents & Assets" as a residency project, because it would maximize community involvement in the performance and public conversations. We also decided that we wanted to work with drug-recovery programs and find the local cast among recovery-program participants. We'd previously worked with recovery programs in Miami and consistently for four or five years in Los Angeles. We knew that often times you can go miles in minutes in performance work with people in recovery, because of the openness that is part of the recovery process. We also wanted to make the link between people actively concerned with recovery, program participants and staff, in a conversation with policy-reform advocates and with the community at large.

Buzz Alexander and Gillian Eaton, friends from the Ann Arbor-based Prison Creative Arts Program, suggested I contact

Ron Allen, a poet and playwright who was producing events at the First Unitarian Church on the edge of Detroit's Cass Corridor, Detroit's version of Skid Row LA.

Ron Allen—an African-American, a veteran, a Buddhist monk in training, and a 10-year recovery veteran—was engaged in teaching writing and self-esteem workshops for men at three central Detroit recovery organizations. The residents and staff of one of those programs, Mariner's Inn, became the cast members for "Agents & Assets" in Detroit. Sobriety House and Neighborhood Recovery Services (NRS) also participated in the project. Their participation included the insightful participation of staff members in our community conversations: Jim Grimmett from Sobriety House and Chris Parks, the director of NRS.

The treatment versus incarceration reform initiative in Michigan never made it to the ballot; it was bumped off on a technicality. Though we'd scheduled our residency to coincide with the run-up to the election, we learned that some things are beyond our strategic planning. Nevertheless, though the initiative went away, the issues it addressed did not, and in fact, were more visible due to the controversy surrounding the disqualification of the ballot initiative. Shortly after the election, many of the objectives of the initiative were achieved in the Michigan State Legislature, through a package of bills sponsored by Rep. Bill McConico.

With strong community contacts, recovery community contacts and strong contacts with policy reform advocates, we were able to construct a dynamic residency and series of events. Several of the events addressed the impact of the war on drugs on the people of Detroit, 90 percent of whom are African-American.

— **John Malpede**

Topic:
The War on Drugs, The Effect on Our Community, and on The African-American Community in Detroit and Throughout the Nation
Thursday, October 17, 2002

Timeline:

October, 2001 — Michigan Supreme Court Throws Out Ballot Initiative on a Technicality

October, 2001 — Congress Writes Bush a Blank Check To Go to War in Iraq, Inciting Worldwide Protests

January, 2002 — Michigan State Legislature Passes Drug Reform That Eliminates Mandatory Minimum Drug Sentencing, and Brings Equity to Criminal Drug Sentencing

Panelists:

Deborah Peterson Small: Director of Public Policy and Community Outreach for Drug Policy Alliance

Jeff Edison: Defense Attorney, Detroit

Felix Sirls: Public Health Worker for the City of Detroit

Ron Allen: Moderator

Attorney Jeff Edison:

The CIA, the relationship with the Contras and their involvement with drug trafficking, it didn't just end with the exposé, the darker lines. Tthe activity of the government in drug trafficking continues. And the devastating impact that this trafficking has had on our community certainly is coming to fruition, and the effects are long-standing effects.

It's interesting that one of the references in the play that the government agents were using is that "the end justified the means." With that reference, it's important for us to try to identify exactly what the "end" was, or is. What is or was the objective of the government? And certainly to many of us, one of the objectives certainly had to be the destabilization and destruction of African communities here in North America.

I'd like to reference some statistics because I think that they really speak for themselves in terms of the impact that the drug trafficking—particularly the government's so-called "war on drugs" policy—had on our communities. Because to many of us it wasn't actually a war on drugs, but rather a war on the African community.

Bear with me, because I have to read them to you. The statistics are on the internet at the Sentencing Project site. There's an abundance of statistics, particularly as it relates to the sentencing disparities and prison development and prison population. And you can get it at the sentencingproject.org.

Let me just say this: the number of inmates in state and federal prisons increased more than six-fold, from 200,000 in 1970 to 1,324,465 by the year 2001. That's in the combined state and federal prisons. In addition to that, there are 631,240 persons in jails—that is, people awaiting sentence.

There are now 6.6 million Americans incarcerated or on probation or parole, which is an increase of more than 258 percent since 1980. Now, of course, the whole influx of particularly cocaine into our communities climaxed in the '80s and the early '90s. Heroin was the drug that was in our communities in the early or late '60s, and early '70s. And now there's a kind of resurgence of heroin, and it's interesting they're talking about chemical warfare that they think Iraq engaged in. But this certainly was chemical warfare in our country. Nearly one in seven black males aged between 25–29 were in prison or in jail in 2001. That was 13.4 percent of black males. Hispanics was 4.1 percent, and for white males 1.8 percent. So you see that huge disparity by race. Of course, the U.S. has the highest incarceration rate of individuals on this planet. Nowhere in this world are people incarcerated at a higher rate than in the U.S.

In terms of the racial composition: 46 percent of prison inmates were black, 16 percent were Hispanic. Some other statistics: 68 percent of state prison inmates in 1997 had not completed high school. Some 36 percent of jailed inmates in 1996 were unemployed prior to entering jail. Some 64 percent of jailed inmates in 1996 had monthly incomes under $1,000.00. About 70 percent of those sentenced to state prisons in '98 were convicted of nonviolent crimes, including 31 percent for drug offenses and 26 percent is property offenses.

So, in essence, we're not dealing with violence in terms of the largest population in the prisons. It's predominantly nonviolent individuals and so it speaks directly to the drug policy. We talk about the influx of drugs into the community by way of the Contras. At the same time, there was an influx of assault weapons and automatic weapons at a higher rate than our communities have ever experienced before—in terms of accessibility. So, you had the opportunity to deal with these more violent weapons—in terms of assault weapons and automatic weapons—together with the drugs. [*Applause*]

FELIX SIRLS:

Well, working for the Detroit Health Department, I had all these wonderful statistics. Thank you, brother. I want to come from another viewpoint—and that is—very personal. Having grown up in Compton, in LA, and moving to San Francisco—as a teenager I experienced first-hand much of the devastation the American government has profited from: the devastation that allows $56,000 to be made per year from every inmate that is in prison, and as long as they are on parole, with the county they're incarcerated in receiving those funds. The fact is that drugs in the minority communities comes in the commodity of crack cocaine and heroin. It comes in the commodity that the most prison time is given for—crack, rather than powder cocaine—which is not emanating from the minority communities of this country and which receives less time. More time. There have been several bills put before Congress and this state, to give equal time for powder and rock cocaine. They are still fighting this. Why? Because it takes money to have powder. The folks who usually get crack cocaine are in the lower-echelon levels of society, generally. It is the last resort—there's very little cocaine in it. But it causes the most devastation, the most mental, physical devastation, the most disruption of family. I see it as the continuance of the Willie Lynch syndrome—which is to destroy and turn human beings against themselves. I want to save my comments for later on, but that's my opening. Thank you. [*Applause*]

DEBORAH SMALL:

Hi. I'm Deborah Small. Don't like microphones. If anyone can't hear me, wave your hand and I'll speak louder. But I'm gonna try not to do that. I'll try to stay seated, but I can't promise that I will, because of what it is I want to say. I want to really drop some knowledge on people, and talk about some things that don't get talked about that often. The first thing is, that the war on drugs has nothing to do with drugs. It never has. It never will. The war on drugs is all about providing the justification for growing and keeping the prison-industrial complex going. And if you look at American history, you would find from the time they brought the first black person over here in chains, our public policy has been designed to keep us in chains—whether it be the chains that were inflicted on us by slave-owners or the chains that we put on our own minds. Okay?

I came here early today because I wanted to go to the African-American History Museum here in Detroit, which I always find to be a fascinating place to go. And the thing that I find fascinating about going there, is looking at the replica of the slave ship and seeing what it was that was on that ship. Because before I ever came to Detroit, I believed that people were brought here as slaves as family members—moms, dad, children. When I came here what I saw was young people—primarily young men. And it was a mind opening for me, because I got: "Oh yeah, this is the same stuff they're doing now." They targeted young, African men and women. Why? Because they were the easiest ones to re-acculturate. They were the ones they could get the most value from. They were the ones who were the most productive and who offered the least resistance.

History has not changed in 400 years. There is a quote by Harriet Tubman that I like to keep in the front of my mind all the time. She talked about later in her life that… in the course of her life, she freed hundreds of slaves. Now she'd have been able to free thousands more, if they only knew that they were slaves.

That reality is still true today. We are mentally and psychologically enslaved by the propaganda that we have believed, that's come down from our government for the past 20 years. We believed that the majority of crack users are from inner-city communities. That is not true. It has never been true. It never will be true. Every survey that the government does every year on drug use in America demonstrates that the majority of people who use crack cocaine are white. This is not a lie. If you don't believe me, go to the U.S. government's website and read their national survey on household drug use. You will see that from the time they first started taking the survey till today, the majority of people who self-report using crack cocaine are white people. And yet there are states in this country like Massachusetts that have never prosecuted one white person for a crack offense. Why is that? Because prosecutors and judges and police do not want them to be subject to the same disproportionate sentencing that black people and brown people are subject to when they are convicted of crack-cocaine offenses. We believe that crack is a more dangerous drug than cocaine. It is not more dangerous than cocaine—crack is cocaine. The only difference between powder and crack—between powder cocaine and crack cocaine—is the way in which you administer it. Any drug, any drug is more dangerous when it's smoked than when it is ingested or sniffed. I don't give a damn what it is. Crack cocaine represented marketing, an expansion of the drug market—in the same way that multinational corporations looked to expand their markets.

By the time we reached the mid-'80s, the market for powder cocaine had been saturated, because there were only so many people in America who could afford to pay the price for it. So people who were involved in the drug-trafficking business, they wanted to see how they could make more money, they wanted to see how they could produce the drug in a cheaper way. Crack cocaine allowed them to expand their market, because it made cocaine available to people who could not afford it before. And the consequences of smoking it—as opposed to sniffing it—produced the kind of behavioral changes we see in our community. But it has nothing to do with race.

And our government was as willing to turn a blind eye to the involvement of people that they had as their partners engaged in distributing drugs in our society, in the same way they turned a blind eye to the people still bringing slaves here after 1805 when the boss said you couldn't do it anymore!

Why would we be surprised, or even shocked, to hear that somehow we were willing to ignore illegal activity? When is it that our government has ever really gone after prosecuting illegal activity that was not in its own interest? Why would this be any different? Why do we not look at what it was that we did with our policies politically that had nothing to do with drugs?

Having a disparity in sentencing for crack versus powder cocaine offenses has nothing to do with the drug, has nothing to do with the criminality associated with the drug. What it does do, is provide an easy justification for locking up tens of thousands of people of color, putting them away in prison for 10, 20, 30 years and allowing other people to derive profits from their enslavement.

I don't know how many people have been watching the series that's been on PBS: "The Rise & Fall of Jim Crow." If you haven't, you need to check it out. Nothing that we are talking about is new. A hundred years ago, black people were being locked up in prison at the same rate that they are being locked up today. Why? Because there was no longer a legal way to exploit their labor—by calling them slaves. But the 13th Amendment, which freed the slaves, had an exception. And the exception was for people who were convicted of a crime. Anyone who is convicted of a crime is subject to the same type of treatment as a person who's a slave.

So, if you're looking for a way to exploit people's labor and to be able to use it in a way that allows you to be immune from any kind of criticism, all you have to do is convict them of a crime and call them a criminal, and then you can treat them however you want to—and no one's going to protest. If you watch that series, they will talk about the fact that 100 years ago, tens of thousands of black men were put in prison for minor offenses, like vagrancy, and they died. They died from health consequences. They were worked to death. They died from lack of adequate health care.

Drugs are just the newest excuse to re-enslave us, and we need to really break free of the chains in our mind that sees the problem as being the drugs, and not the policies that we put in place to deal with it. And that sees the problem as being those countries over there—that if they just stop growing these plants, we wouldn't have these problems. That is not the problem, okay?

I'm gonna stop right here and ask you all to ask some questions about this later. But I urge you all to watch that series, and see if you see much difference between what was happening in the late 19th century and what's happening now in the early 21st century. [*Applause*]

Jim Grimmett:

Good evening. My name is Jim Grimmett. I am a grateful, recovering alcoholic. I was born a member of this community and I can remember the struggles in terms of trying to survive a broken home, a dysfunctional family, and being told you got to do something with your life. Education. Come from that dysfunctional family, low-income... Not to brag, but I'm the first of 27 grandchildren to complete high school. I can remember from the age of 14, 15 years of age, developing an attitude of a government conspiracy to keep black folk—as well as poor folk—in their place.

Somehow—through curiosity and experimentation—I got involved with the use of heroin. I got involved with the abuse of alcohol and really lost touch with reality. Well, over the last 22 years of having gotten my head on straight, I started to try to give back to the community what I could do as one individual. I heard a lot of positive things being shared. I look at substance abuse and drug use in this country as one that is destroying communities—a family at a time. I also view it as a health issue. I also view at it as legal issue.

You know, spend a few minutes talking from the legal perspective. There's this debate going on in our society right now in terms of treatment versus institutionalization. This brother spoke earlier, giving a bunch of good statistics. I just happened to think of some things today, and some of the things that came to mind to me in regard to the prison issue. In most cases, most drug offenders that are arrested never go to jail. And of those who do, few of them ever receive treatment. Without treatment, while incarcerated, most drug offenders quickly return to their bad habits and end up earning more hard time.

I do believe that forced treatment can work at times. Drug courts work. Generally, with most offenders, they are probably forced for the very first time in their lives to become accountable for their own actions. I think it has to be attacked on another front as well, and that we have a need for more research to motivate addicts to enter treatment. A change in the social attitudes will help us to recognize that dealing with the number one health disease in this country should become a priority, while we stop stigmatizing addicts and treating them as modern-day lepers.

I think the last time I looked at some statistics in terms of "should we incarcerate an addict or treat them?" sort of ended up showing that we're willing to say, well: "Send them to treatment twice and then incarcerate." I struggled with that personally but you know, some of our elected officials today have had one or two useful…

DEBORAH SMALL:

…or five or 10…

JIM GRIMMETT:

…experiences in the past, and they didn't get incarcerated.

DEBORAH SMALL:

…and never will.

JIM GRIMMETT:

State of Michigan…just a few stats. In 1999, the state of Michigan, Michigan Department of Corrections appropriated a budget of $21 million. Some 26 percent of that budget was spent on outpatient services, 56 percent of the budget went for residential services and 18 percent for drug tests. Prisoners in the state of Michigan at that time: a little in excess of 46,000. There were 13,000 parolees, 50,000 probations. Receiving treatment altogether: 18,600.

They spend more money than that throwing social parties in Congress. They spend more money than that flying around the country in jets with corporate America. Why can't we take the time to spend that kind of money rebuilding our families and communities? I want you to think about that. [*Applause*]

RON ALLEN:

Now, that is a different kind of panel than you experienced earlier. And you'll have an opportunity to come to the mike if you have an interest or to make a statement or response. What does this bring up to you? So what do you do about it?

AUDIENCE MEMBER:

I want to know, from somebody on the panel, do the inner-city communities have certain institutions in it, and is there an indication that the institutions foster choice in terms of finding a means to a better life, and how to find a purpose, and how to find what success is? What do you think? Is it lack of institutions in the inner-city communities? What does that mean in terms of incidence of drug use, and criminalization of citizens who do drugs?

DEBORAH SMALL:

I just want to restate what I said before. We look at our communities and we see people who are suffering from addiction and alcoholism and we think that's a problem that's primarily, predominantly taking place in our communities. That is just not true. Less black people proportionally abuse drugs and alcohol than in the rest of the population.

I think that it's the way we enforce our drug laws, the way that we deal with issues like shoplifting. Every single one of us of color have had the experience of going into a store and having security people follow us around because they believe that we're stealing. While they're busy following us around, five and six white people steal and never get caught because nobody's looking at them. So therefore they don't steal, because they don't get arrested for it, they don't get convicted for it.

Drug law enforcement is exactly the same way. I guarantee you, that if we put police in suburban affluent communities to go after drugs the same way that they do in our communities, they would produce 10 times more people abusing it than they do in ours, because more of them are doing it than us. But because we only look in poor, inner-city communities, those are the fish that we bring in. Those are the people who go to jail, and it re-enforces our belief that this is primarily our problem.

We actually don't suffer from this any worse than anyone else. But because we don't have national health insurance, because we don't have treatment on request, the consequences for us of having a substance-abuse problem are much worse than it is for other Americans.

What we need to be demanding is not more police, not more law enforcement, but more opportunity for treatment, a national health-insurance policy that allows everyone to get health care as they need it, and an educational system that does not create the circumstance that allows the drug dealer be the only equal-opportunity employer in our community. [*Applause*]

Jeff Edison:

I think that the resolution of your question ultimately gets to a question of empowerment. We have to be empowered individually, so that we can go beyond ourselves to empower ourselves, and our community collectively. We have to have the spiritual power to recognize our whole greatness and majesty so we can have vision. We can be visionary. We can tap into our creativity to create the institutions that are going to uplift us, so that we are less likely to fall into the problems of what the brother calls dysfunction, or to see the need to indulge ourselves with substances to make us feel whole. So it's an educational piece, if we can. If we're empowered to control our education. And gets back to throwing off the shackles of Willie Lynch, that my brother talked about. And it's about divisiveness in our communities amongst ourselves. It's all of these things.

It's going to take a holistic approach to our own well-being. But the essence of it all, I think, is that we have to empower ourselves so that we can realize our own true spiritual and human potential.

FELIX SIRLS:

In regard to your question, having been an addict, having been a dealer, having been in the community and experiencing it, one of the first things we need is long-term treatment centers, rather than this door-in-door-out, you go... you jump from one treatment center to another, you can stay there for 30 days and then you're out. It usually takes an addict practicing for a couple of years to become an addict, but in 30 days they don't recover.

So, number one, we need to get long-term treatment centers. Yes, I would love for the patient to look at himself in a mirror to see how everyone else is involved, but I know how I am involved. I cannot change the federal government and overthrow it at this time, which is what it would take to have the policy changes that we need euphorically to happen. But, the reality of what is happening....

When I was born, we were 15 percent of the American population as African-Americans; now we represent 12 percent. You gonna keep—you gonna look for a mirror—when we gonna become eight percent, six percent?

HIV, STDs, syphilis is the leading infection in Detroit. Now Detroit leads the nation in syphilis infection. African-Americans are dying from eating the wrong foods, smoking the wrong things. They are dying from a lot of things, and it's based on self-esteem, the lack of self-esteem, the lack of self-control, the lack of love for oneself.

We need to attack churches that attack other human beings through their religion. We need to engage people in caring and knowing what a family is, finding families. Once we had communities, but when something called "integration" came along, we decided to give our money away.

Money. In the 1940s, a dollar stayed in the African-American community for two years. Now it leaves the African-American community in 10 minutes. We need to look at the realities of what we can do now—not a euphoric afterlife. Part of that—if we want to save our people—we need to look at long-term recovery. We need to look at self-esteem programs, artistic and art programs. We need to become involved in the schools and stop using them as baby-sitting centers. We need to go to our schools and learn the names of the teachers whose classrooms our children are in. And we need to start saving our children. [*Applause*]

Again, to go back to the brother's question, we need to go back looking at our own moral fiber. One thing that I've heard years ago, and I still subscribe to, is that "It takes a village to save a child." That same village can reunite a family. So sometimes it's about reach one to teach one, to heal one. We have those resources, the churches, the schools. It's just in learning how to empower ourselves to use those community resources to our advantage.

I don't want to end this night without hearing from more of you, because what we hear from listening to each other is that there is no one method, and that each of us has a role to play.

Evan:

Hello. My name is Evan, and I'm a recovering addict. I would like to say that lately I've heard police forces are stealing drug money, and money out of the evidence rooms. And I wondered why the government couldn't take drug money that they were confiscating and use that money towards rehabilitation and treatment centers. [*Applause*]

PAULA SIRLS:

I would just like to make a comment. I'm Paula Sirls, Felix's wife. When you use "dysfunctional"... I speak to a lot of people, I've met a thousand people from all over. I do not know one person who did not come from a family with no function, or dysfunctional—however you want to put it. Cause if we're all connected, and I know we are—we are from a dysfunctional family somewhere down the line. That's partly because we define "functional" based on some mythical TV family that none of us came from. And that's what they made up. But most of what we base our society on and our mental truths on has a lot to do with fantasy. Very little has to do with reality. We have a lot of formulas and philosophies that don't exist, such as "fairness," honesty" and "justice" that don't exist.

AUDIENCE MEMBER:

I just wanted to know: how does the community deal with drug dealers? Has anybody addressed that?

DEBORAH SMALL:

How do they, or how should they?

AUDIENCE MEMBER:

Well, has anybody addressed that? How should they? How do they? I'm talking about, do you wait for the police force to deal with it and get them arrested? They go in, they come back out. They go back doing what they were doing. How involved does the community become? Because...obviously, we don't fly the drugs in here. But, once they get in here, they have to be distributed by somebody, okay? So how do we deal with drug dealers?

DEBORAH SMALL:

I live in New York, and I don't know how many of you all are familiar with the Rockefeller drug laws, that have been on the books for 30 years. They are basically designed to target drug dealers. And the notion was that if you had harsh, mandatory sentences, that it would deter people from selling drugs.

We've had thirty years of this law. Drug dealing has not been deterred. Drug abuse has not been deterred. But we've threefold increased our prison population with people of color charged with drug dealing. Some 94 percent of all people incarcerated for drug offenses in New York are African-American or Latino. No one has ever argued that 94 percent of the people who sell drugs in New York are African-American or Latino. I think we need to have a different discussion about drug dealers.

I think we need to get real about drugs. We need to deal with the fact that drugs are a commodity, just like any other commodity, and as long as there is a demand for them, there will be someone to supply them. We don't blame liquor-store owners for the fact that some of their customers are alcoholics. We understand that they are in business selling a product there is a demand for, and some of the people who come to buy the product will have a problem with that drug—with that thing that they're buying. And we help them by getting them into alcohol clinics, and helping them to dry out. But we don't lock up the person who sold them the liquor for 15 or 20 years and say that person is wrong.

I think that it's not an accident that the war on drugs started at the same time that we decided to end the war on poverty, and what we have done is criminalized two or three generations of color for engaging in the only types of economic activities that were available to them.

The Kennedys made their money selling illegal liquor, and now they're considered America's First Family. Why are they less criminal than the Ricky Ross's or other people of the world that are trying to do the same thing that America tells you to do, which is to try to make as much money as you can. Let's start looking at what is actually happening in our community and stop scapegoating certain groups of people and writing them off.

You know, we are the only group of people—and I believe this is part of the legacy of slavery—that have become so conditioned to receiving harsh punishment for whatever-the-hell we do, that we think it's okay for our people to be carted away every year and thrown in these prisons to make more jobs for rural white people to make up for the factory jobs that they lost. Let's stop making an industry out of our men and women and saying that there's something inevitably wrong with them because they're doing what economic necessity is forcing them to do. If drugs were not illegal, there wouldn't be so much damn profits in it in the first place. And in America, there's only one color that counts, and it's not black, it's not white, it's not red, it's green. And as long as there's green in drugs, there gonna be people out there getting that green, because that's what we tell them that they oughta do.

DEBRA WRIGHT:

If I could just make a quick statement, my name is Debra Wright. I'm with the Drug Policy Forum of Michigan, and one thing you can do is to get involved with our group. We meet monthly in Detroit. We advocate for changes in drug laws, because there is no justice in the war on drugs. Be sure you pick up a pamphlet and become active. We have a website: www.drugpolicy.org.

I just want to say that our organization put a ballot initiative on the ballot in this state that would have required treatment over incarceration for first- and second-time nonviolent drug offenders. Your state department got us kicked off. So, you all won't have the opportunity to vote on this initiative in 2002. But I promise you, that we will be back to put it back on the initiative in 2004. When I come back here in 2004 I want to see this church, and other churches like it, filled with people in the community who've been affected by the drug war who are committed to voting for more humane policies instead of voting for a continuation of the same that we've had.

And I want to thank the Unitarian Universalist Church for hosting this, for taking a position as a church to combat drug prohibition in America. And I think that they need to be commended for that, and that more organizations need to understand that that's one of the ways you fulfill a spiritual mission, by fighting injustice wherever you see it. And this is about injustice.

DEBORAH SMALL:

Until 2004, which means that we have the rest of 2002 and 2003 to do some work, so when she comes back in 2004, we will have not only this room, but other sanctuaries, filled, right?

RON ALLEN:

Tomorrow night we have another panel discussion. Thanks for coming down. Have a good night.

Topic:
The Rhetoric of War
Sunday, October 20, 2002

Panelists:

Chris Parks: Clinical Psychologist and Director, Neighborhood Recovery Services, Detroit
Peter Sellars: Theater, Opera and Arts Festival Director
Regina Schwartz: Professor, Northwestern University, Illinois
John Malpede: Moderator

Introduction:

While we were in Detroit, the Congress of the U.S., the same ones whose behavior is staged in "Agents & Assets," gave carte blanche support to President Bush's impending pre-emptive war on Iraq. We reached out to the peace community and organized a public conversation on "The Rhetoric of War."

— **John Malpede**

John Malpede:

So we're going to start the discussion. And, why don't you come closer, people in the back? We invite you to come up closer. As you can see, there's a microphone here, and the real idea is to have a discussion that everybody participates in together.

My name is John Malpede and I directed the play, which is a word-for-word transcript from the U.S. House of Representatives, although I edited it for time—even though they only allotted two hours and 15 minutes for the hearing, we only gave them an hour and 15 minutes. But I edited scrupulously, so that no one's position was distorted, and any distortions reside with the people who said the words in the first place.

I want to introduce our panel and then I want to tell a little bit more about what happened after this hearing. On my far right is Chris Parks, who is on the faculty of the University of Detroit and runs two drug-rehabilitation programs here in the city of Detroit and is an expert in arts used in recovery as well.

CHRIS PARKS:

Strong word.

JOHN MALPEDE:

Well, he's not an expert because he's the person who's figuring it out. So, he's more of a pioneer.

And next to me is my very good friend and outstanding troublemaker worldwide, Peter Sellars. Peter is a renowned theater and opera and festival creator and deconstructor. It's really wonderful that Peter's here. And on my left is Regina Shwartz, who is a Professor in the English Department at Northwestern University, and also an outstanding troublemaker in her own right, having authored a book on the violent legacy of monotheism. So every day after the show, we've been having a panel about drug policy, the devastation of drugs to the communities and the citizens of this country, and about the drug policy that makes it all happen. And we wanted to do this show in Detroit because we heard through the grapevine that there was going to be an initiative on the November 5th ballot about treatment versus incarceration. Regrettably, we were not able to control the fact of this actually making it to the ballot. And some other people on the canvassing board and the Michigan Supreme Court decided that it wasn't going to be on the ballot. Nevertheless, the issue doesn't go away, and there's also a legislative initiative introduced by State Representative Bill McConico in your state legislature that addresses many of the concerns of the ballot initiative.

Today's discussion spirals out from that very particular beginning, to look at not just the drug war, but why "war" is the metaphor for so many things. Alfred McCoy, who was here last night, is a seminal historian of the drug war, and he pointed out the first time we did this show, in Los Angeles, that the drug war during the Nixon era employed the military metaphor and that it was first applied overseas and then, eventually, over the course of 30 years, it became applied in this country. So the military metaphor was applied here. And that is the war on drugs, which has resulted in enormous incarceration of our citizens, etc. So today, we're going to look at the metaphor itself. That's the idea. And since there's a lot of talk of war these days, and it seems to be imminent, this is a good time to do that.

Before we get going, I want to say a little bit about what happened after the hearing that we just witnessed in "Agents & Assets." What happened after this hearing was that, ultimately, this committee signed off on Mr. Hitz's report. So even though there seemed to be a lot of inconsistencies that showed up in the hearing, nevertheless they signed off on the report and concluded the CIA was not involved in any way in the activities made in the allegations.

So, who would like to speak first? We didn't determine that. Peter did volunteer to go last. That was very generous and wise of him. So Regina, how about you?

REGINA SCHWARTZ:

Sure.

JOHN MALPEDE:

That would be great.

REGINA SCHWARTZ:

I'll just begin. I won't say everything I've got to say about this right now. I'll just say a little bit, so everybody can get involved.

JOHN MALPEDE:

And when you want to say something, just come up to the microphone and we can have a dialogue.

REGINA SCHWARTZ:

I want to start with your interest in metaphor, and the issue of the war on drugs being a metaphor. Susan Sontag, after September 11th wrote a really amazing article called "Real Battles, Empty Metaphors," in which she was talking about not only the war on drugs, but the war on poverty and the war on terrorism and the way in which our government is so freely bandying about these terms. She made the important point that a war is something which has an end. And that these things don't end. Poverty, unfortunately, doesn't seem to be going away. The problem with drugs doesn't seem to be going away. Terrorism doesn't go away. So it's completely inappropriate in any way to call it a war. Why then is this rhetoric used, she asks. And the answer that she gives is that it's because the government wants to mobilize lots of resources. So, if it declares war, it can claim a lot of resources, just as they do for their military expeditions, and use them. In this case however, the war on drugs is a war on our own citizens, obviously. It's not only a war on our citizens, it's a war on some citizens, and not others. Because important distinctions really have to be made, even in the issue of drugs. Because it's an upper-middle class white problem on the one hand, where it seems to be sort of tolerated, sort of condoned. Then, on the other hand, it's something that is visiting the poor and wreaking havoc there and that's not okay! And so in a lot of ways, the War on Drugs is really a class war. And as many writers have said, it's a race war, an opportunity to incarcerate a hell of a lot of black youths who are behind bars now. So I'm going to stop with these provocative statements just to point out how dangerous this rhetoric really is.

JOHN MALPEDE:

Great.

CHRIS PARKS:

I wasn't really expecting to be one of the people to make one of the more provocative statements on this panel, and in teaching ethics courses to other clinicians—something that I was doing yesterday. I didn't know that this was going to be the topic that we were going to be discussing today. But yesterday I was teaching an ethics course to other clinicians, and I made a comment to them about how we view the people that we work with. I told the therapists that they needed to give up the rhetoric of the war on drugs, because we declare war for historical purposes when we are about to commit atrocities. And this rhetoric brings about the idea that great losses are okay for the final victory. And this is inconsistent with a therapeutic approach to treating a health problem that affects so many people. If we are trying to treat a health problem and people are lost in our attempt to treat that problem, we see each loss as a failure.

In a war, we see casualties—even "collateral damage"—as potential for "final victory." And I think that's one of the biggest problems that I see with the whole rhetoric with the war on drugs, a war on poverty: people become numbers who are added up in the final summation of our coming out on the other side victorious, and as Regina said, ending. Whereas, if we simply see it as health problem, the struggle for better and better health is a never-ending struggle, and something we do not need to see all the way to resolution and then say: "our job is done, and history will judge us."

PETER SELLARS:

Hi everyone. Thanks for coming over. Hello great cast. That was awesome. Thank you. An awesome performance. Thank you. Thank you. That was so fine.

Just a couple of quick things. Just dealing with the fact you have a 25-, 30-year war on drugs which over 30 years triples the flow of drugs into the United States. Hello? Hello? Like what is that? Like you fight this war for 30 years and you triple the drug flow. War is usually just about one thing and one thing only and that is profit. And the people conducting it are making the biggest profit. You make a car, hello, in Detroit, you make an eight percent profit. You make a weapon, you make a 27 percent profit. That's why America's economy is based on making weapons. And that's why we're the biggest arms dealer in the world, by far. And that is why, obviously, we can support any irritating dictator that looks like they'll buy more weapons because, of course, we perfected this whole thing, this illusion of independence. And, of course, the beautiful thing about granting independence to an African nation is that then it's their army enforcing your economics. And so you profit double. Because you continue to rape the country and all its resources, you do not pay real money for the resources you're getting—for all the aluminum that you're wrapping your tuna fish sandwich in—that comes from the bauxite that comes from Guinea. No way that Guinea's going to see any of that. Meanwhile, in case the workers want a raise, they're not going to complain because the army of Guinea is right there. Anyone who wants a raise gets shot. And the army of Guinea is buying our weapons. So we're just doubling our profit with the independence movement.

And another thing that is going on with the war thing is that it also lets everything be about "good guys" and "bad guys." Because the "good guys" are on the "good side," and the "bad guys" are on the "bad side." And declaring war means that we all know who the "good guys" are. That would be us. Always. And then the "bad guys" are just "bad." We don't have to know anything about them. They're just "bad." And that's enough. And so whatever destroys them, they're just "bad." And there's no other questions to be asked, right? And it's not like there's a structural thing in place that's going on, nobody has to ask: "Wait a minute. Like, where's this coming from and who's involved?"

And obviously if a 25- or 30-year war on drugs triples the flow of drugs, that means that obviously somebody is being paid off big. That means we're not seeing the real money. The real money's doing just fine. The real money's doing just fine by people in very high places. Hello. I mean, George, Jr. was just like dangling on his father's knee when his father was running the drug trade in the United States out of the vice president's office. The reason that you're not going to hear from Manuel Noriega is because he has to be eighty-sixed. Because he knows too much. Because he was in the vice president's office every other week when the vice president was George Bush, Sr., former CIA director. Hello.

So, in fact, the whole Contra thing was run through George Bush, Sr.'s office, which is why George Bush, Jr. is going to take the whole thing to the next step because, obviously, the drug war is very good at silencing certain people who are inconvenient to the people who are making the most profit. And that's why it has to be prosecuted, and why it particularly has to be prosecuted with unbelievable severity on people making a tiny profit on the street. And, meanwhile, why the people making the real money are not saying one thing about that. Unless somebody betrays somebody because they want to get them out of the way for competition, and then you can always phone up and get somebody in the newspaper and increase your profit margin.

And obviously, we know if drugs were declared legal, certain young men and young women in lots of communities would be leading businessmen. And, obviously, it's also about not allowing a lot of America to participate in any kind of real economy. And so the only economy that is allowed in large sections of America is an illegal economy.

So for me a lot of the war image is also about the violence that's necessary to sustain the drug trade, because if it wasn't for this violence, the price would go down. And because of the violence you can keep the prices jacked way, way, way up. The other thing that is really important is, in a war and it's just like prisons: You are attacking one segment of the population, but meanwhile all the money goes into another segment. And so you are building jobs in whole communities of prison guards. You are building jobs for police. You are building jobs for special agents. One whole segment of the community has a paycheck and the declaration of war means that you can just have an open checkbook. Cause war is about an open checkbook, and holding a gun to people's head and saying, "We need this now!"

So Congress isn't allowed to say anything against a war. Whereas you pay for your kids' education on a day when you are feeling good, and then on another day well, it's not so important. You can get America to spend money on anything negative. You can spend any kind of money to hurt someone. It's really hard to find the money to help anyone. And that's the reality. And that's why it's not just a war metaphor. It's a reality. It's about hurting, not helping. Every day when you get up you have a choice, you can help, or you can hurt. And this country chose to hurt.

John Malpede:

Thank you, Peter. [*Applause*]

Audience Member:

I was really shaken by your comments about the war on drugs as a class war. Yesterday, in the paper, a Michigan appeals court ruled that it was proper to subject people on welfare to random drug tests in order for them to receive their payment. Now, they're not insisting that judges and legislators and other people who receive their money from the government are held to the same scrutiny. The justification, of course, was that we have to protect the children, the same old, sorry excuse when they don't actually do it. This proves that this is all about establishing who's "thems" and who's "us-es", and who's powerful and who's not. It's just proof positive that you're sustaining and maintaining power by setting up these categories for control and condemnation.

JOHN MALPEDE:

Thanks. Who else wants to say something?

AUDIENCE MEMBER:

Hello. My name is Barbara Stevenson. I'm a member of this church and I want to thank you for picking this place to have this play, because I think that Unitarian Universalists themselves are independent thinkers, which makes us, right now, unfortunately, dangerous people. And as somebody who works with children teaching peace, I really thought about this a lot and one of the things that bothers me is we have gang-ism everywhere in our society. And gang-ism is sort of what you are describing in terms of how the work of the drug lord gets done. But it's also how the work of politics gets done. It's also unfortunately how public schools are run. And I think that—and I have to give credit to Michael Moore for this insight—but we're the majority, damn it, and we keep acting like we're not. The people who want a different kind of life in this country are really in the majority, and I wonder if you can speak to how we can have the guts to stand up, because we're in a dangerous place right now.

PETER SELLARS:

Actually, I'm sorry if I have to contradict you, but most people on the planet really want a war right away and are very anxious for World War III, as soon as possible. Just kidding. No, that's the thing. Nobody wants it. Everybody knows we don't need it. It's again like World War I. Nobody asked for it. It was a handful of people that decided they could make a whole lot of money, and did. And we redrew some map lines that were irritating them. And the world is still fighing wars, permanent war zones, where a drunken British diplomat drew a line on a map in 1920. And so we're dealing with people who really feel they can carve up the planet to suit their own needs. And make borderlines where normal citizens are not allowed cross the border, but big business can move anywhere it wants.

I think that one of big issues about this drug war is that the second biggest economy in the world is drugs. The amount of money that is moving all over the planet, that's not just funding Contras, it's funding all kinds of stuff. The question is, where's this money going? Who's really collecting it? There's a whole huge economy out there, right now. And that is very useful for some people. So that's why they keep it going and keep it flowing. And the other thing that's going on, the other end of the drug war, because everything has a connection somewhere, is where the drugs are coming from. And who's growing them. And of course, it's mostly indigenous people in all over the world, who have no other way to survive. And then these governments can use it as war against the indigenous people that speak some other language they just want to eliminate. And so it's about sending in the government force also to eliminate indigenous people. So at either end of the drug war is violence against people who are struggling to survive everyday. And in the middle of it is a lot of profit.

Audience Member:

Hi. In Detroit we have a really unique situation. We have a very dynamic organization called Drug Policy Forum of Michigan, and myself and several other people here today are members. We had a conference last weekend where Congressman

John Conyers and Congresswoman Kilpatrick spoke. We also have a police chief who has come out against the war on drugs. Both the *Detroit News* and the *Detroit Free Press* editorialize consistently, as do their journalists, against the war on drugs. So we have an opportunity that's very unique. And I find it very frustrating, I'm sure that many of you do too, that there's a war on a plant. And this, the most best-ist plant on the whole planet, is also considered to be the worst plant by them. If you ever wondered why the environmental or peace movements never took off as they should have, it's because the government went after us not because of our politics, they went after us because we sought to use this plant as a relaxant.

Since 1960, over 20 million of us have been arrested, decimated, and we're all afraid to speak up to say, you know: "I smoked marijuana" because our jobs are in jeopardy and the freedom of a society is being jeopardized because of a plant. We're the people of the planet. It's almost like a cosmic joke. I speak at Hash Bash, by the way. I'm Martin Harmon. I'm so proud of you guys. You have the courage to come out, especially after 9/11, because so many people are afraid to come out. Millions are afraid to come out.

And finally, I want to acknowledge our government that they don't come on over and take us away for being here today. That's great. Thank you.

REGINA SCHWARTZ:

Real quickly, I just want to add that it's not just the plant, it's something's going on with human nature and human values. The problem of greed that Peter keeps talking about, that some people are making so much profit from the drug war, and, on the other hand, the lack of responsibility. One of the ironies of all this rhetoric about drugs is that the government so often says: "Gee, everybody should be more responsible for him and herself. Everybody should be more self-caring and more self-reliant." It's sort of the rhetoric in self-help books. "And this is what's wrong. This is why we don't like drug users, because these people aren't self-caring and self-helping." But, this is a real perversion of the whole concept of responsibility, because what responsibility is, is concern for somebody else. In fact, it's for your neighbor. And since I'm in a church, I might as well say that the Bible's real clear, it says: "Love thy neighbor." It says, "Take care of the widow, the orphan and the poor." What's going on with this drug problem is that we're creating essentially widows by incarcerating so many people. We're creating orphans and we're creating the poor. And then we're turning around and blaming them for being widows, orphans and poor. That's far from taking responsibility and taking care.

So with all this money floating around that we have for destruction, as Peter was saying, it seems like pouring that money into education and care-taking and forms of welfare that will really make a difference, is something that we all should really be vocal about and it sounds like Detroit is a place that it could potentially happen.

AUDIENCE MEMBER:

I have a question for Chris about the association between this sort of a production and performance process and the connection between art and recovery.

CHRIS PARKS:

How many people who are here, when you were young, stood in your backyard and spun around until you fell down?

[*Laughter*] And then when you were done, you got up and did it again?

I am an addiction counselor, and, certainly, I know the pressures of public forums to talk about my own feelings about drug use, drug abuse and addiction, which are three separate things.

Altering your consciousness is a common human experience; it's something that everybody does. For example, everybody raised their hand when I asked if you spun yourself 'till you fell down. It's a natural human drive. Drug use is an extension of that, whether we think it's good or bad, it's an extension of that. It's a way to explore. It's a way to examine. It's a way to look for new ways to view things and new ways to feel things.

Addiction is a pathology. A pathology by its very nature is a rigid structure that is resistant to change. And that's all we're talking about here. Now, when the gentleman said that there is a war against the plant, I disagree. Nobody wants that plant to stay around more than the people that are locking people up. The reason why we won't seriously talk about the fact there are 2 million people behind bars is because it is profitable for certain segments of the population and it vilifies other segments of the population. So it remains a way of thinking that is resistant to change—in essence, pathological. They are as addicted to the marijuana plant as they claim that some people become.

So I want everyone to understand this is in answer to the question. Art and things such as this play, they push at the borders, and sometimes crack the boundaries that are so rigid, allowing things to flow through, allowing communication to go from one place to another. And that is the purpose of any type of good therapy. And I think if we looked at this as a health problem more than as an instance of war, we would have the ability to find all kinds of creative ways to do things.

Ron Allen works of course with many of the addicts around the city with his poetry and that's part of what I'm doing the studies on. And there's Dr. Mandingo, who uses drama therapy to work with addicts. The whole idea of art and treatment is that art frees up and extends boundaries, makes them more permeable, makes them less rigid. And that's what I think things like this do. Because rigid boundaries keep people from finding that thing within them with the most creative potential, which is the healing part of themselves.

AUDIENCE MEMBER:

My name is Linda Smith, and I'm a member of this church and I'm really grateful that you chose our church to do your performance. It's really helped me put together some pieces of the puzzle, especially on the national and international scene.

You were talking about the whole connection between people in power and people at the bottom, the class war idea. And then you added the piece about the jail industry. My mother lives in a little town in Arkansas. It was almost dying and now they've gone through this big economic revitalization because they built this new prison. With all these insidious forces, how are we going to do something to change the system?

When I put all the pieces of the puzzle together, it almost seems like somebody, some group, is orchestrating this. We get these little additional pieces falling in place that seem to stabilize the system. So it can't just be that our roots are Puritanical and Calvinistic. What it begins to look like is that there's some kind of conspiracy going on. And is this even a useful question to ask, to deal with this problem? Or is that going to make other people think that we're crazy and they'll blow us off and say you're paranoid?

John Malpede:

Why don't we have one more question and then we'll sort of respond to both of them. The short answer is that it's bigger than a conspiracy. [*Laughter*]

Audience Member:

I want to comment about something and it's directed to the black community and black women particularly. Black women hear the same thing from their men their whole life. Things like, "I'm tired of the police holding me up all the time." I get pulled over pretty regularly. They ask you questions like: "Do you work?" They don't say: "Let me see your license." First they say things like: "Do you work? Where are you coming from? Where are you going? How long are going to you be there?" What's that have to do with making a right on a red light? So, if I come home and I'm bent to the woman I'm with, then she says, "You black men complain all the time about this and that. Why don't you be more responsible and not make a right turn on red?" You know what I mean?

The point is, these things are real, the things that happen to people on the street. They are real. And if you hear a story being told to you from the time you were a little girl everyday and you heard the same thing from any number of black men today, you have to consider something is happening in your life that you need to pay attention to and not say to that man: "You know, why don't you be just more responsible."

John Malpede:

Thanks. So let's go back to, either someone here responding to that question or the question about: Is it a conspiracy? Dan, why don't you go up and identify yourself?

Dan Solano:

My name is Dan Solano. I'm a retired Detroit police officer. I'm president of Police Officers for Drug Law Reform. I'm also a board member of LEAP, which is "Law Enforcement Against Prohibition." To answer your question about whether police specifically target ethnic communities in particular in the war on drugs: that's a fact. Our executive director is a retired New Jersey police lieutenant, and one of his jobs was to go around the country and teach other state police agencies to stem the flow of drugs. And one of their methods of stemming the flow of drugs was to target people of a perceived nationality. If you were brown or black and in particular a male, as you were driving north to south, east to west, or west to east, it didn't matter, you were stopped, investigated and searched. So, yes, it is a fact. You were targeted. It's still a problem today, but it's being addressed. We, as police officers, find that to be offensive in the worst kind of sense. And we're dealing with that issue. So it's being addressed.

Chris Parks:

I'm not too big on conspiracy theories, but if you want to call secrets and hiding things a conspiracy, then I can talk to that. In an alcoholic family, the family members cover up the alcoholism of the person who is using. Is that a conspiracy? I guess if you want to add a political flavor to it, you can call it that. I think if it more as a pathology. John said it was larger. I think it is much more a pathology of our society than it is any kind of organized conspiracy and organized cover-up. I think it's just a general attitude in which we approach things. If you call something a "war," like I said at the beginning, the idea of collateral damage is an acceptable loss, in a war in which you're attempting to win. So the attitude with which some of these people may or may not have sold drugs or participated in the selling of drugs to get money to finance the war is the real problem. It's the attitude that's the problem. It's not that there's some hidden, hidden chamber of dark secrets. All families have their shadow members that we attribute all of our negative things to. The way that we deal with our shadows in our family is by shining light on them. So it sometimes is much easier to fight an organized conspiracy than to fight a disorganized pathology.

PETER SELLARS:

Wow. I'd like to keep going with that. Who's gonna tell his dad what he doesn't want to hear? There's a big issue in every family. But also the fact is, and what the Freedom of Information Act is starting to show, and what you get from, for example, the book that just came out by this guy, David Brock, *Confessions of a Conservative,* is stuff so much darker than you would ever guess.

And what about the stuff that they're still not letting out on freedom of information? Why can't they let that out? And you get these pages and there's still stuff all blacked out. Stuff that they're not telling you, when what they're starting to show you is already so scary. So what did they do that they're not showing you? And so I have to say there's a really healthy case of paranoia.

And I also have to say, when you look at how the money-making is organized… it is organized. That's why they call it organized crime. And the key to organized crime is its penetration to high levels of government, cause that's what lets it be possible. And we're dealing with the biggest organized crime in the history of the planet, at its highest penetration into the levels of government at any time in the history of the planet. And yes, these people have been working on this thing. They're serious about it. They're way more serious than we are, and that's the problem, because they are serious every day all day. They are working and they're working hard, and they mean it. And these right-wing think tanks have been going for 30 years to plan the takeover of the United States.

You know, say anything you want about George W. Bush except that he was elected. Hello. This is Argentina now. And you are in the middle of a right-wing military coup, and these people are organized, they are planning it, and it is happening. Anyone who is against them is a criminal or an enemy.If it's a war, that means anyone who is opposed to them is just an enemy, and the war on drugs means anyone who has anything to say is a criminal. And we know criminals are not human beings. Enemies are not human beings. And once they've dehumanized you, then they can do anything they want and then open up all the prisons, work camps and death camps you want. And we are at the one of lowest ebbs in the history of the human race. And it's official.

JOHN MALPEDE:

And that's all happening at an undisclosed location at this moment. [*Laughter*] The term "crack addict" is exactly what Peter was just talking about. Nobody is a "crack addict." I mean, no one's essence is that they are a "crack addict." But if you define someone as a "crack addict," then they become the enemy. And then, you know, etc.... Regina, did you want to say something?

REGINA SCHWARTZ:

Yes, I just wanted to add my two cents. Your question about conspiracy—I would just call it politics instead of conspiracy, to cut to the chase. And the reason I do was so beautifully exemplified by this performance, because what was this performance about? It was a hearing that was designed to bring to light information, bring to light facts, bring to light evidence, bring to light, dare I say the word "Truth"?

And it didn't make a damn bit of difference. It didn't make any difference. It didn't matter at all. I mean, it was all silenced altogether. Why is that? Why does information not matter? Why does evidence not matter? Why are people silenced? Why aren't the right people interviewed? The answer is politics. The fancy word for that is "ideology." But it just means it's not in the interest of the ruling party to bring that evidence to light. So I think it's definitely true. It's conspiracy and more.

AUDIENCE MEMBER:

I think you're more right in saying that it was race or class, more than politics, because we've got to recognize that there are 8 million individuals now tied up in the prison industry, whether they are in jail, prison, parole. But it's not just 8 million individuals. They have brothers. They have sisters. They have mothers. They have kids. They have fathers. And so a huge amount of people are tied up in it. And the other side of it, there's 2 million people who are police, FBI agents, ATF, prison guards. There's 2 million out there right now employed watching us. But it's not that simple. There are not 2 million people watching 6 million people, or, even counting the families, 20 million people watching each other.

It's one of the larger conflicts around race since the Civil War. In the Civil War the white northerners were able to tell themselves a lie, that only the white southerners were into the slave trade, but the entire northern economy was tied up with producing the goods, the services that a lot of the slave trade helped perpetuate.

What I'm trying to get to is that we have a similar situation now. Arizona has seven prisons! Three quarters of the population of the state is tied up in prisons. They get to use that as tax write-offs, they get to use that in census drawings, they get to use that for jobs. There are people involved in this on the outside. All the people who are in the communities where these jails are prevalent. And also, the people who buy stuff from Eddie Bauer, which is one of the companies who contract stuff out from Unicor, the government corporation that makes products for Bauer using prison labor. And if we're going "this is cheaper"—whether it's the prisoner in Texas who made some product, or an Indonesian girl—if we're getting excited saying, "This is cheaper," then we're all complicit in our own destruction. So it isn't a conspiracy, because people buy into it. It does affect us all.

Audience Member:

I'd like to add on to that, that the language politicians use to talk to us has changed over the last 30 years, and now we are usually called "taxpayers," in other words, "consumers" in political language. We're only called "citizens" when we're asked to volunteer to pick up the pieces of government programs that didn't last or have been cut. When you're called a "citizen" it means that you are asked to do something. When you are called a taxpayer, your question is: "What's in it for me?" And for the last 30 years, that's what we've been being called: taxpayers and consumers. So we're all stuck in this role, of living in, on the outskirts of activity in our own country, our own government.

John Malpede:

Thank you, and I want to thank everyone here for sharing so much deep thought, as citizens, and not taxpayers or consumers here today.

Public Conversation
Cleveland, 2004

LAPD arrived in Cleveland two days after the November election. Ohio had been the pivotal state in deciding the presidential election. It had put George Bush over the top. The city of Cleveland and Cuyahoga County had gone strongly Democratic, as expected. When we flew out of Los Angeles the mood was grim, and when we arrived Cleveland the mood was grimmer.

We traveled with the same LAPD contingent as had gone to Detroit; Alexander Anderson, Melina Bielefelt, Henriëitte Brouwers, John Malpede, Rick Mantley and Tony Parker.

In Cleveland, we partnered with Cleveland Public Theater (CPT), located in what was a working-class neighborhood—back when there was a working class—near Lake Eire, just west of downtown. The current state of the neighborhood included elements of stability, decay and gentrification efforts.

James Levin, the founder and former artistic director of CPT, had invited us. Prior to founding CPT James had worked as a criminal defense attorney. In 1999, he had established a link to Y-Haven Homeless Recovery program. Y-Haven's Westside location is five or six blocks from the theater, and around the corner from James' home, a converted factory loft.

Each year, James and CPT worked with the residents of Y-Haven and produced a show that played at CPT and traveled to schools and shelters in the area. We arrived just after the completion of a 2004 project, an original, autobiographical show, called "The House Within." James had officially left CPT by that time, and the show had been developed and directed by Raymond Bobgan, CPT education director, and resident director at the theater.

In 2002, a drug-reform initiative in Ohio had gone down to defeat, after extensive and legally questionable politicking against it by the governor's office. Among our invited speakers were Ed Orlett, the manager of the defeated proposition, and Dan Forbes, a freelance journalist from New York who had written extensively about what the Taft administration had done in defeating the proposition. It revealed the lengths to which the drug warriors would go when faced with the prospect of successful reform.

While we were there, Cleveland earned the dubious distinction of being designated as America's poorest city. In addition to holding public conversations about the impact of the drug war on poverty in Cleveland, I conducted interviews with Terry Luria, head of the clinical staff of Y-Haven and with our cast members from Y-Haven. An interview with cast member Johnny Mack is included here, along with an interview with Rufus Sims, a lawyer working with the organization Racial Fairness for reform of the criminal justice system. These interviews follow the transcript of a panel that included Dan Forbes and the director of the Northeast Ohio Coalition for the Homeless, Brian Davis. Taken together they provide a good picture of the obstacles that confront people trying to get out of homelessness, addiction or the criminal justice system.

Also, I interviewed LAPD's Rickey Mantley about his organizing work in Los Angeles with the LA Community Action Network. I include this here, not only because in took place while we were in Cleveland, but also because it articulates a means for homeless people to gain a voice in representing their own interests in public policy discussions. —**JOHN MALPEDE**

Thursday, November 27, 2004

PANELISTS:

DAN FORBES: Freelance Journalist based in New York who has written extensively on drug policy

BRIAN DAVIS: Director, Northeast Ohio Coalition for the Homeless

JOHN MALPEDE: Director, LA Poverty Department

JAMES LEVIN: Moderator, Defense Attorney and Founder, Cleveland Public Theater

JAMES LEVIN:

It's interesting to note that if the government was sophisticated enough to pull off the Iran hostage situation, that the possibility of an election fix should be secondhand. And I am completely convinced that the election fraud of 2004, when it comes out, will be an even greater scandal than Iran Contra. The question is whether it will happen before January or not.

Okay. We have a wonderful panel today. I'd like to welcome the director of this show, John Malpede, and also, to my right, Dan Forbes. Dan Forbes is a noted freelance journalist who has done much work related to social policy and drugs, and he will tell you about that. To my left is Brian Davis, who is sort of a local hero to the progressive community. He is now the executive director for NEOCH, the Northeast Ohio Coalition for the Homeless. They will both present a short expression of what they're working on now, and how it might pertain to this play, and then we'll be open to a dialogue with you. Please welcome Dan Forbes.

DAN FORBES:

Well, thanks a bunch to Cleveland Public Theater and to James, and of course to John and the LAPD for bringing me here. I'm a freelance reporter out of New York, journalist—that's a newfangled phrase. I'm an old-fashioned reporter, that's good enough for me. Such outlets as *Slate, Salon, Village Voice, The Nation,* etc. When John got in touch with me, it was primarily because of a report on some real snakey, snarky secret stuff that happened here in Ohio, you'll be shocked to hear, with the election of 2002. In 2001, of the people sent to prison here in Ohio for the first time, that's almost 5,000 people, 65 percent of them were sent for drug possession alone, at a cost of about $22,000 an inmate. Half of those prisoners are African-American, even though only 12 percent of the state's population is. There have been calls for years to halt this needless and self-destructive incarceration. They just sat on it. That's why the need for a constitutional amendment was recognized. It was called the Ohio Constitutional Amendment for Treatment of Substance Abuse Offenders. By no means a "Get Out of Jail Free" card, it was open to a very narrow range of offenders: only those with first- or second-time possession offenses, no weapons, no dealing, no crimes of violence. It was modeled on Proposition 36 which passed with 60 percent of the vote in 2000, in California. It was designed, basically, for folks on the corner who are popped for extremely small amounts of drugs. Why are we putting them in a box, a graduate school for crime, embittering them, giving them a record that really sends their life inexorably on a downward path? A trio of billionaires pushed it, George Soros, the New York financier; Peter Lewis, a local Cleveland boy made good with Progressive Insurance; and John Sperling, who founded the University of Phoenix. That's on one side of the equation.

On the other side of the equation we found the Taft Administration, with about $106 million spent on community services, control of that budget, a lot of jobs, sentencing policies, and frankly a paternalistic notion of government. A "we mean best, and also, we know best" approach, and also, a resentment of this rich trio of outsiders coming in. The Taft administration started their campaign to defeat this initiative, at first attempting to secretly sway the voters of this state, and then in the last couple of months to overtly campaign against it. They started this 18 months before the election, and they didn't pull any punches.

Bob Taft, his wife, Hope, who was very much the prime mover of this, his chief of staff, his top criminal abuse official, a substance abuse official, all worked on this. It added up to hundreds of hours of state-paid time invested in defeating this ballot initiative, because the top four or five officials in criminal abuse and substance abuse departments were all secretly on this. This came to the attention of the campaign manager for the initiative, a man named Ed Orlett, a former state legislator. Someone slipped him a single memo of talking points for this. And he thought, "Well, gosh, the governor is having talking points to defeat this, let me do a freedom of information request. And Ohio actually has a pretty good open government act. Orlett was astounded when his request was met a couple of months later with a stack of memos, some 300 pages total, on the Taft activities just in the first several months. And I got ahold of them, wrote up a 20,000 word report on that was published by the Institute for Policy Studies.

Like any good politician, this administration sought to frame this issue, rather than have it be a debate on what should be done with these low-level possession offenders. They said, let's lie. Let's make it seem as if everyone in the field is against it. And they tried to bribe. There was talk of trying to bribe the treatment providers with a new excise tax on beer and wine, and saying, "Your budgets will be much increased if you go against this."

So they had the intellectual parameters, and then they had the sheer logistical—if not strictly illegal, that's open to discussion, but certainly unethical—use of public employees who were supposedly on the clock, working for the citizens of Ohio. The strategy sessions… they couldn't hold them in government offices, so they secreted themselves away in the governor's residence. It wasn't on official calendars, just, "Okay, 3 o'clock we're going over there." That they did weekly. They also had a high-level session. As there was talk of similar ballot initiatives in Florida and Michigan, they brought the criminal justice officials from there, and had the number two official in the White House drug czar's office come out to a strategy session. Ohio taxpayers paid for these out-of-town trips, with DEA agents involved. They had outcomes from such strategy sessions, with such talk as "beat the initiative back in the entire country, not just this one state." All sorts of really sophisticated or blatant politicking. I only managed to get one official on the phone, the criminal justice chief —everybody else ducked me—and he referred to this sort of activity as "fact-finding" because the Taft administration needed to inform themselves of the implications.

Another thing that really sticks in my craw is a strategy session held in the U.S. Capitol building. The one with the dome that is toured by school children every day, and is referred to as "the people's house." It was hosted by the top Republican staffer on the international narcotics caucus. Why he was involved in a session for an Ohio initiative I'll let you figure out; I never quite did. His main role there was that he had an "in" with the Partnership for a Drug Free America, the folks that started out with the ad saying: "This is your brain on drugs," with the image of an egg frying in a pan. He got their four top executives in this meeting with Hope Taft and all of her minions, and, interestingly enough, the wife of George Bush's chief fundraiser, who is now the ambassador to Italy. He started out as the ambassador to Australia, but I guess the food's better in Italy. And there was a lot of talk about creating ads indicating how good the situation in Ohio was, that there was no need to change the status quo.

The Partnership woke up at the last minute, after a lot of back-and-forth meetings in New York, and just said, "Wait a minute, what if this comes out in the memos? Oh my God, Ohio has an open government law. Maybe we shouldn't do this." So they pulled back at the last moment, and that marked the first half of the campaign.

Then the Tafts, both Bob and Hope, got on their high horse and were running around the state saying that this initiative would legalize drugs, even though if you failed more than two drug tests on it, you'd be sent to jail for 90 days. Taft himself appeared right here in Cleveland at the Circle for Treatment Center, talking against it. The backers of the initiative sought, once this came out, to sanction Taft, to get him to stop doing this. But with a Republican-dominated secretary of state's office and judiciary, that obviously went nowhere.

But the *coup de grace* for the initiative, what really killed it, was the ballot summary language. There was a gubernatorial election in 2002, and most voters... they go in the voting booth to cast their vote for governor. Most likely they haven't given any thought to the ballot initiatives. "What's this, a ballot initiative?" That's the way it is for many voters. On the ballot there's ballot-summary language, a paragraph or two, and that's really the whole ball of wax for a number of voters. And astonishingly enough, with a Republican-dominated state board approving the ballot language, the language confronting voters said, "If you pass this initiative, it will cost the taxpayers of Ohio $250 million bucks over seven years"—even though treatment costs $4,000 a year or less, while jail will cost $22,000. The language was absurd on its face. Yes, it would cost that amount, $35 million bucks a year for seven years. But it would save at least $60 million bucks a year by keeping 4,000 or 5,000 or 6,000 people a year out of prison. That tiny detail was not mentioned. With that language summary confronting voters, the measure lost overwhelmingly. Based on that tax expenditure, that fraudulent language, 67 percent voted against it. As one paper said, most voters never heard of the net savings, but saw only that $250 million highlight, and that was pretty much it.

And so the racial disparity in Ohio, as far as incarceration will continue, and it's getting worse, it's getting worse around the country, with the exception of a few states which, primarily for fiscal reasons, are pulling back from this. Pennsylvania just did. But still the overall trend is for ever-increasing prison sentences. The average prison term is now 50 months; a decade or two ago it was 25 months. For blacks it's six years, for whites it's four years, and the insanity continues. The powerful chairman of the House Judiciary Committee has just introduced legislation that if you so much as pass a joint to someone who has ever been in treatment—so in other words, if you're involved with your friends, your family who have been in treatment, if you give them any drug at all—it's a five-year mandatory minimum sentence. I give you this pill and boom, you're gone for five years. It'll cost you and the country $100,000.

JAMES LEVIN:

Brian Davis, okay?

BRIAN DAVIS:

I thought the performance was wonderful. I thought all of the performers were amazing. Especially I thought Congresswoman Waters was good in the middle. I thought she was going to stand up and say, "I don't care if no Senator has signed the discharge petition from *Fahrenheit 911*," but she didn't.

I'm going to give you some impact on the war on drugs, Cleveland specifically. I'm from the Northeast Ohio Coalition for the Homeless. And we see thousands of people coming back every year, into Cleveland, because they were put away for possession and other offenses, and they wind up in the shelters. Every shelter in Cleveland is full. Every shelter in Cleveland has been full for at least 10 years now. When individuals return to our community from jail, usually their family has been taken away. If they had children, they were taken away. Therefore, they qualify for nothing in our community. They qualify for no cash assistance. They have a very hard time qualifying for medical care. They have to wait for two years to qualify for any housing assistance in our community, and they're usually confined to the plantation that we call temporary labor in our downtown community, because they can't get a job that pays any decent wage. We also have the reality that all of our treatment beds in our community were purchased by corrections facilities. The incentive is to go to jail in order to find treatment in our community. And as I said, the shelter beds are full, and the racial composition of the homeless is that about 75 percent of the homeless are African-American in Cleveland, far above the population that exists in Cleveland, considering the fact that many of the homeless population come from outside the city of Cleveland. Many are returning to Cleveland, and are told to stay away from their families. They are told to stay away from the neighborhood that got them in trouble, and so they have nowhere else to go but the shelter. We've increased the size of the shelters. We now have an overflow shelter. The shelter at 2100 Lakeshore is the largest shelter for homeless in Cleveland, and it is full every night. They had to open a secondary shelter because it was full every night. That's the impact that we see from the war on drugs in our community. We see people that are without housing and have no ability to find housing. They cannot make enough money to make the housing that exists in our community, and have a hard time spending nine to 24 hours in our emergency rooms waiting for health care. That's really the reality that the war on drugs has brought to Cleveland and to Cuyahoga County.

JAMES LEVIN:

There are so many issues here to deal with, we just need to hear from you, what you want to talk about.

AUDIENCE MEMBER:

An actual interesting Cleveland connection with the show had to do with the Arthur Feckner case in the 1980s. It involved literally the drug sales by Arthur Feckner right outside public housing in Cleveland in 1985. Arthur Feckner sold cocaine and handed the money from it over to the police, hundreds of thousands of dollars, and the money was then stored in a safe. They were very patient with this. They were going to take this money and use it to do a drug bust in Miami. The Cleveland police literally drove it down to Florida for a drug bust. It was a big scandal. This is documented, covered in *The Cleveland Plain Dealer.* Right after this was going on, crack cocaine really started to increase. There were reports from local substance-abuse clinics that were issued simultaneous to this operation, that substance abuse was increasing. Then, right after the police–Feckner operation, Police Chief Mike White decides he's going to do a major crackdown on drugs. And so they started to do a massive series of arrests, of neighborhood users and small-time dealers.

Audience Member:

You haven't said a lot about this, but I'm wondering what do the tax man and the Bush administration and all of these forces have in continuing the status of the way it is. What is their interest in allowing for all of this?

Dan Forbes:

Well, it's bureaucratic inertia and absolute power corrupting absolutely. Why would they allow outsiders to tell them how to run their sentencing policy? Also there have been vast sums of money invested in building and running both public and private prisons. The California prison guards union is the single most powerful lobby in that state. In the state of New York there's been so many people emptied from the city of New York to upstate New York; they're actually counted in the census for getting political power, congressional representation, and all sorts of funding. Those folks swell the population of these little counties by 20 percent or 30 percent, even though they're not allowed to vote.

JAMES LEVIN:

On a local level, as one that does some defense law, I go to the Justice Center maybe twice a week, and the criminal justice system is absolutely addicted to drugs. It's totally clear, in any courtroom in the county, and there are about 30 some, every docket is probably 80 percent to 85 percent minor drug cases, primarily African-American. If there weren't this constant fuel of the criminal justice system, we wouldn't need all of this. We wouldn't need all of these prosecutors. We wouldn't need all these bailiffs. We wouldn't need all of these court reporters. We wouldn't need all of these defense lawyers. And God knows we wouldn't need all of these prisons that we do. I mean, they're all over southern Ohio. It's a primary industry. It's a very vital industry in central and southern Ohio. The prison contractors, the people like the prison guards.... I mean, God knows what these people would do if they weren't prison guards. The concessions people, the amount of food that goes in.... The concessions people are just serving the prisoners. It's a huge industry in this state, and it is itself addicted to drugs. I mean it's crystal clear that we can't possibly decriminalize drugs because the system is addicted to it. It's feeding too many people.

AUDIENCE MEMBER:

I just wanted to say that with a lot of the arrests being concentrated in the black community, I think you have to look historically. United States capitalism has built itself on the trans-Atlantic slave trade, and it still is doing such things today. Mario Van Peebles made a semi-documentary on the Black Panther Party. He talked about how after the U.S. military government defeated the Panthers, they bloodied that community with cheap heroin. And now what they've done is they've taken over the rap thing, when it first started out in the mid-80s, early 80s, it was all about empowerment in the inner city. And now it's all about drug dealing and all that. So there's still a conscious effort by the United States government to keep people doped up, and not political and fighting for their freedom.

BRIAN DAVIS:

I think that policy locally certainly makes it very difficult for local people to organize, for people to realize that we're spending millions and millions to shelter people, to incarcerate them, to go through the legal system. It's gonna take a lot to overturn that.

AUDIENCE MEMBER:

So what is it going to take to change the tide? What about the propaganda machine, how can we fight it? How about, what are we going to do? How can we organize? How can we inform the communities?

JOHN MALPEDE:

I know Dan wants to talk to the propaganda machine, and can, but I do think what you just said ties into the propaganda machine. Because I think it's true, there are disincentives. It's true that rap music did raise a lot of political awareness at the beginning, going all the way back to "The Message," Fab Freddie and the Furious Five. And at a certain point, that was less acceptable to the people that were making money in the recording industry than it was to be talking about, you know, gangsta stuff and all of that kind of stuff. So on some level social justice is less acceptable than a proliferation of drugs and the destruction of communities. Absolutely.

DAN FORBES:

A lot of people are saying, "All right, it's time to start getting resolutions, initiatives, laws passed on the local level," even though it doesn't have a great deal of effect on actual enforcement, especially at the federal level. The city of Oakland, say, the city of Cleveland could do it. Detroit just recently passed a medical marijuana initiative, "legalizing" that for seriously ill people in Detroit. Now that will not keep people in the DEA from busting people in Detroit, should they wish. But it does have an effect. And, it does put pressure on the state government to consider that. It's very hard to see change happening on the federal level. It's certainly possible on the city level. A lot of that has been happening in Ann Arbor, and obviously cities known for their liberal populations. On the other hand, that may be something of a feel-good exercise, I'm afraid.

JAMES LEVIN:

These panel discussions, or any discussion you might have in a bar or a café, often lead to the question, "What does one do?" Any ideas on that?

"AGENTS & ASSETS" CAST MEMBER RICKEY MANTLEY:

I got a comment directed for the "What do we do?" I feel a sense of optimism. Despite the reelection of Bush, despite both houses of Congress controlled by the Republicans. What makes me optimistic is that we've come a long way in raising awareness of these issues in our states and our communities. We've opted for more treatment programs, and those programs have a lot of tradition. I recall the time when people who have substance-abuse problems were fairly ostracized in our society. There were no treatment programs. If you had a job, you lost your job. We've come to recognize that people who have these problems, and who are willing to go into treatment, there's a treatment program for them, like Y-Haven. In California, in the downtown Skid Row area, I remember a time when there were no treatment programs for addicts and alcoholics. These programs have proliferated over the years. Our awareness has been raised that it's a health issue, and even though our government continues to treat it as a criminal issue, the public is slowly becoming aware that it's a health issue. And somehow the tide is going to turn, because it's through forums like this, and it's through propositions like Prop. 36, that we're going to slowly bring about change and common acceptance that this is not a criminal issue, it's a health issue.

DAN FORBES:

One possible crack in the armor is, of course, when it starts affecting the middle class (i.e., the white population). And one of the very few out-and-out victories on the federal legislative level is that the Bush Administration has agreed to roll back the Higher Education Act that was denying federal student loans to anyone who had had the most minor possession or misdemeanor arrest. As a 15-year-old caught in the parking lot with a joint, you were ineligible for a federal loan. Well, this started affecting more and more middle-class, white folks. And they actually are going to rescind that and say it's only if you're caught while you're actually in college. Of course we can't have you in college, which is also ridiculous.

JOHN MALPEDE:

I think there are a lot of different opportunities to organize around change on this issue. When you can talk about prison labor or the prison construction industry or the music industry, you are identifying special interests that do benefit, and which could be targeted for these kinds of campaigns. When we started to work on this performance, it was during the time that the treatment vs. incarceration issue was on the ballot in California. It passed right before we actually did the performance, and at that point there was a lot of optimism about future initiatives passing in other states. In 2004, everything is pretty different. When they lost the initiatives in 2002, everyone said it was going to be back on the ballot in 2004. In fact it wasn't back on the ballot in 2004, because there was a perception that things had changed for the worse. So the steam has sort of gone out of the initiative, but even so, there are a gazillion other ways of organizing around drug reform.

Brian Davis:

I'm not as optimistic as Rickey is after November 2, so I think that a few state bankruptcies, a few urban school-district bankruptcies, and when states stubbornly refuse to take away any middle-class tax cuts, it'll start impacting the entire community. And then things will start changing, because we have this drag on our system because we incarcerate one-seventh of the African-American male population and keep building prisons, and keep having to build shelters, and eventually that will affect all of us, to the extent that there will be some change.

Dan Forbes:

Not the initiative process, but the actual state legislators have gone somewhat for treatment rather than jail. It was costing them countless millions in Philadelphia and Pittsburgh and, you know, the state governments are in a hell of a financial bind, and it's only going to get worse. So there is some shoot-yourself-in-the-foot optimism there.

JAMES LEVIN:

Well, Ohio State beat Michigan. It's hard to come up with something hopeful. This has been a very upbeat discussion, and I'd like to end it in a little bit of an upbeat way, but I can't think of any way to do that at the moment. Come back to CPT some time, we'll have more hilarity and good times. Thank you very much.

EXCERPT OF INTERVIEW WITH DAN FORBES

The night's conversation never did get back to Dan Forbes' account of the propaganda campaign in support of the war on drugs, emanating from the Clinton White House and then the Bush White House. Dan Forbes' account is offered here, taken from an interview I did with him earlier that day.

—JOHN MALPEDE

JOHN MALPEDE:

How long have you been writing about drug policy?

DAN FORBES:

I was doing some work for a trade magazine in the marketing and advertising world, a magazine called *Brand Week,* which is sister to *Ad Week* and well-known in those circles. I was friendly with the editor, and he said: "You know, the White House is doing something odd with the anti-drug ads that have been given donated media time and space for the past seven or eight years." All of a sudden the government is jumping on board, contributing close to 200 million bucks a year in taxpayer funding. He said that he's been in that general field for years, and he doesn't have any idea whether these ads work or not. "Why don't you do some digging around and get into the social science, talk to some of the public health professionals and find out if this is just money down the tubes or what?"

So I said, "fine," and found out that there was no indication that they worked at all. The whole thing was just a feel-good enterprise. It was money donated by people just trying to do some good. The government had far more nefarious intent, but the funny thing was that it was based on just about no social science whatsoever. So I wrote up a big feature on that, and on what I found under some of the rocks I kicked aside. And it was off to the races from there.

JOHN MALPEDE:

What were some of the more nefarious governmental motives?

DAN FORBES:

The government was not involved until the passage of the first drug-reform initiatives, medical-marijuana initiatives passed in California and Arizona in 1996. And in just about a week Clinton's drug czar, an ex-general named Barry McCaffery, who had his own checkered military history, had convened a meeting of 40 top government officials and some private sector senior folks as well, to basically say that we got blindsided by this private money leading to the passage of a medical-marijuana initiative. The medical-marijuana initiatives were written for cancer patients to overcome the nausea of chemotherapy, or MS patients to stop their tremors, or people in wheelchairs to not have spasms that will literally throw them out of their wheelchairs onto the floor.

Well, McCaffery said the government certainly can't allow that. So they kicked off a propaganda campaign, not to mince words. As notes of that meeting that I obtained from a lawsuit put it, their campaign intended "to make sure that no reform initiatives pass ever again," and to roll back the two that had already passed. At lightning speed, by Washington standards, this whole media campaign was born. The Clinton White House got its toes wet with ads that were only slightly over the top. Since Bush has come in, there's no restraint whatsoever in the content. It's almost a self-parody. But that can be said perhaps of the entire Bush Administration.

But just to finish the story, it's quite funny working at a trade magazine. I had access to the government officials, and I was talking to the guy who had oversight, day-to-day oversight, over the media campaign. And he said: Okay, we're going to X and Y and Z and have ads in magazines and on television. And by the way we're going to have government content in TV shows. And this was as the campaign was starting off; he was looking forward six or eight months. I didn't bat an eye. Internally, my doppleganger was racing around the room saying, "Oh my God, is this happening?" and "Wow, is this a scoop." I sat on that knowledge. It took well over a year to go from his prospective planning, to starting to appear on TV screens. But then, lo and behold, they had government-approved content in—I'm remembering off the top of my head here—50, 60 shows, the biggest dramas and sitcoms on TV at that time.

John Malpede:

So, is that still going on?

DAN FORBES:

No, I kept waiting for somebody—a staffer somewhere—to nail the story, but nobody did. I was lucky enough to expose that. It led to a big outcry. There were next-day front-page stories on every paper in the country, pretty much. There were editorials condemning it. There were articles in every daily. There were four Congressional hearings. I was invited to testify before two, which was quite an experience.

"Agents & Assets" certainly took me back. I'll say, parenthetically, you raise your hand to testify before Congress, and you think you're blasé, and you really do get choked up when you raise your hand in Congress. It's like, here you are, just a schlump—freelance writer/citizen, with just a few shekels in your pocket—and here you are testifying before Congress and raising your hand to say that you're going to tell nothing but the truth and you know you're sitting next to governmental officials who are there expressly to lie, and you do get pretty choked up.

But to answer your question, it was curtailed under Clinton, and then Bush discontinued it because the whole thing was done as social marketing to influence peoples' views. It became too obvious: "Oh, here's another government message embedded in a TV show." Of course, they're still doing paid advertising in spades.

JOHN MALPEDE:

Did government input into content have to do with Clinton's rapport with Hollywood?

DAN FORBES:

No, it didn't have to, because Congress mandated it. Here's

what happened. Congress appropriated a new pile of money, $200 million a year, which is a nice chunk of change, for anti-drug advertising. Congress said, we are not going to give that money unless it's done on a two-for-one basis. The networks, newspaper or magazines have to contribute their time: 50 cents on the dollar. And that was fine when it was first instituted, because there was actually an advertising slump around '98–'99. But then when the "dot-com" boom exploded in '99 and advertising time became much more valuable, and the TV networks started screaming.

There's only so many 30-second slots on a show, and they owed some of those slots to the government on that two-for-one basis. So they worked out a deal to allow government input into the content of the shows, where it wasn't eating into Hollywood's advertising revenues. They had White House consultants on the phone with conference calls to the Hollywood script writers, saying, "Okay, I like the first half of the show here, but you need to punch up the anti-drug message in the second half. There need to be much more dire consequences." Or even, just for instance, one I recall, they said: "The kid who smoked pot is a really good-looking kid. He seems popular with the female students in his class. You've really got to cross that out and make him seem like a buffoon." And the scriptwriters are taking all this down. So with the program as it unfolded, Hollywood was delighted. They were able to trade the slot for input into the content. They were released from that agreement, and they could turn around and sell a 30-second spot for half a million bucks. And when you add it all up, it was many million dollars more in their pockets, so it wasn't hard to convince them.

INTERVIEW WITH RUFUS SIMS

Rufus Sims is an attorney and a board member of the Racial Fairness Project in Cleveland. Due to a schedule conflict he was unable to join one of our panels. He was gracious enough to squeeze in an interview on the Saturday morning of Thanksgiving weekend. He immediately mentioned the Feckner case that audience members brought up more than once during our public conversations in Cleveland. —**JOHN MALPEDE**

RUFUS SIMS:

I think with any discussion of drugs, I'm gonna focus on the black community, because that's where most of my work is done. It would be remiss unless you discuss a guy named Arthur Feckner. Arthur Feckner was a small-time drug dealer back in the 1980s, who became a big-time drug dealer. The Cleveland police department set up a drug house in the heart of the black community, right next to a housing project at 105th and Woodlawn. And Feckner was allowed to sell drugs—crack cocaine—out of that house that was set up. And by his own admission and by his own testimony he sold 13 pounds of cocaine. And for those of you that don't know, 13 pounds of cocaine, that's a lot of dope. And it impacted a lot of peoples' lives. And when it got back to the community that this guy was an operative of the police department, and was functioning under the auspices of the narcotics division of the police department, the you-know-what hit the fan. And he was prosecuted by the county for selling drugs. He spent about five years in prison. They also indicted five narcotics detectives. This was in 1985. All five detectives were acquitted of any illegal activity.

Feckner's testimony during the proceedings was that he gave the police department $432,000, and this money was to be used to fund a drug sting in Florida. And when the word got out to the community that our own police department was funding a drug house, there was outrage. And we are still suffering the effects of that experience. A lot of people got hooked. A lot of children, meaning people under 18, got hooked. And they bought drugs directly from Arthur Feckner's drug house. And I think that if you understand that, you understand what's going on today. That's the point I want to make to you. The system, meaning the authorities, have a vested interest in promoting the drug trafficking that's happening, particularly in the African-American community.

JOHN MALPEDE:

When they said, "We're just raising money for a drug sting in Florida," that was their total explanation?

RUFUS SIMS:

Yes, to use a small fish to catch a bigger fish.

JOHN MALPEDE:

But they were going to catch the big fish some place else, down in Florida?

RUFUS SIMS:

Right. But they didn't set this house up in the wealthy, white communities. It was brought down to the inner city, where we live. To this day people are very upset about that experience and that case.

John Malpede:

So why is this agenda in place with the police?

Rufus Sims:

It's business. Drugs represent business, and if you look at what's really going on in our society, particularly our state, they're building more prisons than schools. The drug trafficking and the drug business is profitable for a lot of people. Today, in our county, where I work, Cuyahoga County, 80 percent of the indictments are drug-related. So of our roughly 40,000 indictments a year, 80 percent are related to drugs. That's a lot of cases directly related to illegal drug sales, and the number's not going down.

John Malpede:

So it results in a huge investment not only in prisons, but police.

Rufus Sims:

More prisons, more police, better surveillance, a lessening of civil liberties. But things are happening now. It's not all gloom and doom. There's a drug court now today that's funded by the Cleveland municipal court. You have a shot at treatment in the drug court at the municipal level. If you're a first-time offender, you can get a chance of treatment at the felony level. They are doing what they can to try and combat the drug problem. Given the enormity of this problem, the drug court is a very small but positive result.

John Malpede:

Is there any momentum to expand the drug court.

RUFUS SIMS:

There's no money to expand the drug court. In fact, just the reverse. There's discussion now to eliminate the drug court.

JOHN MALPEDE:

This would be in the city budget or the state?

RUFUS SIMS:

City. I think there's some funds available through the federal government. Right now, the city has the drug court. The larger county didn't want to have the drug court, but the city said this is something we have to have for our citizens.

JOHN MALPEDE:

What avenues are you pursuing to make change here?

RUFUS SIMS:

I deal with a lot of drug cases in my practice, and one of the moves we're trying to make, at the grassroots level, is to have residue, cocaine residue, considered a misdemeanor and not a felony. I mean you're in your car, you're driving, something happens, there's a crack pipe in your car.... They don't have crack in there, just the residue of the crack, and why that's indicted as a felony that blows my mind. People that use need help. The punitive stuff is not working, not working, and so we're pushing to make residue a misdemeanor, rather than a more punitive felony. Because what happens with a felony, if you get a felony conviction, then you can't get certain funding to go to college. You can't get certain public housing. You can't get certain jobs with the city, the state, the county. You're eliminated from the job market to a certain extent with that felony conviction. It's a downward spiral.

We think that the only way for it to be changed is through the state legislature. We think we have to get the Ohio state legislature to agree that drug residue should be a misdemeanor and not a felony. There are some discussions going on in that area. But we have not been successful till this day. For the most part the politicians in Columbus really don't care what happens to the inner-city people. I think that's the reality. There's an attitude of, "Hey, we don't really care what happens in certain neighborhoods." And we think that if this problem had been taking place in some of the whiter communities, if this had been taking place in the suburbs, something would have been done. That's what we think.

JOHN MALPEDE:

Alfred McCoy, who's one of the foremost historians of the drug war, has said that our incarceration rate has gone so high that it can't possibly keep going on in that direction. He calls the current drug policy "a doomsday machine."

RUFUS SIMS:

We incarcerate more people than in any place in the world and it costs $40,000 per year for one person to be in prison, So just imagine you multiply that by hundreds of thousands. And now in Ohio, there are so many women in prison, they're talking of building a second women's prison. We only have one right now, for women: Marysville. But Marysville is busting at the seams. So now they're discussing building a second prison for women in the Cleveland area. So again, building prisons. And look at the educational system. It's the worst in the country.

JOHN MALPEDE:

You're saying the legislature isn't really interested in seeing the light, making the changes?

RUFUS SIMS:

No, they don't think that minority people are worth spending the money on. They'll spend it on the war or some other budgetary expense. But our city's going to hell. It really is. The legislators don't care about minority people. Now they've just made it legal, given people permission, to carry concealed weapons. So the answer is: if you're approached by someone, just shoot 'em.

JOHN MALPEDE:

Everything is fear-driven. Like the war, as you brought up, or gay marriage.

RUFUS SIMS:

That's a non-issue. The whole gay marriage issue is a smokescreen. I'm not even going to discuss that issue, when our schools are in this condition and we're in an epidemic with the crack cocaine. We're in a crack cocaine epidemic in our community right now. That's what's happening now, which leads to all kinds of other problems, like the breakdown of the family, the destruction of the school system, that kind of thing.

This is a very conservative state. In general, Ohio is a very conservative state. We are.

JOHN MALPEDE:

So much of it is rural. And that's the most conservative part of the state.

RUFUS SIMS:

Yes. I would say the areas below Mansfield.

JOHN MALPEDE:

So then they have a short-sighted notion of what their interest is with regard to the welfare of the cities.

RUFUS SIMS:

A lot of people have the idea that if you violate the law, we just lock 'em up. If we say that's not the problem, then there are people that answer, "Well, we just haven't locked up enough of them yet." So we just keep locking people up, building more prisons, hiring more police, hiring more prosecutors, building another women's prison. That's the answer that a lot of people have to the drug problem. And it's not going to work. It cannot work.

JOHN MALPEDE:

I know that when the drug-reform initiative was on the ballot here in 2002, the churches here in town and the African-American newspapers were the only ones that supported the reform.

RUFUS SIMS:

Yes, because I think that in our community we're impacted by drugs more than any other community. So we understand the need for treatment over punishment. We understand it more than anyone.

JOHN MALPEDE:

Lobbying the legislature, is that something Racial Fairness is doing? Is that something a lot of other groups are doing?

RUFUS SIMS:

That's something that a lot of groups are doing, but it has to be done on a more consistent, umbrella-type basis. Racial Fairness is an excellent vehicle and other groups can come up under it. Lobbying the legislature is one of our activities. Sometimes you get very frustrated because the politicians are not listening. People in Columbus are not listening. We have to come up with a solution for people who use, because people who use need help. And they're crying out for help. We deal with racial fairness in the justice system. For example, Cuyahoga County is 23 percent African-American, but the indictments that come down are about 75 percent African-American. We're being indicted three times higher than our representation in the population of the county. And, again, 80 percent of the indictments are drug cases and most of them are for possession.

In Ohio, with half a gram of crack in your possession, there's a presumption that you go to prison. I said possession. I didn't say you were out trafficking or dealing drugs, just on your person. There's a presumption, and that presumption is rebuttable. But I'm talking legal gobbledegook. What I mean is that if you go to court and your lawyer can't plea bargain you down, and you are convicted of half a gram, there's a presumption that you go to jail to six to 18 months for possession. We need to do something about that. That's the low-level stuff. The higher stuff is even more serious.

JOHN MALPEDE:

In this project we're working with Y-Haven; half the cast is from the Y-Haven program. There was an African-American minister here last night and he was saying that so many of the programs are only three months long and that they're inadequate. The Y-Haven program is a two-year residential program with continued ties after that.

RUFUS SIMS:

People who use will be addicts for the rest of their lives. You will be an addict till the day you die. That's why these longer-term programs are necessary for it to be effective.

We know it's not working. What we have right now is the revolving door. Catch a case, go to court, get pled down, get probation. You use, you violate probation, you go to the penitentiary. You go there, come out, use again, you go back. I mean it's the revolving-door system that we have. Most of the guys that have been in the penitentiary, they've been there two, three times. There are very few first-time offenders in the penitentiary. And as a general rule, they don't send first offenders. Why? There's no room. There's no room for first offenders.

JOHN MALPEDE:

What about mandatory minimums in this state?

RUFUS SIMS:

Again, depending on the amount of drugs you have, you can be indicted by the federal grand jury or the state grand jury. In the larger cases, where people are dealing with kilos of cocaine, those cases are dealt with by the federal system. And that's a whole different ball game. And when you mention mandatory minimums, that applies more to the federal system of indictment rather than the state system, which in this state gives the judge some leeway. In the federal system, the judge has less leeway, less flexibility, when it comes to sentencing.

JOHN MALPEDE:

It's being challenged right now isn't it?

RUFUS SIMS:

Yes. A lot of my colleagues are out there fighting, because it doesn't give the judge enough flexibility to deal with individual cases. So a lot of my colleagues are fighting that, that's happening.

JOHN MALPEDE:

What about stacked sentences?

RUFUS SIMS:

You mean consecutive sentences? Consecutive sentences are somewhat rare. They're rare in the state court because you have to meet certain criteria in order to be subject to consecutive sentences. These are sentences in which a person has been a repeat offender, when he's been in the penitentiary before, when he's used a weapon in committing a crime, when maybe he's injured someone. So these are the more violent repeat offenders who are subject to consecutive or stacked sentences.

However, in the federal system, you don't have to be a repeat or violent offender because the amount you have could put you in the mandatory minimums. It's their version of a stacked sentence. When you get 50 years in the federal system for possessing so many kilos of cocaine, that's equivalent to the consecutive sentences at the state court.

JOHN MALPEDE:

I know the Racial Fairness Project was working in the jails prior to the election. Could you tell me about that work?

Rufus Sims:

One of the things we did was we filed a lawsuit during the elections. Well, what some of the county boards of elections were doing is that they were telling people leaving the penitentiary that you can't vote. Now there are 88 counties in Ohio, and about 30 to 40 county boards of elections were telling released inmates from the penitentiary that they were not eligible to vote in the election for president. Of course, under Ohio law you can vote if you're released from prison, if you're registered. The only ones in Ohio who can't vote are the ones in the penitentiary. They're the only ones who can't vote.

John Malpede:

You can vote if you're in county jail?

Rufus Sims:

Absolutely. And some did vote by absentee ballot. As a matter of fact, Racial Fairness Project went into the county jail and registered people at the county jail and at the local jail called the house of corrections. So a lawsuit was filed suing various county boards of election that were denying felons the right to vote. The case was settled. Secretary of State Ken Blackwell issued an edict, a public order, stating that felons can vote if registered, and that made the airwaves and the papers across the state of Ohio. But the damage had been done already. You tell people "you can't vote," they say "okay." Now we have to reverse what has been said. Which we think.... We don't know if it was done by accident. We have our doubts. We have our concerns.

John Malpede:

How does crack use compare to 10 years ago?

Rufus Sims:

Probably higher, if we judge it by the number of indictments. We have more indictments than 10 years ago. We're still suffering the effects of what happened in 1985. Because those people who got addicted had children and the addiction was passed to the children. That's what happened. That's what we're suffering from today. That community where Feckner sold drugs is still destitute, still poor, still a gang-ridden community. Feckner's sales contributed to that, with the sanction of the Cleveland police department.

It was a very emotional time in our city. The black community was in an uproar that this happened, and that this man was allowed to do this and bring drugs into the community, cocaine, and just devastate a lot of lives. The only one that took the fall for this was Feckner. The cops walked away scott-free.

John Malpede:

Did he get into this because he was in trouble with the cops and he made a deal?

Rufus Sims:

Dealing? Yes, that happens every day. "Fine I'm a small-time guy, but I can get you someone bigger." "Yeah, we'll cut you some slack." That happens every day. Louis Stokes was the mayor at that time and George Forbes was the city council president. So we had African-Americans in significant positions, and this happened under their watch.

John Malpede:

You said that the five police officers that got indicted, all of them got off?

RUFUS SIMS:

They indicted them and took a look at their involvement. They concluded that they were acting in their official elected capacity, and under Ohio you are immune for certain crimes if you are acting in your official capacity. Now that's a bunch of gobbledeegook. But still, that was the government's rationale as they went forward with the prosecution, that they were acting in their official capacity as police officers.

JOHN MALPEDE:

So the whole thing came to a really unsatisfactory end, from the point of view of justice.

RUFUS SIMS:

Absolutely. Feckner did five years, but what's that?

JOHN MALPEDE:

What's the most hopeful sign, in terms of dealing with these issues?

RUFUS SIMS:

Well, I think people are taking a real hard look at treatment alternatives. A lot of people are understanding that punishment is not the answer to the drug problem. Punishment gets us into a downward spiraling cycle. We think we've got to put more emphasis on the treatment end, particularly for the users. I'm from an addictive house. My dad was an addict. So I understand on a personal level what's involved with that on a daily basis. We've got to push for treatment, money for treatment. We've just got to keep pushing and lobbying our representatives.

Thanks for the opportunity. It's good to know that there are people interested in the struggle. We've just got to keep getting the word out that treatment is better than punishment in terms of using.

John Malpede:

Thank you.

Interview with Terry Luria

Terry Luria is the Clinical Director of Y-Haven Recovery Program. Seven Y-Haven program participants made up half the cast of our "Agents & Assets" production in Cleveland.

—John Malpede

Terry Luria:

My name is Terry Luria, and in my professional life I'm the clinical supervisor at Y-Haven transitional housing for homeless men. We house 135 men and they can stay with us for up to two years. We have three different sites. What you need to come into Y-Haven is to be over 18, to be a male and to want to make some changes. It's up to two years, and for the first four months they come in we do substance-abuse treatment. They have to be in group every day, and they have to meet with their counselors regularly. Our groups go from nine in the morning, to two in the afternoon, with a break, of course. They are required to be active in a 12-step program. They have to go to a minimum of five meetings a week. They have to have a sponsor. They have to do all that kind of stuff.

The first four months is treatment. Then they're in phase two. That's where we go to the next phase of their life, which is to get them a GED, send them to college, if they have a high school diploma. Send them to job training, or if they're trained, they can even start working at that point. Most of them, though, need something in between. And then at the end of that part of it, in the next phase, we then try to help them find a job, or go on with school, whatever it is that they're interested in. Generally at that point they look for a job, and we help them with that. And then we help them find permanent housing. So if they leave Y-Haven a success story, they are sober, they have gainful employment, they are in permanent housing, at least more permanent housing.

We feel that these guys, in order to be homeless, and coming to us for transitional housing, they have had a lot go wrong in their life, obviously. To get to a place in your life where your family says, "you can no longer live here," and you're homeless… things have to have gotten pretty bad. And I would say 98 percent of our clients have substance abuse as an issue.

JOHN MALPEDE:

What are the other two percent? What are the other issues?

TERRY LURIA:

We are very fortunate in that we have a full-time psychiatrist that works at Y-Haven now. It's been in the last year, which has just been an incredible help for us. I should say that 98 percent of people have substance-abuse and/or mental-health problems. The two percent that you're talking about… We have a gentleman with us now who does not have a substance-abuse problem, nor does he have a mental-health problem, but he's been incarcerated for 27 years over a crime that he committed when he was a young kid.

So he is a perfect candidate, because what we're really about is: How do you change your life and function in society? How do you become a worthwhile citizen? Coming out of a 27-year prison term—I think he's in his late 30s or mid 40s—he has a lot of issues about how to live in the world. So there's a very small percentage of people who come in, who are like he is.

Our treatment component is based on 12 steps and it always returns to that, but what we try to do in treatment is to get these men to get in touch with their feelings. All the ones who have substance-abuse problems have buried their feelings by using. And we want them, now that they're not using anymore, to start to deal with the issues that got them into so much trouble to begin with. We believe that chemical dependency, substance abuse is a disease. And as a disease, we treat it as a disease. It's a chronic disease, because it never goes away. We try to let our men understand that, as long as they're alive, they're going to need to go to 12-step meetings.

JOHN MALPEDE:

It's like an allergy of some sort.

TERRY LURIA:

Well, I don't know if it's an allergy. I think of it more as diabetes, for example. If someone has diabetes they can ignore it and get sicker, which is the same thing with substance abuse. They can treat it and get better, but they can never not treat it. And they also can't talk it away, or reason it away. You have to treat it, and in the case of somebody with substance-abuse issues, they have to remain abstinent for the rest of their lives, one day at a time. They have to continue to work on the issues that have been problems for them. So in the 12-steps, the only mention of drugs or alcohol is in the first step. The rest of the steps are all about how to change your life and become a better person. So really with a substance like crack cocaine, which many of our men have problems with, within three days the substance is out of them, or anybody's system for that matter. So now what? What are you left with? What you're left with are the issues that you had before they started using, the issues that they tried to forget about and cover up with their use. And now we have to start to try and deal with that. And that's what we try to do with group therapy. That's what we do with individual counseling, to guide them to where they begin to bury what was going on.

JOHN MALPEDE:

So those can be traumatic issues?

TERRY LURIA:

Many of our men have been abused. Many of them have been through sexual, physical, and emotional abuse. Not all. Some actually came from good, solid families and got mixed up with the wrong people. Or chose the wrong people, and because of the fact that they have this disease of addiction, as soon as they began to use, they were off and running, because it's a progressive disease. So if someone—no matter what kind of family they've come from—uses, it's going to progress, if they have the disease of addiction or chemical dependency. So some of the guys will tell you, "I ran around with a lot of guys who used, but they just quit when it came time to quit." But they didn't. They continued to get into more and more trouble, because it progresses and it gets worse. Absolutely. If untreated, it will invariably become a bigger and bigger problem. And a person dies from it, if it goes untreated.

JOHN MALPEDE:

Now how does the group start? What is the dynamic there?

TERRY LURIA:

You mean, how the actual group goes? When we meet, they all introduce themselves, they all say their name, describing themselves as an addict or an alcoholic. Or if it's someone who isn't, they would just say their name. And they say how they're feeling today. We try to start with the feelings. Our guys on the east side, we try to do what we call a "Yeah, me!" They say something that happened in the last 24 hours that they feel good about. The goal is to not only talk about what got them here, but to also to begin to build on the things that are good about themselves.

For them to even walk through our door, indicates things that are good about them. It means they want to change. It means they have a desire to do something different. We have different subjects on different days. But we always start off with, "Do we have any sobriety-threatening issues?" And then if anyone has anything that they're struggling with, hopefully they'll talk about it, that's how they get better. So someone might say, "I had to use in a dream last night, and it scared me. I thought I was getting high again." And this person may feel that he's alone, and that this hasn't happened to anyone else.

Then the group starts to share, and he finds that so many others have had those using dreams, and have been just as frightened by them. We talk a little bit about what that means, and why dreams go back to ways we used to cope. It's common and normal. And then we talk about what we can do about it, being grateful that it isn't true, or whatever. They get a lot of feedback.

It's all about identifying with the men in the group. For example, if someone ever shares in the group that they were molested as a child, and they feel very alone, what they find in the group is that people then say, "It happened to me, too." They find that other people have experiences of that kind of pain, and that together they can talk about it.

JOHN MALPEDE:

What a discovery. It really shifts their affect at that moment.

TERRY LURIA:

That's right. So that's what we try to do. That's our goal in group, to find common ground, to help each other. Learn to talk about how we really feel, not just what we think. They have a very difficult time initially talking about feelings, and they say, "Well, I think this." And I often say, "Well how does that make you feel?"

Somebody the other day, in the group, we had a white guy that had made a comment to the group: "You people." And I happened to come into group that day, and I asked the group, "How does that make you feel? When someone calls you 'You people'?" And they were trying to say to him, it's not the right thing to say. And I would keep saying to them, "How does that make you feel?" And they would say, finally, "hurt, sad, angry." The white guy could hear that, and he could understand that he hurt someone's feelings, and they were angry at him. And as the group went on, what we discovered was that he just felt insecure because he was in the minority, and he just wanted to fit in. And everybody ended up being able to share past experiences when they've felt prejudiced. And he was able to share experiences where he felt prejudice, and by the end of the group they were hugging and being able to work together. It doesn't always end up that way, so fast. We were able to tie a pretty neat bow on it, and it was a pretty neat package at the end. Sometimes it takes a lot more than one group. This was just sort of an easy one.

JOHN MALPEDE:

Are people sober when they come in?

TERRY LURIA:

They have to be. We drug test them when they come in. We let them know they need to be sober. They do an intake, and then they're put on a waiting list. Unfortunately, even with 135 beds, we have a pretty long waiting list. We often can't take people right away. Unless it's an easy thing where three people have left the night before, and we can't reach anybody on the list. We keep a list, and by virtue of the fact that they're often homeless, it's often difficult to find them, unfortunately. The ones that really want to get in call regularly. In the winter, the list is usually a couple months long, because of the cold, but in the summer, they're not quite as motivated. But they come in for the intake, and as soon as there's a bed available at one of our sites, we let them know, and they come in. And then we do a whole assessment at that time, an entire site-social assessment. And then we assign them to a counselor and then we get started.

JOHN MALPEDE:

With regard to drug use in the community, is it trending up, is it trending down? Is it impossible to really see a difference?

TERRY LURIA:

I don't really know those statistics. I really do look at it as one man at a time. A lot of people ask me about statistics, and it's hard for us. We do a follow up after six months and a follow up after a year. We call the last-known number. But as you can imagine, just because of our population, sometimes it's very hard. Some of these guys may be doing beautifully, we just can't find them. But we do our best to find them.

And many of them do continue to come back to Y-Haven. We have a whole after-care component that they can continue to come back to for the rest of their lives. Some of them have been sober six or seven years and still come back once a week for the after-care component. So obviously we know a lot about the ones that stay connected. I think that one man staying connected, staying sober, going to meetings, and doing what he's supposed to do, affects so many people. His family, his children, his children's children, everybody. It's like a little pebble and the wave that comes after that. And so the fact that we have as many men as we do who successfully complete the program and stay sober, even if it's... I don't know if it's 40 percent or 50 percent, it makes a huge impact on society. So if we had one guy I would tell you that we were successful. Fortunately we have a lot more than that, but every one that can go out and be a father, a husband, a contributing member of society is just huge. So I don't know if drugs are up or down in the Cleveland community, but I do know that we just work on our little niche.

JOHN MALPEDE:

That image of the pebble, that's really beautiful. It makes total sense.

TERRY LURIA:

What we see each day is so uplifting, and so incredible. We see guys that come in that are broken down physically, mentally, emotionally, spiritually, literally some are close to being on their death bed. They've been using heroin for who knows how many years, they weigh 90 pounds and they come in. They've told me they come in so that they would have a bed to die in, that that's what they come for. And six months, 12 months later, they're in school, they're back with their families, taking care of their children. They're doing things that everybody does, and they're saying, "I just can't believe this is me. I love this life." What a miracle that is.

JOHN MALPEDE:

We were talking about 12-step programs. So many times, I've been in a meeting, a 12-step meeting or a group meeting, and it's such an uplifting experience that I think there aren't really that many outlets for such real caring and sharing, in the... I don't know what you call it... well, the "normative" society.

TERRY LURIA:

"Earth people" we call it. I always say that 12-step works for everybody. First of all I'm convinced that everybody has some addiction or another. You might argue with me, but a big percentage of the population—whether it's eating, or relationships, or sex, overworking—whatever it is, people have things that they overdo. So there's a place for everybody in the 12-step program. Again, only the first step mentions anything about what the substance is, or, the abuse is, whatever the group is. Then the other eleven steps are just about living right. And it's amazing. Y-Haven views treatment as discovery. And continuing in the 12-step meetings, really, they just learn about themselves. It's a little corner of the world. But if they don't stay connected, their success rate diminishes. That's where they really learn how to live.

JOHN MALPEDE:

So tell me about when the LAPD'ers—Rickey and Alexander and Henriëtte—came to Y-Haven to talk about the issues raised by our play.

TERRY LURIA:

It was wonderful. Henriëtte called and asked, "Can we come up and talk about "Agents & Assets?" And I said sure, great, come to the east side. They came into group, and they talked to the guys. Then they did the same thing the next day on the west side. I was so taken. I'm sure Henriëtte and Rickey and Alexander can tell you this too, but the knowledge they had about all this was amazing. I was in awe. The men at Y-Haven, they knew a million times more than I did. I just knew the basics, but they knew so much. It was very moving, it was profound, the things that they knew.

JOHN MALPEDE:

What did they know about?

TERRY LURIA:

They knew about the hearings, they just knew everything. I learned so much that day from them. And the thing that was most interesting was that it was clear that Alexander was very convinced about the CIA's role. And also clear that Rickey was not as convinced, or if he was as convinced, he didn't let on. The thing is there are two schools of thought here. There are people who do not believe this actually happened in the way that others think that it did happen. So it was really food for thought. And I think the most interesting thing that happened was the men who had a lot of information about it were saying, "We were abused, and we were put upon, and the drugs came into the black community and it was a terrible thing," which everyone was agreeing with.

And then there was this one guy in the group who said, "But wait a minute, what are we going to do now? We cannot live in the past, and we cannot live saying how taken advantage of we were. We must do something to get ourselves out of this."

And to me it was a total analogy to substance abuse, in the sense that we can sit in groups and we can talk about all of the terrible things that happened to us when we were growing up, and all the terrible abuses, and all of the terrible parenting, all the things that went on.

Yes, that's important. But what are you going to do about it? It's the same thing with this. Yes, these things probably happened, and yes, the government was probably responsible or mainly responsible. I'll know more by tonight when I see the show. But the reality is, this guy was the voice of reason, saying, "I can't live on what's been done to black people, thinking about the abuses. I have to move on from here, saying, "Where am I going to go now that I know better?" Really enlightening.

JOHN MALPEDE:

Rickey, Alexander, and Henriëtte were all really excited about how it went.

TERRY LURIA:

It went so beautifully. I was just in awe, as I often am with our men.

INTERVIEW WITH JOHNNY MACK

Johnny Mack is a resident of Y-Haven Recovery Program and was a cast member of "Agents & Assets" when we produced it in Cleveland. Just before our arrival he'd also performed in the "The House Within," a show developed with Cleveland Public Theater from autobiographical material of Y-Haven program members. —JOHN MALPEDE

JOHNNY MACK:

My name is Johnny Mack. I am a drug addict. I live at Y-Haven.

JOHN MALPEDE:

How did you get involved with the Cleveland Public Theater?

JOHNNY MACK:

A guy named James Levin came to Y-Haven and he had a play. So I was in the play called "The House Within."

JOHN MALPEDE:

So obviously not everyone in the program gets into the play. How many are in the program?

JOHNNY MACK:

Sixty on the west side and 60 on the east side. They had the opportunity to get involved in the play when he came up with the idea for the play for this year. But just 10 of us got involved.

JOHN MALPEDE:

Why did you get involved?

JOHNNY MACK:

Well, I tried it last year. And then I had to work, and I could not keep up with this schedule. Then I got laid off. So this time I had the opportunity to do so.

JOHN MALPEDE:

What were you working at last year?

JOHNNY MACK:

I worked at this construction company called Hayden. And I got laid off.

JOHN MALPEDE:

At the Y-Haven do they pay for your room and board and stuff?

JOHNNY MACK:

When you first get there you get a little subsidized, paid to stay there. And then by six months they cut off your check. Then you get to go to work or go to school. And from there it depends. If you work you get to pay a little something. Or if you go to school they'll lend it to you out of payment.

JOHN MALPEDE:

If you go to school do you get some money from the government to pay for that?

JOHNNY MACK:

You get a grand. But you've still got to pay for your room and board. They just want you to be active in the program. That's county welfare.

JOHN MALPEDE:

How does the county welfare work here?

JOHNNY MACK:

Well, it's like I said. Me being in the drug-rehab program, they give me subsidized pay for at least six months.

JOHN MALPEDE:

What if you are a homeless person who is not in a program?

JOHNNY MACK:

You have to be in a shelter. Then all they give you is food stamps for three months. After three months you are cut off. You are still homeless, but you eat a little better, if you know what I'm saying. But other than that, when they cut you off you are back just like you were.

JOHN MALPEDE:

But if you are in a shelter, is there any program that tries to get you into something more permanent?

JOHNNY MACK:

Yes. I came from 2100 Lakeshore. There I went to an in-house program. I went to meetings there and then I went to Recovery Resources. That's how I got into Y-Haven.

JOHN MALPEDE:

2100 Lakeshore—that's a big municipal shelter, right? How many people were there at the time?

JOHNNY MACK:

Approximately 700 people at the time.

JOHN MALPEDE:

And how long did you stay there?

JOHNNY MACK:

It depends on you, you know what I'm saying? If you want to live like that, they don't force you to get into a program.

JOHN MALPEDE:

So. You chose to get into the program.

JOHNNY MACK:

Yes.

JOHN MALPEDE:

Is Recovery Resources another program? How does that work?

JOHNNY MACK:

That's another program to get you into independent housing. You go there for about three months, under supervision. You've got to have meetings. You've got to have random drug tests. From there they get you into Y-Haven, Pass or Salvation Army. They've got three different programs, you know. And from there on it's an extensive program.

What I'm saying is like I am at Y-Haven. I had to be in the house for at least 30 days. I cannot have any visitors. I cannot go nowhere by myself. And then after the 30 days I have treatment for four months. And after four months, when I get out of the group, I can either get a job or go to school.

JOHN MALPEDE:

So, how long have you been in the Y-Haven program now?

JOHNNY MACK:

Going on March 19, I'll be there two years.

JOHN MALPEDE:

So that's the end of the program right?

JOHNNY MACK:

Yeah, that's the end of the program. Like, right now, I am looking for a house. When I've got my house I will have successfully completed the program. So now I'm looking for a house. Within the next month I should have found a place.

JOHN MALPEDE:

And then you are looking for a job, too?

JOHNNY MACK:

I'm working right now. I work for the YMCA, right up at

Y-Haven, in security. There are a couple more programs they send the guys to when they get out of the group. Like job training, you know, situations like that.

JOHN MALPEDE:

So the program has worked pretty good for you, right? What is it about the program that works?

JOHNNY MACK:

Yeah, it worked pretty good for me. Well, to be frank with you, I have been through three programs before this. And it is the thing that… sometimes you get into these programs and they just… people don't care. All they do is look for the funding from the government, or the people they are getting it from. But Y-Haven cares, you know what I'm saying? They let you know what you need to do to stay sober. And give you some kind of idea about yourself. Before, all they wanted you to do is go to meetings. The places I went before wanted me to go to meetings and come back in. But what about me identifying myself with me? You know what I'm saying?

JOHN MALPEDE:

How do they achieve that over at Y-Haven?

JOHNNY MACK:

They give you the opportunity to tell about your lifestyle from the time as a child up until you leave. And by that time you have some idea of how to work your program, you know what I'm saying? In other words you have to be honest with yourself. You don't have to be afraid to tell somebody else about yourself. Like my situation…. I lost my mother when I was young. My father did not know how to tell me. I was raised with five sisters, and as I got older I got into trouble. And at the age of 23 I committed a crime that… you know, I'm not proud of that. A crime with murder. And I got out of the penitentiary and the government don't have too many places where a fellow like me can get a job. So I turned to drugs. I started selling drugs, you know what I'm saying? And I went in and out of prison. But this time they turned me around in this program. Because I didn't have to go out, you know. I could talk to you about what I did, and not feel bad behind it. And they gave me hope.

JOHN MALPEDE:

So that when you could not talk about it, it made you feel bad, and that there was no way out of it?

JOHNNY MACK:

True. No way out of it. Because like I was saying, the government does not have a lot of places where a guy like me could go to. If I fill out an application they tell you to be honest on the application. So when I put that down, they read it. And I can guarantee you that the moment I walk out of that door they throw my application in the garbage.

For the last couple of years—I say six, seven years—there are some companies that are hiring ex-felons. But not too many of them. And for a person to be homeless, and be out on the street, they are going to survive. And if they sell drugs, they are going to sell the drugs until they get tired.

JOHN MALPEDE:

So it sounds like you quit selling drugs and then went into the shelter?

JOHNNY MACK:

Well, I quit selling drugs in the last two years, because the last time I was in the penitentiary it was for selling drugs. And it was stated to me that if I ever come back I would be in it for the rest of my life. And that is no place I want to be to live, to die in.

I had a choice. And when I came home this last time a friend of mine came by, and the first thing he did was he gave me some drugs. Because I'm well known in the city. I knew how to make money by selling drugs. But I had to ponder it: Do I want to go back to the penitentiary for the rest of my life? Do I want to sell drugs? Eventually I would fall or kill. Either way, because not only did I sell drugs, I used drugs. So it was time for me to give up. So, I gave up. Went down to 2100. Stayed there a couple of months. When I was at 2100 I went to Recovery Resources through a young lady who came to that like a counselor, you know. At Recovery Resources then, she got me into that. Then she got me into Y-Haven. Right now she is working at Y-Haven. But like I say, the counselors there, they treat you like somebody, they don't treat you like a scumbag. They know what it is like out there with the homeless people, just the lifestyle. The majority of the counselors there are alcoholics and addicts, because they have been in the system.

JOHN MALPEDE:

Right. They have been in recovery for x number of years.

JOHNNY MACK:

Right. And the way it was before, when I was in a recovery program, I did not run into somebody who was in recovery, even the counselors. So how are they knowing what I am going through? They were just there to collect this money, you know what I'm saying?

JOHN MALPEDE:

You said that when you come out of jail the government does not do much for you. What exactly do they do for you? What happens when you get out?

JOHNNY MACK:

Years ago, if you got out of jail you could get on welfare. Nowadays when you get out of jail all they are gon do is send you down to 2100.

JOHN MALPEDE:

Before you could get a check which allows you to get a place to live and stuff like that.

JOHNNY MACK:

You could live off welfare and live off that, but now a couple of years ago, or something like 10 years ago, they just cut completely the welfare office. And now you get out of prison and you cannot get on welfare unless for three months, and that's the end of it.

JOHN MALPEDE:

How much is welfare?

JOHNNY MACK:

$115. And the cost of living is way more than that. You cannot even get a motel room for $115 a month. So you are out on the street, or in 2100, or you are back to what you were doing. It is totally on you to get out of the situation. Because, you know,

I don't know how I did it. But I thank God I did. Cause before, like I said, I was in and out of the penitentiary. And I'm just tired.

JOHN MALPEDE:

How was it like in the penitentiary?

JOHNNY MACK:

Chaos! I have seen one of my cellmates get killed. I was in the cell, but they set my whole cell on fire because he owed somebody. You stayed to yourself and did what you need to do. Survive, you know. Then it was all right. It's like out on the streets. They've got more alcohol and drugs in the penitentiary. I could find more drugs out in the penitentiary than I could out here, at one point.

JOHN MALPEDE:

Were you using in the penitentiary?

JOHNNY MACK:

Not very often because it would cost you a arm and a leg in the penitentiary.

JOHN MALPEDE:

So last year you were not in the play because it conflicted with your work and now you are in "The House Within," and you are going to do that some more after this play is done. And now you are doing "Agents & Assets." What do you think you get out of these shows?

JOHNNY MACK:

"The House Within" I portrayed myself as a little kid and

to me that was something that might needed to be said. To get adults aware of situations like that, you know, losing a loved one and you to be able to tell your kids. "Agents & Assets"—I always thought that the government was involved. But at one point I was high and I see it on TV and I did not give a heck because I was making money at that point. But now the country needs to be woken up to this. Because all it is doing is destroying us. You know, as they were saying last night, there is more penitentiaries here in the state of Ohio than there are schools. And at one point there were not. And it is a big business. When we lock them up, we make more money. The last time that I qualified, or knew about it, the government was getting like $38,000 a person by penalizing, by putting a person in prison. And the money they are getting from the drug dealers that they bust with big quantities of dope and lots of money. Where is that money going to? You never hear about that.

And now the kids in school, they are losing all these sports events, they are closing all that down. They are losing all their activities. They are closing down them schools. They crowd them in. And then the government is saying, "We are going overseas to fight." That makes me mad. Because they are going over there to destroy something, and then rebuild it, but not rebuilding their own country. So there has got to be a wake-up with this here. I know that you put it together a couple of years ago. But you really…it's got to get brought back, brought back up. Because like I said the other night, they are spending all this money over in Iraq, then they have about this much money left over for bin Laden. But then yet, what about the people in the U.S.? I guess in Cleveland alone you might have over 20,000 or 30,000 homeless people that they don't even know about. Because when you go out in town any time at night you can find them laying down in the street. They don't go into shelters, you know. And then you've got to realize, they are single and they don't have a job. They are homeless, too, regardless if they've a place to live, not with your family. Because if they don't have a job, they are out of money and you have to do some kind of dirt, you know.

JOHN MALPEDE:

It has been great working with you and having you in the show. Anything else you want to say?

JOHNNY MACK:

No.

EXCERPT OF INTERVIEW WITH RICKEY MANTLEY

Since we were interviewing all the Cleveland cast members, I took the opportunity to have official sit-down conversations with the LAPDers as well. What follows is an excerpt from my conversation with Rickey Mantley, who has a huge role in the show as CIA Inspector General Fred Hitz. Rickey Mantley has been one of the people at the very heart of the "Agents & Assets" project. One of the people whose participation defined the project's character. Not only because he played a main role in the show, but, more importantly, because of his understanding of the issues and his personal commitment to social justice. For a number of years Rick has done important community organizing work with Los Angeles Community Action Network. I wanted to talk with him about that work and also about the conversations he, Alexander Anderson and Henriëtte Brouwers had conducted with all the residents of the two Y-Haven Recovery Program sites.

–JOHN MALPEDE

RICK MANTLEY:

My name is Rick Mantley. I became a member of the LAPD in 1999, before I joined the Homeless Writers Coalition, which is now defunct. And from the Homeless Writers Coalition, I went to work, at first as a volunteer, for the LA Community Action Network. I started there as a volunteer and now I'm on staff. And I'm also the editor of the Community Action's newsletter, which has now been re-termed a newspaper because we are a member of the North American Association of Street Newspapers. I've been the editor there for roughly four years. I would describe myself as an organizer, an editor with the LA CAN, and also I am a founding member of the Downtown Women's Action Coalition (DWAC). I work with DWAC to advocate the problem of homeless women and children who are being forced through economics or personal situations to migrate downtown where there is sort of a last stash of affordable housing in LA. In some cases there is no housing at all, because again a lot of women and children are forced to reside in shelters or very substandard residential hotels. Doing my work, I work closely with the LA Coalition to End Hunger and Homelessness.

JOHN MALPEDE:

I am really impressed with the work of LA CAN. How does LA CAN decide what issues they work around? And how do they go about creating an effective strategy for the issues they do choose?

RICK MANTLEY:

First, I'll give a little background of how LA CAN came into being. The founder is Pete White. He was formerly a civil-rights organizer with the Coalition to End Hunger and Homelessness. They are advocates. They try to change policy. They are not service providers. They focus on policy and advocating on behalf of those who are homeless or dealing with the issues of poverty. Pete spent ten years as an advocate with the Coalition to End Hunger and Homelessness and he saw this gap, this disconnect between the people who they were advocating on behalf of homeless and very poor people, and the fact that these people were not in the room with the policy-makers and decision-makers. He felt that had to be addressed. That there had to be an organization created to get the people who were dealing with poverty, the people who are homeless, people who are formerly homeless who had no voice in the decision-making process. He felt that there had to be something put in place to get them to the table. And when LA CAN was put together it was decided how to get the people to the table, and that was to go out and to meet them, to go out to where they were living, or where they were staying, and talk to them about issues that were effecting their lives and to get their input or their suggestions. And when politicians or policy-makers had meetings or hearings, public forums, it was all about getting a lot of the people to these forums so that they could add their voice to that process.

Right. We go to the Community Redevelopment Agency hearings and meetings that are about redevelopment policies. We go to City Hall meetings, which also include policy about redevelopment and any ordinance that is going to affect how people live on the street. We are trying to steer municipal ordinances away from what we call the "criminalization of poverty," ordinances that make it basically illegal to be poor, to sleep on the street, to get food. I mean if you are poor and you have no means to eat and someone comes down to give you a sandwich there have been laws proposed and passed—and Santa Monica is notorious for this—making it a civil infraction to feed poor and hungry people. So, whenever there are public policy hearings on these type of issues, we get people there to get them to lobby the legislators who are going to vote on these ordinances, these laws, these policies. We give them our side of the issue. And I think we have been very persuasive and very effective in at least getting our message out there, and at least letting them know that we exist and cannot just be shrugged off.

JOHN MALPEDE:

What are the main issues that LA CAN is working on now?

RICKEY MANTLEY:

We aligned ourselves with an organization called SAJE, which is Strategic Actions for a Just Economy and also several other organizations, Figueroa Corridor and Coalition for Economic Justice. And their base is a core group of the Latino poor and working-class population. We have aligned ourselves with them and we have an initiative that is called "Share the Wealth." Because Downtown LA, as well as other areas of the city, were slated to be redeveloped, there was a plan put together by the Community Redevelopment Agency (CRA), a 30-year, two-billion-dollar plan. It was called a Central City Downtown Area Plan.

Well, I forgot the exact term, but it was a huge plan. And we looked at the plan, the nuts and bolts of it, and we did not see anything in terms of jobs, we did not see any truly affordable housing, we did not see anything in terms of building wealth and assets for renters or alternative living in Downtown. They were totally slighted and left out of this huge redevelopment plan. And we wrote what we called the "Share the Wealth" plan, and had alternatives for some of the proposals in the regular plan.

As it turns out, the regular plan was shut down in court. The judge invalidated it. The CRA was sued by the County of LA. They were sued by former LA City Council member Ernani Bernardi, and they were sued by the "Share the Wealth" Coalition. Ernani Bernardi's lawsuit prevailed because Bernardi had sued and gotten a development cap on the previous CRA plan. The judge ruled that the new plan was invalid because it was put on top of a plan that was yet to expire.

JOHN MALPEDE:

Has any of LA CAN's work has been focused around drug policies or drug issues?

RICKEY MANTLEY:

We support the reform issues. But we have not really focused on the drug issues because we need affordable housing and we need jobs. What goes on with the drug issues is another example of the criminalization of poor people. And of course, the drug laws by and large adversely effect someone who is poor, who is homeless, and who has a substance-abuse problem.

Although we have not addressed this issue directly, it is implicit in our stand against any ordinance that seeks to criminalize behavior, or that seeks to put criminal sanctions on situations that result from economic circumstances—for example, losing your job, or not being able to find a place to stay. Of course, a lot of times people do resort to using drugs when they are under such stress and it is a really complicated issue. So, we have not come out on the drug-reform issue per se. We have sort of indirectly addressed that issue.

JOHN MALPEDE:

You and Alexander and Henriëtte have done a couple of presentations at the Y-Haven. You all came back pretty excited about that. Also Y-Haven was excited.

RICKEY MANTLEY:

It was a very freewheeling discussion. At first we told what the play was about. A lot of people were animated by the issues raised in the play. A lot of people became excited. A lot of people were unaware of government complicity or involvement on whatever level. Some people thought the government was entirely responsible. And there was a lot of back-and-forth about whether this was a personal issue. I mean, are you personally responsible for the fact that you use drugs, or is this government agency responsible for bringing drugs in here? Sort of putting together a conspiracy or plan: We'll flood this community with drugs and make it so cheap and available that, again, as they say in the play, that there was a plan to undermine the black, the African-American community, the women and children in that community. They are bringing the drugs in to undermine the family structure. Well, we talked about that.

And at the end of the discussion at the Y-Haven West I tried to steer it back to drug reform as an issue and as a movement. Tried to make the point that the drug laws and policies that are now in place adversely affect African Americans. They have a lot of incarceration, do a lot of jail time, get criminal records and that can basically leave a black mark for your entire life. And I talked about the Drug Reform Forum for Michigan, and about how we got to know a lot of the drug-reform activists in Detroit. And about how they fought against the mandatory-sentencing laws and how they managed to get those repealed—even after the ballot initiative there was defeated. And I talked about grass-roots organizing. I talked about how something has to start from somewhere. This is an issue that has largely impacted the black community. You cannot wait for a savior to come down from the mountain to bring this issue before politicians and policy-makers and say this is a health issue and not a criminal issue. It has to come from the grassroots up, from people who are most being affected by this. And they have to go out and make their voices heard. I talked about organizing. I talked about forming coalitions. I talked about delegation visits, lobbying, going out to the state legislators and going to the offices of your con-gresspersons. And going there with papers, armed with a lot of information, passion, and a lot of personal stories. This is how you become effective, at least in terms of getting people to sit up and take notice of you, however they feel on the issue. And it is sort of a slow grinding process, to sort of whittle away a lot of the opposition or the antagonism to any type of drug-reform initiative or measure. This is a public health issue. It is not really a criminal issue, and people's lives are being needlessly ruined. Why do you throw people with a health problem in jail?

JOHN MALPEDE:

Were people at the Y-Haven sites responsive to these suggestions about organizing? Were they involved or even aware of such efforts going on?

RICKEY MANTLEY:

One guy said, "Point me in the right direction, I want to get started today." I'm saying, "Well, how you get started is, you just form groups." OK. You get a core group of people and you meet over this issue, and you talk about it. And you talk about the next steps, and you talk about, Where do we go from here? And you talk about, How can we get others involved? And, again, you form alliances and coalitions and you go out and get on the soapbox. But, the basic thing that I stressed about this is, get a core group of committed people to get the ball rolling. I mean people that feel so strongly that something has to be done that they are not going to be easily discouraged. That's what I talked about.

Public Conversation

Los Angeles, 2005

"Amnesty International, in its campaign against torture, has effectively been following the footsteps of the CIA, picking up their pieces. In 1983, the manual we got was the so-called Human Resources Exploitation Manual of 1983, a CIA training session with the Honduran military. And, by the way, Honduras was the forward base area for the Contras that this play is discussing. So in fighting the Contra war, we were allying with drug lords, and as another part of it, training the Honduran military in torture techniques for the pacification of the local population. So the two things are actually operating in the same space. These are the visible and invisible aspects of the play." — Alfred McCoy

"And so you get to the period of this presidency, George W. Bush, and the idea of critical analysis, independent information, going against the grain. Those traditions were lost, at least in areas that I deal with: national security and those sorts of things. I'm not saying that there were not parts where the press was doing a fine job. But in these areas the independence of the American press had been broken. The reporters were now conveyer belts. And the American people have paid a very high price for that reality. But, it does go back to this Contra drug problem in some ways and other issues that you can see coming out of what this show was about. Even what was admitted to in the first, in Volume 1 of this report was quite damning." — BOB PARRY

Los Angeles, 2005

In May 2005 we had a second round of "Agents & Assets" performances in Los Angeles. We held two performances in Downtown and one at Compton Community College, the site of a heated community meeting that led to the governmental investigation into CIA-connected Contra drug-dealing. The performances occurred amidst revelations of torture of prisoners in Afghanistan.

—JOHN MALPEDE

TOPIC:
THE WAR ON DRUGS AND THE WAR ON TERROR
May 21, 2005
REDCAT Theater at Disney Hall
Post-Performance Discussion

TIMELINE:

May, 2005 —Torture Uncovered in US-Run Prisons in Afghanistan

May, 2005 — LA County Seeks to Close Drew Medical Center in Watts

PANELISTS:

ALFRED MCCOY: History Professor, University of Wisconsin, author, *The Politics of Heroin* and *A Question of Terror*

RAMONA RIPSTON: Executive Director, American Civil Liberties Union, Southern California

RICK MANTLEY: Moderator, LAPD Performer, Inspector General Frederick P. Hitz in "Agents & Assets"

AL MCCOY:

The hearing dramatized in "Agents & Assets" took place in March 1998, on the occasion of the release of Volume 1 of Inspector General Hitz's report. Volume 2 of the report came out the following October — October 1998. When you read Volume 2 of Hitz's report, and get to paragraph 913 — which nobody in *The New York Times* or *LA Times* or any of the nation's media did, and which therefore went completely unreported — what you find is the most sensational, detailed and amazing revelations about the CIA alliance with drug lords imaginable. What you learn in this report from direct quotes from CIA cables with interviews with CIA operatives, from field operatives in the Caribbean right up to the director of the CIA itself went like this: From 1986 to 1992 at the height of the crack cocaine epidemic, when cocaine was flooding north from Colombia through Central America to the United States through our communities and neighborhoods, the CIA was allied with the largest cocaine smuggler in the Caribbean, a man named Allan Hyde. He controlled a port in the Bay Islands. He didn't control one plane, one boat; he had thirty-five ships on the high seas, one of them on consignment, owned by the drug kingpin Pablo Escobar, smuggling cocaine into the United States in bulk quantities. At the time the CIA alliance with Allan Hyde started, there was detailed intelligence from the Drug Enforcement Administration, the CIA, the Department of Defense, the U.S. Coast Guard; every major U.S. government agency involved in the drug war knew that this guy was a class-A violator, one of the biggest, if not the biggest, trafficker. And from 1986 to 1992, in order to gain access to his facilities to give arms to the Contras, the CIA protected Allan Hyde from any investigation by Honduran or U.S. authorities.

So what happened? From 1930 to 1980 the United States had 100 prisoners per 100,000 population. By the end of the Reagan era, in 1988, we had 400 prisoners per 100,000 population; it was a four-fold increase in our prison population. Why? Because the logic of the war on drugs is the logic of a doomsday machine. Cocaine flooded into the communities. People are buying it and using it. People are being arrested. Under federal government legislation there are more officers and each officer is making more arrests. They're going to court.

Under mandatory minimums they're being automatically sentenced. The prisons are filling up. Today where are we? We're at 700 prisoners per 100,000 of population; we've crossed the 2 million mark and there's no end to it because of the doomsday machine. It happens. The drugs flood in, the cops arrest the people, they're going before the courts, they're put into jail. That's the empirical issue. It's worse than we imagined. It's not some fantasy; it's not some conspiracy. It's documented in Part 2 of the inspector general's report that came out in October, after the only public hearing on the matter — the March 18, 1998 hearing that's dramatized in "Agents & Assets."

Now what can we draw from this? After September 11, 2001, all changed. The consequences of the war on drugs was cast into the dark past. How did everything change? What we can see is that in the 200-year history of the American republic, with many wars, we have only declared war on the invisible, the inanimate, the impersonal twice. We declared war on drugs beginning with President Richard Nixon in 1971–72. And this play, "Agents & Assets," is a chapter in the ongoing, endless war on drugs.

We've recently, since September 11, 2001, declared a war on terror. Now think about what we're doing. Drugs are infinite. Illicit drugs are, according to the U.N., eight percent of world trade. The illicit-drug traffic is larger than the trade in textiles, steel and automobiles. The illicit-drug users are 180 million people; they're four percent of the world population. According to the U.N., there are 3.5 million full-time organized-crime figures around the world involved in the drug traffic. So this is endless. A war on drugs is like declaring a war on textiles. It's like declaring a war on steel; it's infinite, it's endless. And I can go into why it doesn't work, and so it will never end. What does that mean? Think about other wars that we've fought. There is an inherent rationality of the battlefield. Commanders faced with taking actual physical real objectives with finite materiel and manpower are extraordinarily judicious and rational, because society says it's their children that they're sending out to fight. They demand this rationality because for every drop of blood spilled there must be an objective gain. There is rationality to the battlefield that we don't even think about. War, in its ultimate irrationality, is nevertheless quite rational in the way it is fought. There are spatial, real, territorial objectives.

But when you declare war on the inanimate, the invisible, the impossible, you enter into a realm of total irrationality where the usual constraints are eliminated. What are the manifestations of the irrationality? We're fighting this irrational war against drugs; we're filling up our prisons doing incredible damage to people that are still incarcerated, exhausting our social-welfare dollars, which should be going to everything else but prison, on this infinite, endless expansion toward incarceration.

Let's now look at the war on terror. Again, another one of these wars on something invisible, a war that very quickly goes into the irrational. What is the irrational manifestation of the war on terror? Torture. The whole Abu Ghraib incident is an irrational manifestation of this other war, this other impersonal war. And when you think about torture, it is done in the belief that we can exercise surgical torture to extract judicious intelligence, but it spreads through the irrationality that torture always involves. Torture taps into the deepest, darkest recesses where life and death, pain and pleasure all converge in the darkest recesses of our consciousness. You unleash torture and you unleash something unimaginable, something that, well … we can call it evil. And this society, in unleashing torture to fight the war on terror, as the French found in Algeria, and, as we should have found in Vietnam, as every society that ever does it always learns that, yes, it can work. You can get a bit of information. You can even get a lot of information; but, in effect, the larger objective is lost. You are so stained, you are so stigmatized, by your practice of torture that whatever morality, whatever legitimacy our war on terror might have commanded, in the world beyond us, is gone.

So, in effect, it's irrational. We engage in a tactic to fight the war on terror that is making it impossible for us to win this war on terror. So I think there is a clear kind of connection that we can explore in this discussion between these two endless, indecent wars that we've now been fighting for many, many years.

RAMONA RIPSTON:

We talk about a war on drugs. War on drugs: drugs won. Now we talk about a war on terror, and terrorism is winning. First we have to look at the statistics. The overwhelming percentage of people who have gone to prison between 1985 and 1995 were convicted of using drugs. And remember that the people who used drugs are getting longer sentences than the people who are the kingpins. Because if you are a kingpin, you hire a good lawyer, you know the right people. You then get off in a way that the small user — often someone who is an addict — doesn't get off.

Women and people of color have been disproportionably hurt and injured by this war on drugs. I want to tell you that from 1986 to 1996 there was a 421 percent increase in the prison population of women who were convicted of drug use or drug sales. The same is true of blacks. We have imprisoned more people for drug use than any country in the world. We have imprisoned more people for drug use than the rest of the democratic countries of the world. So you can see what this has done to our population. Also you should know that Proposition 36, which we passed here in California—which was supposed to help drug users who were convicted for the first time, to get therapy and treatment—hasn't been used effectively. It's important to realize, too, that treating people for drug use is a lot less expensive than sending them to prison.

The American Civil Liberties Union (ACLU) here in Los Angeles won a lawsuit back in 1978 because of the conditions in the LA county jail. A large percentage of people in the LA county jail are there because of drug use. Conditions there are terrible. I cannot describe to you how bad they are. Yet there is very little that even a legal organization like the ACLU can do to help people get medical care, which is abysmal. About two weeks ago I went through the jail again and there were six men to a cell. In a cell there was a toilet and a sink and a bed on the floor, because we're putting into county jail more people than we have room for. And the toilet was leaking. Someone is sleeping on the floor and the toilet is leaking.

You've read about conditions in the prisons throughout California, and they are not any better. When I started my job, we used to talk about rehabilitation, but rehabilitation doesn't exist anymore. One thing that's happening here in Los Angeles, is that the LAPD — not the Poverty Department, but the Police Department — picks up homeless people and often puts them into the county jail. An officer will often ask you whether you are on parole or probation. If you don't answer honestly, you can be thrown into the county jail, and if you do answer honestly, the LAPD has a right to further question you. It is a very serious situation.

Now, for a moment, let's talk about the war on terror, and what has happened to that. We've heard a little bit about how people have been tortured. I think many people in America found it very difficult to believe that Americans could be involved in torturing people, and yet we know that it is true. We know that while there was torture that was psychological, that they were torturing people psychologically, we know that it was more than psychological. We've learned about waterboarding. I had never heard about waterboarding until this information came out. The soldiers, the people who were there in Iraq and in Cuba, are certainly guilty of torturing people. They were the ones who were waterboarding people. They were the ones who put black hoods on people and attached wires, piled naked bodies with leashed dogs, put leashes on men.

But what is not often talked about is: Who is primarily responsible for this? The Freedom of Information Act (FOIA) is a federal law, which is supposed to give the right to citizens and organizations to get information about what its government is involved in. For three years the ACLU filed under the Freedom of Information Act and — after court hearing, after court hearing, after court hearing, because the government resisted all along — we finally received some documents. We received lots of information and we now know that many of the higher-ups in the Justice Department, and in the CIA, were responsible for the torture. The soldiers and the people that you see being put on trial did it, but they were doing it at the behest of the people who were involved in our government. We know many of the people who were involved, including a judge who is now on the 9th Circuit, who wrote a memo condoning torture while working in the Justice Department. The rationalization for the torture was that we were not involved with a war against another country, therefore all of the covenants against torture didn't apply. This was a war, as we heard, about people out there, or about things out there that can't be named or seen. Therefore, it is okay to torture people who were involved in this war. One of the persons who was rewarded now sits on the Ninth Circuit. His memo, the memo that he wrote for the Justice Department, did not come to light until after his confirmation. He was rewarded with a lifetime appointment to the 9th Circuit Court of Appeals. We know that a law professor at a law school up north was in the same position, and that he has been rewarded with a position at that law school. We know that people who were higher-ups were rewarded by appointments, with promotions. The ACLU lawsuit has been filed against Mr. Rumsfeld. Now, will we get Mr. Rumsfeld convicted? Probably not. But what we hope to do is bring to light that America itself is responsible for what is going on.

We also have learned in the last two days that in Afghanistan also there was torture, promulgated by the same people who were responsible for it at Abu Ghraib, where we are holding hundreds of men. Some of the people tortured in Afghanistan really have had little connection with the war on terror. One was a taxi driver who was beaten so savagely that he died. Tomorrow's *New York Times* will give details of that. So I think that we as Americans have much to be ashamed for. I think we have to petition our government and tell our government that we as Americans don't want to go along with this kind of activity. I think we all feel a modicum of shame, that we are embarrassed by what our government has done, but I suspect this is not the first time in our history that this has happened. And I hope that through our litigation, through evenings like tonight, that we will learn the truth about terror and the truth about the war on drugs. Thank you.

Rickey Mantley:

Now we come to the question-and-answer portion of our discussion, and I'd just like to set some parameters to strengthen the discussion. It would be very helpful if you could be clear, if you'd like to stand up and make a statement in response to what Professor McCoy or Ms. Ripston have said, or if you'd like to ask them a question directly.

Audience Member:

This is primarily for Professor McCoy. I'm wondering why the Democratic Party so far hasn't made more of an issue with respect to torture. And I'm wondering if the answer is that torture has been used, even under Democratic administrations, ever since Kennedy, as well as the Republican administrations.

Al McCoy:

Let me address the statement first, and then I'll address the question. The statement is: "Does this go deeper back, does this go further back?" Yes, it does. After having spent 30 years working on the relationship between the CIA and international narcotics trafficking, a few years ago, I began to turn my research to another legacy of the cold war. There are many aspects that came out of this covert dimension of America in the 1950s. One was the start of a series of alliances with drug lords, with drug lords in the Third World. Beginning with Burma in the 1960s to Afghanistan right up till the present, the CIA has a long history of alliances with powerful tribal warlords that can mobilize mercenary armies in far-away, difficult terrains. And through the protection of the CIA, plus the arms, logistics and political backing, these tribal warlords are quickly transformed into powerful drug lords. Their localized traffic becomes internationalized. They become linked to the international circuits of illicit traffic that bring their commodities to Europe and to the United States. In part, that's what this play is about.

During this same period, and as the CIA was reaching beyond our boundaries, and exercising American power in continents where it had never been exercised before, they actually began an exploration of the most remote, the most obscure, the most difficult terrain that there is: the human consciousness. From 1959 to 1962, the CIA conducted a mind-control project; the parts that we all know, the LSD experiments, those are the roads not taken, the failed parts. Those are the null researches. But an obscure US–UK project in McGill University discovered the impact of sensory deprivation, and with that discovery, they crafted basically the first revolution in the cruel science of torture in 500 years. They transformed the paradigm from physical to psychological, and they codified these researches in a 1963 manual that you can find on the Internet, KUBARK. Type in K-U-B-A-R-K and read it, okay? And then, in 1983, you have a second manual, and this method is very distinctive. What they basically came up with is a method of attacking every human sense and sensibility without touching. Bombard sight and sound, confuse the human clock; it's a total attack on the existential platforms of human existence, and it has the potential to destroy people. And they propagated this transnationally.

Amnesty International, in its campaign against torture, has effectively been following the footsteps of the CIA, picking up their pieces. In 1983, the manual we got was the so-called Human Resources Exploitation Manual, a CIA-training session with the Honduran military. And, by the way, Honduras was the forward base area for the Contras that this play is discussing.

So in fighting the Contra war, we were allying with drug lords, and as another part of it, training the Honduran military in torture techniques for the pacification of the local population. So the two things are actually operating in the same space. These are the visible and invisible aspects of the play.

Then the ACLU, among these many documents as Ramona was telling us that they uncovered, a couple of weeks ago, they hit it. They came up with — or me, in the book I just finished on torture — the most revealing document. They actually got Ricardo Sanchez' September, 2003 document, his instructions for interrogation at Abu Ghraib. Now if you take those three documents: the CIA KUBARK report, 1963; go online and get it. Type in Human Resources Exploitation Manual, 1983; and then type in the Sanchez memo. I want you to see it's the same method, okay? Verbatim, exactly the same thing. How does a black-boots combat commander like Ricardo Sanchez understand the techniques for attacking the existential platforms for human existence? He's able to, because this is deeply embedded in the intelligence community. This is part of war-fighting doctrine.

KEVIN MICHAEL KEY:

I have a question for Mr. McCoy, and it has to do with that second CIA report, and what was the media's response to that report, and what steps are being taken to, you know, further publicize it, if it's as clear as you say it is?

AL MCCOY:

When the first report came out, the one that we see in the play, March of 1998, the Hitz report, they played up the Executive Summary very strongly. All of the exculpatory, exclamatory portions of that report say, basically, there's nothing to answer. They played that up. When the second report came out in October of 1998, they made a few references to the Executive Summary of that report, which was more of the same, no big case to answer. Now, I've googled this; I've checked it on microfilm; I've checked it on hard copy. And as far as I can determine, there was no press coverage whatsoever of the material contained from paragraph 913 onward.

Everything that I talked about earlier was not reported in the press. There are only two places where it was reported, to the best of my knowledge… and forgive the tendentious nature of this remark. One is in the CIA report, and the other is in my own book. We edited the third edition of my book in 2003. In the first two editions of my book, I'd reported about the CIA complicity with drug lords from external sources, observing their operations, talking to their people, but I'd never had internal documentation. Finally, for the first time, with the publication of Volume 2 of the Hitz report, I had internal documentation. It corroborated not only CIA complicity with the Contras, but indeed a whole mindset, the mentality and the CIA's operational doctrine that led them into an alliance with the drug lords beginning in the 1950s.

So for me, it was a smoking-gun document and I go into it in great detail. But *The New York Times, The Washington Post,* all of the people who had faulted Gary Webb, that had tracked the report, ignored this evidence, even though it was incredibly newsworthy: "CIA Confesses to Protecting Top Drug Trafficker at Height of Cocaine Epidemic." You know, that's gotta be a headline. But it didn't happen. No headline, okay?

Ramona mentioned earlier that *The New York Times* was coming out with this story on the murder in the prison in

Afghanistan. Part One was yesterday about the murder; it's two pages of *The New York Times,* its incredibly detailed. Now, two things: I mentioned that there were three reports in *The Washington Post, The New York Times,* and in the *LA Times* that attacked the "Dark Alliance" story, and I mentioned that the *New York Times* story talked about African-American frenzy, African-American paranoia. That was written by Tim Golden.

Now Tim Golden is one of these guys… they're police reporters, I'm sure you know them, Ramona. They're guys who get the police story. They know everything, they say nothing. But they rely upon the police. They get the call, "there's a body here. Come over." They write it up. It's a very complicitous relationship with the agency they should be reporting critically. Tim Golden is, I think, an intelligence reporter who has that kind of relationship with the CIA. And so, whenever Tim Golden is writing a major story in *The New York Times,* whether it's about the "Dark Alliance" case or now about Afghan murder, you've got to read it very carefully.

Read Tim Golden's story very carefully when it comes out tomorrow. And here's what you're going to find: You're gonna find these hillbilly guards are a bunch of savage brutes, and that there'll be no mention of where they learned this. For example, in Part One, we have descriptions of these hillbilly guards behaving in this savage way: of beating a man's legs so badly that they pulverize the flesh, that if he'd survived, actually been autopsied by the army, the leg would have had to be amputated. It was that badly beaten.

Now you read this, and you get so angry. But what you don't see is what he's not telling us. He says for example, that prisoners were shackled for days. Superior officers wandered through cells; there was no report, no reprimand. This would have been from colonel up to general, not stopping this. Why not? And then what they don't get into are the psychological methods. They focus on the abuses. They don't talk about what's really going on, and that is the method I described earlier on, that there are also CIA operatives in that same facility that are helping to direct this procedure, training these officers in these techniques. That's all left out of that report. You'll find very little mention of the CIA. That's what I predict tomorrow. So it's Tim Golden. Watch it, read your text very carefully when it's a Tim Golden report.

AUDIENCE MEMBER:

During the '80s, in the Solidarity movement that happened at that time, people just assumed that the connection between the Iran-Contras was there. There were bumper stickers: "Support the Contras, buy your drugs from a Republican." There were posters, Robbie Conal's "Contra Cocaine." Why did it take ten years before it suddenly got involved in hearings and the press?

AL MCCOY:

Well, as the hearing dramatized tonight, which took place in 1998, mentions, Senator Kerry in 1989 actually released a major report, which I think was corroborated by the later findings, so it actually came out more quickly than you might imagine. Kerry actually took a lot of political risk with that report. In the campaign coverage, they all talked about how Senator Kerry was a man that never took risks, that he never took a position, that he didn't have the requisite strength of character. But actually, if you look at the sustained investigation that he did in Central America, under that Committee on International Terrorism, it was actually really a gutsy report. He found and documented, for example, that four corporations hired by the U.S. State Department to provide humanitarian relief supplies to Central America were controlled by criminals, and that they were flying cocaine back to the United States from Central America. They were offloading humanitarian relief supplies to the Contras, loading on Contra cocaine, and flying directly into the United States. He had testimony from the pilots that were involved with the flights. And, it's one of those reports where the executive summary and the contents actually closely correspond; he didn't hold back. He didn't package the report to make it more palatable. It's very gutsy. And it got very little coverage in the *Times,* and what you would call the corporate media, what I would call the national media.

Ramona Ripston:

I would like to answer that as well. It's very difficult to get information out. The fact that the ACLU filed a lawsuit, in which Mr. Rumsfeld was a defendant, really did not get a lot of coverage. We had thought, when we filed the lawsuit that it would be front page. It was not front page. There's documentation that backs it up. Very few people have read it.

Audience Member:

Professor McCoy, in your opening statement you mentioned Pablo Escobar as being one of the stopping points for the drugs. And I was wondering what was the CIA's participation in the final hunt down and absolute decimation of this man, which has now become a film documentary. Isn't that kind of playing the role of the hypocrite? Were they involved with that after using him as a drug dealer for them, and allowing him to run things and make sure that drugs pass through?

Al McCoy:

Actually, that's very consistent with the Agency's policy. For example, we used Noriega, and he's now in jail. The latest, the most stunning example of all is Gulbuddin Hekmatyar, a name that probably most of you don't know. It doesn't flow trippingly off the tongue. Let's all say it three times: Gulbuddin Hekmatyar. Who was he? Well, he was the recipient of about $1.5 to $2 billion of U.S. funds, in the secret war in Afghanistan from 1979–1989. Hekmatyar received over half of the approximately $3 billion that went to the Mujahideen resistance. He was the client war lord of Pakistan's Inner Service Intelligence, and when the operation started under President Carter and was continued by President Reagan, he became the primary vehicle.

There were a number of other contenders. There were actually some liberal, more democratic, secular Afghani politicians who were contending for the leadership. They were frozen out of the funding. Hekmatyar was an extremely right-wing Islamic fundamentalist who in the 1960s made a reputation in Kabul by throwing acid in the faces of women who weren't wearing veils at the Kabul University.

This was the man who we picked to be our guy in Afghanistan. Now you may have read that after the events of 9/11, Gulbuddin Hekmatyar came back to Afghanistan to revive his movement, and the CIA nearly got him with a predator drone. They hit his cavalcade, they blew up a couple of his cars, but they missed him. They are trying desperately to murder Gulbuddin Hekmatyar, a man who they turned into this powerful figure, transformed from acid thrower and petty, failed, revolutionary bandit figure into this major force. Actually, in 1992 he became prime minister of Afghanistan as a result of all the CIA funding. This was our guy and now we're trying to kill them. So that's a very clear pattern. We use them when we need them, but when we don't we dispose of them.

AUDIENCE MEMBER:

Well, given that this is the second war on drugs—we went through a war on alcohol, which was an unmitigated disaster, it created organized crime for the FBI—I have sort of a simple question: Why are we in the middle of a war on drugs? Could you help me understand that from a historical perspective, and also from a legal, bureaucratic, political perspective. What are we doing in the middle of a war on drugs?

AL MCCOY:

This is actually a very old war; in fact we're about to have our centennial. Nobody's going to celebrate it, we're going to miss it, don't look for the commemorative stamps. But the first international conference on drugs, which launched our drug diplomacy, was held in the Philippines in 1909. That was actually part of a global, Protestant, moral movement that culminated in an attempt to ban narcotics. You have to remember that beginning in the 18th and throughout the 19th century, opium became a major global commodity, because it was shipped from British India to China. By 1907, China had 27 percent of its adult male population as opium addicts. China's opium harvest was 35,000 tons, which was about the scale of Colombia's coffee harvest. It was this vast political enterprise. British Malaya had over 50 percent of its tax revenues from licensed opium dens. And for the Protestant clergy, this was an abomination. The state was using its power to promote addiction in Asia, largely among Chinese and overseas Chinese in Southeast Asia.

This gave rise to a reform movement, which was the prohibition movement. At the same time as the United States prohibited drugs in the Philippines in 1908, Britain and China concluded a treaty that was a mutual Prohibition Treaty with a total prohibition of any exports of Chinese opium.

So this is now a century-long movement that is deeply embedded within our theology and our political ideology. Moreover it is not an easy thing to undo, because of the legal layers of the prohibition regime. First of all, there are U.N. conventions that ban 245 drugs at last count in the 1990s. There may be a few more added since. Then there are federal laws, there are state laws. This is deeply embedded, it can't be easily undone. That, I think, was the genius of Proposition 36; it didn't try to undo the whole apparatus, it simply made the punishment appropriate to the crime. If you're a drug user and you need treatment, you get treatment, you don't get incarcerated. That was the genius of Prop. 36. It didn't try to undo the whole apparatus which would take years to do, should we be inclined to do so.

AUDIENCE MEMBER:

Following up on that though, the question included the question, Why do we not treat alcohol and tobacco in the same regard? I think that there's an interesting story there.

AL MCCOY:

We did initially treat alcohol as such, I mean, the prohibition of alcohol and narcotics were simultaneous. Indeed, the prohibition unit of the U.S. Treasury Department had two arms. One was narcotics, the other was alcohol. And we maintained that prohibition until 1930. It became unworkable. The whole repeal movement of prohibition is not something that's been well studied. It's actually a major nationwide movement, from which my own family, personal disclosure, benefited enormously. My mother is Margarita Piel McCoy. Piel's beer at one time was a very popular New York beer. We suffered mightily during the 1920s. As mother said, we got our depression early. But then, with the repeal in 1933, things looked up, and we did much better after that. So the repeal movement was, in effect, an ethnic policy in the United States, and German-American brewers—of which there were 1,420—were displaced momentarily. Italian-Americans, Jewish-Americans moved in, took over the enterprise, and the repeal was basically a complex ethnic-political battle in which the brewers won the right back. When you look at the repeal of the prohibition against alcohol, you realize you've got contending drug forces at work. Well, one of the problems with getting rid of the drug war is—how should I put it—the repeal of drug prohibition doesn't have a lobby. There isn't any "Cocaine Manufacturers Association of America"; in terms of a movement, there isn't a contending force. When you weigh up the people that are concerned with ephemeral issues like civil liberties and social justice in America, this is a weak lobby compared to the prison-industrial complex: all the prison guards in the communities that depend upon them, the whole apparatus of law and justice that's got a stake in this incarceration of America. So in looking at the contending forces, if you want to be a kind of materialist, drug-law repeal doesn't have the same force behind it as did alcohol repeal in the late 1930s.

Melina Bielefelt:

Ramona, in your introduction you said Proposition 36 is not working. Could you speak to that treatment-versus-incarceration proposition, and why you don't believe it's working?

RAMONA RIPSTON:

Oh, because not everybody who is eligible for Prop. 36 gets the benefit of it. You have to be certified by a judge that you are entitled to be treated rather than to be sentenced to prison. And I suspect that it's not being funded in the way that we had hoped that it would be. Some few people are benefiting, but not everybody who is a first-time offender has received the benefits of Prop. 36, and I think it's probably funding that is responsible for that.

AUDIENCE MEMBER:

What's the position of the ACLU on homelessness, their freedom and rights particularly?

RAMONA RIPSTON:

Well, we filed a lawsuit that said that homeless people have the right to sleep on sidewalks, that when a society, when a city and county does not provide enough shelters for homeless people, where do you expect homeless people to go? Clearly a judge didn't agree, but neither did he answer where he expected those people to sleep. The homeless population is very large. In Los Angeles, we have the largest homeless population in the country. Often they'll throw away the belongings of homeless people who are sleeping on public property. We represented people who received money from the county because they were mentally ill, unemployed, and they were drug addicted, alcoholics or just down on their luck. Some homeless people are just people who don't have enough money to get a month's security deposit. Housing in Los Angeles, as you all know, is very expensive. So we represented people and we were very careful about who the plaintiffs in this lawsuit were. People who would spend half the month in one of these SRO's, these hotels, but then the other half of the month on the street, not because they like living on the street, but because they didn't have the money to be in a hotel, or to be in any place for that long. And yet, the judge decided that that was something that the Constitution didn't protect. The people who need treatment find it very difficult, whether it's treatment if you're an alcoholic, or if you're drug-addicted. The services offered to people like this are really negligible. As we become a more mechanized society, you have to know how to use a computer. We have a growing population of people who just didn't learn how to do that. They didn't go to school. Now suddenly they're unemployed.

So the homeless population has people across the board with a variety of problems. And we try. We also brought a law suit, as I mentioned earlier, to stop police officers from asking people whether they are on probation or whether they are on parole. That litigation is still going on. It's very difficult. I worked with Chief Bratton to try to get him to stop putting homeless people into jail. Because if you remember reading, there are many illnesses that make their way through the county jail, and medical treatment is very poor. So if you are a reasonably healthy person who is homeless, and you're thrown into county jail, your crime being that you are homeless, you come out in far worse condition than when you went in. It would be much more profitable for us as a society to treat people, rather than housing them in county jails or in prison.

AUDIENCE MEMBER:

Certainly, what John's doing is transforming people's lives. What are the other ideas that are out there?

RAMONA RIPSTON:

Well, I think being involved is important, letting the people who represent you know this. We have a new mayor here in Los Angeles, it's a splendid opportunity to let Antonio Villaraigosa know about the part that the city can play in this. Most of what happens in the jails here in Los Angeles is a responsibility of the county; so we have five county supervisors, somebody represents you here in the city. Also education is important. People need to know about this. There's a lack of interest here on the part of most people.

Most people believe that people who end up in jail, or people who are homeless, are there either because they deserve it, or they want to be there. It's a very tough situation to bring about change, to bring about what is needed, which is rehabilitation and education. We try to tell people that the only way these problems can be solved is for people, for individuals to be involved. We do what we can with litigation. Litigation is becoming more and more difficult. I would suggest you take a look at the ACLU's website. We have a part on our website that tells you where different legislation is being considered, we can generate mail, e-mails, letters to people in the state legislature, people in the city council, people in the board of supervisors. We all have a responsibility to do that, and it's the only way I know to bring about change.

I don't believe we're going to be able to rely on the courts much longer. I think when President Bush gets his appointments or his nominees to the federal courts we're going to see a change in that. Until now, the courts have been pretty good on civil-liberties issues, but I believe these new nominees are going to get through and make it to the court. You're going to see a change in the federal courts, And you will no longer be able to depend on the federal judiciary to vindicate rights. I think it's all going to be up to us for a very long time, because people who get appointed to federal courts, are appointed for a very long time. They'll be there for a long time, and they'll be there long after George Bush is gone and Donald Rumsfeld is gone, and the only way we can change that is to be active as citizens of this country.

RICKEY MANTLEY:

I work with an organization, a downtown-based organization called the Los Angeles Community Action Network. And we work directly with and for homeless individuals in downtown Los Angeles. The mission of our organization is to empower homeless people and formerly homeless individuals, and we're based in downtown Los Angeles in the heart of where homelessness exists. We are directly working with homeless people to empower them and to get them involved in the decision-making process, getting them to the table with decision-makers.

As Ramona talked about, if you have to sleep on the street, if you have nowhere else to go, nowhere else to sleep, and if you're forced to sleep on the sidewalk, why should that be a crime? Why should you go to jail when you have nowhere else to go, when you have no shelters, when you have no affordable housing? It's the necessity defense, and we've worked hard to get people to recognize that. At times, people have nowhere else to go; why should they be penalized for having to use the bathroom in public if there's no public restrooms? Why should they be penalized for sleeping in a tent, or on a sidewalk, or in a cardboard condo when there are no shelters, where again in the downtown area, development of lofts is proceeding at an extremely rapid pace. Every abandoned commercial building is being converted into lofts. Lofts are springing up all over, but not affordable housing, not housing for low income, and extremely low income. That's what we're doing in downtown Los Angeles, we're fighting on several fronts to alleviate the condition of homelessness. Most of all we feel that it's a matter of getting homeless people involved in the political process so that downtown development isn't going to roll over people.

Gentrification is here, and it's here to stay. There's no stopping it; it's a juggernaut. But people are going to fight back for their rights in terms of affordable housing, in terms of health care, and in terms of issues that are impacting their lives, and they're not just going to roll over and play dead for developers who are coming downtown. [*Applause*]

Topic:
The Press, Media Coverage of National Security, Narcotics Trafficking and the CIA
Wednesday, May 25, 2005
The Democracy Forum
of the Japanese American National Museum

Panelists:

Alfred McCoy: History Professor, University of Wisconsin
Robert Parry: Washington journalist, broke first Iran-Contra stories while working for the Associated Press and *Newsweek*
Kevin Michael Key: Moderator

Kevin Michael Key:

We're now going to begin the discussion. To my right, physically but not politically, Mr. Al McCoy. He is the author of *The Politics of Heroin: CIA Complicity in the Global Drug Trade*. He is a professor at the University of Wisconsin and he has interacted with LAPD and "Agents & Assets" on numerous occasions. On my left is Bob Parry. He is a journalist. He's worked for *Newsweek* and Associated Press. He was personally involved in breaking the first the Iran-Contra stories. We're gonna start with Bob on the left.

ROBERT PARRY:

Well, that account of that first hearing is quite amazing. I somehow had forgotten some of the testimony myself. But it's also important to realize that after the presentation by Fredrick Hitz there was a second volume which was even more condemning of what the CIA had known and done during the Contra war.

Of course, it is always the case of how you phrase a question in terms of what kind of answers you'll get. And clearly there was a goal, both in the government and in some of the mainstream press, to frame the question in the most exculpatory way possible for the CIA. If the question were asked, however: "Did the CIA know that the Contras where deeply involved in cocaine trafficking during the 1980s?" the answer to that question based on Hitz's Volume 2 is a categorical "yes."

The agency was aware that fifty or more Contras and Contra entities where implicated in the drug trade. They also did nothing to bring those people to justice. The agency withheld the information from DEA, from the Congress when it was asked, and even from the internal division of the CIA itself. The goal was, as Hitz described in Volume 2, to get the project done. And the project was the CIA's war in Nicaragua. The idea was to oust the Sandinistas. And the way they did it was less important to them than doing it. So there was a tolerance, and this is an acknowledged part of our history now, at least in terms of the public record; that there was a tolerance of this drug trafficking by the Contras as part of the National Security Operation known as the Contra War.

Just very briefly, my connection to the story began in 1985 when I was with the Associated Press. I was one of two reporters — me and Brain Barger — who had investigated this aspect of how the Contras were staying armed and in the field after the Congress had cut off the CIA's support in 1984. We stumbled on this through sources within the Contra movement, who acknowledged there was this problem they were aware of, that some elements of the Contra army had engaged in drug trafficking as a way to raise money. So we prepared that story with a good deal of documentary evidence from Costa Rica, to say that there was this problem and the story moved on the AP wireless in December of 1985. The overall response was not good. The mainstream press largely ignored the story even then, and generally remained hostile to the story throughout. And that includes *The New York Times, The Washington Post,* and the *LA Times*.

As the story moved forward, as we found out more and more, even with admissions of the government at times, the continued way of phrasing the story was that the CIA had not ordered the Contras to do this and was not implicated in that fashion. But there really never was a denial throughout this period by the Contras themselves that they were involved in drug trafficking. And that was really the point that the people cared about. Were we involved with a movement that took part in bringing cocaine into the United States? And we now know that the Contras were involved, not just peripherally, they were involved with pretty much every major drug-trafficking organization that was moving cocaine into the US during this period, including the Medellin Cartel, the Matta Ballesteros operation in Honduras, elements of the Honduran military and the Cuban-American drug trafficking in Miami. These were all part of the Contra movement.

So, while there have been questions raised about the quantities, and it's impossible really to give a specific answer, it is clear that the Contras were not just small players. The drug traffickers at this period had figured out that they could move the drugs under the Contra umbrella, they had a much better chance of getting the drugs into the US and they'd be much less likely to have the whistle blown on them. It didn't mean some of them weren't arrested; some of them were. But this was a plan that the drug traffickers had figured out and to some extent it was successful. Obviously the case moves forward through John Kerry's investigation in the 1988 period, where he discovered a good deal more. The Kerry Report was quite strong in terms of describing the role that the Contras and some of the pilots had in the drug trafficking.

And, again, the story was never taken seriously by the mainstream press. It pops up again in 1991 when there is the trial of Manuel Noriega, where at this point *The Washington Post* does an editorial because the government puts on Carlos Lehder, one of the Colombian traffickers, as a witness against Noriega. And Lehder describes that he provided $10,000,000 to the Contra movement as part of his way of buying his success in getting drugs into the United States. At this point *The Washington Post* says in its editorial that perhaps there should be more attention paid to the Kerry Investigation. But, the *Post* doesn't really acknowledge that part of the problem was that *The Washington Post* itself had not paid much attention to the Kerry Investigation.

And then, of course, it remains pretty much a stagnant issue until 1996 when Gerry Webb revives it for the *San Jose Mercury News*. And at this point, frankly, the CIA becomes much more open. The Hitz investigation turns out to be fairly thorough and reasonably frank. But it remains the role of the mainstream press — *The Washington Post, The New York Times* and the *LA Times* in particular — to discredit Gary Webb's work. And it becomes much more a story of how Gary Webb may have had some nuances of the story wrong, rather than the larger import that the U.S. government was indeed working with drug traffickers, knew it was working with drug traffickers, and protecting them from exposure. That is no longer a disputable fact. But it is not a fact that is well known because the mainstream press chose to protect these secrets even as the CIA exposed them. So that is where we are today and I think that that is in the play. This play provides a certain context and reality to this story that, I think, brings it home.

Alfred McCoy:

Our topic tonight, as we discussed earlier, is really not all of the many, many issues that this play raises about national security, about drug trafficking, about the protests that arose in this city in particular, in South Central Los Angeles, over this particular controversy. What we're supposed to be focusing on is the discussion of the theme that Robert Parry raised for us in his statement: the media coverage of issues of national security and narcotics trafficking and particularly of national security and the CIA. So let me pick up on that theme, and address it in this opening round with three points.

First of all, to compliment some of the things that Robert said, I want talk a bit about the press coverage of the CIA's role in this case:

1. Was it perhaps even worse than we might imagine from the play tonight?

2. Were there other operations going on at exactly the same time, in a very similar pattern, that would have raised larger, deeper questions about the CIA's relationship to drug lords and to global narcotics trafficking?

3. Once we engage these two questions, that raises a question about the coverage of this case in the national press. You know *The Washington Post,* the *Los Angeles Times, The New York Times,* are fine newspapers, and are pillars of democracy in many respects. I would not want to do anything that would diminish the stature and the role of the national press in this society. I cannot imagine what this society would be without it. But, nonetheless, it does behoove us to ask whether or not on every issue they do the best job they can do. And I think this is an issue in which they do — compared to all the other things they do very well — they do miserably. And the question is: "Why is the national press so bad in dealing with the CIA?"

So, let me now go through each of these points. First of all, the particular coverage of this story. Robert mentioned that on October 1998, six months after this hearing, which took place in March of 1998, the CIA inspector general published Part 2 of his report which was, as Robert said, much more damning. Indeed, at paragraph 913, starting at that paragraph, there are forty paragraphs with the most detailed, sensational revelations about the CIA's relationship with Allan Hyde, the largest drug trafficker moving cocaine from Colombia through Central America and the Caribbean to the U.S. In order to get access to Allan Hyde's logistic facilities they formed an alliance with him and they protected him from any investigation by either Honduran or US authorities from 1986 to 1992—the height of the crack cocaine epidemic.

Now, when you are a criminal, what is the one thing you want from the state? Okay, you only want one thing: just immunity from investigation. If I had a connection with LAPD, within three months I'd take over the streets, okay? I would drop my footnotes, forget my erudition and my lecture, and I'd be the drug kingpin of Los Angeles. That's all I need, okay? Three months, that's what anybody needs.

Second, what was the press response to this sensational revelation? I mean this is sensational. If you look at Volume 2, it had interviews from CIA field agents all the way up to the director of Central Intelligence. It's got direct, verbatim quotes from CIA legal memoranda justifying this alliance. It's got direct quotes from documents in which everybody at every level in the agency is signing off on the relationship with a top drug lord. I mean this is sensational, 40 paragraphs of this material, plucked right from the CIA archives. But to my best knowledge there was not one single report in the national press about this sensational revelation. It should have been major headlines: "CIA Reveals Alliance with World's Top Cocaine Drug Lord." "Top Smuggler of Cocaine in the United States Protected for Seven Years by CIA at Height of Crack Cocaine Epidemic." A sensational story, right? They did not cover it.

Next, were there any other instances of CIA alliances with drug lords and CIA protection of drug lords that establish a pattern of behavior, and as they say in police work, a modus operandi on the part of the CIA? And, indeed, in 1979 there where two events that set off such a pattern: one, the Sandinistas took Managua, and two, the Soviets took Kabul. And this then set off two decade-long operations, throughout the 1980s, the Contra operation in Central America and the CIA alliance with the Mujahedddin in Afghanistan and Pakistan.

In both these operations, the same thing happened, exactly the same pattern. The CIA's chosen drug lord on the Afghan–Pakistan border lands, Gulbuddin Hekmatyar, was recipient of over half of the $3 billion of CIA funds distributed to the Mujahideen, and became the largest single trafficker on the borderlands. This alliance between the CIA and the Pakistan Inner Service Intelligence and the Afghan resistance transformed these borderlands from a minor producer of opium for regional markets to the world's largest single source of heroin in just two years. In 1979 zero percent of the U.S. heroin supply came from Afghanistan/Pakistan. Two years later, two years into the CIA covert operation 1981, 60 percent of all U.S. heroin came from Afghanistan/Pakistan. The press didn't report on the Afghan operation until 1990, when *The Washington Post* broke the story about Gulbuddin Hekmatyar and the other Mujahideen being heavily involved in the traffic. Why in 1990? Because the operation ended in 1989. Because they could talk about it then.

Now I would submit, then, that the national press reportage on this issue was consistently deficient. Why? That's a complicated question, and this is something that Robert Parry probably knows better than I. There are two things that I would argue again: First, when I was living in Australia for 12 years... I had a career as a kind of police reporter. I had a desk in the Murdoch press. I used to go down and write stuff about police corruption, organized crime, etc. in Australia. And it was sort of a night job. And the one thing that I was always amazed of, was, that I'd go down to the pub and I'd have beers with the police reporters. And these guys, these are guys that had 10, 20, 30 years of working with the police covering the murders, the robberies and all the rest. They knew everything. They knew all. Their vision of the world was positively demonic. I mean, there was a seventh level of hell that they lived in with the cops, and they knew it all. They had great, sordid, horrible stories, but hey never put out a word in print. Not one word ever got in the press. Why? Because they need the police to do their job as reporters, they're gonna get the call from the cops that tells them where the crime is taking place. They're gonna get the tip, the information they need in order to cover this sealed covered world of police detective operations. They have got to collaborate. They've got to be effective partners. And what I would argue is that this relationship that I saw up close in Sydney, which is not too surprising, probably operates in Washington, DC with the reporters of the national press. Those who cover intelligence, they get into a complicit, symbiotic relationship in which they are unlikely to write anything that offends. Indeed, they serve as conduits for what the CIA wants us to know from the CIA's perspective of the world.

Another feature, in this particular case with the press, was something that my wife Mary McCoy studied. She did it during the course of her doctorate in communications studies at Northwestern University. She published an article in the *Journal of Communication* on the "Dark Alliance" case. And what she argued was that the press had deep institutional reasons for wanting to stifle this story. This was at the time when the Internet was rising up. One of the distinctive aspects of this story was the website, the sensational website, to disseminate the story. The national press has a gatekeeping function. That is to say, they are the ones that serve as the clearinghouse and establish what is the reportorial agenda, what is the agenda of coverage, what is going to be challenged by alternative media. And at this particular point the press was very nervous. There was a kind of informal consensus, a kind of survival reflex, to stifle a story that was deemed to be irresponsible, threatening the reputation and the credibility of the press. So there was kind of an over-reaction, a very aggressive overreaction by the national press to destroy this story and to destroy the reputation of the reporter, Gary Webb, who had reported it.

KEVIN MICHAEL KEY:

Thank you very much, Al. We're going to open it up to questions now and you guys are in trouble because there is a whole row of journalists sitting up there, out-of-town journalists. I have a quick question. Gary Webb died recently. It's alleged that he committed suicide. Am I being paranoid in questioning the determined conclusion that it was a suicide?

ROBERT PARRY:

Well, I think that it was a suicide. I talked to his family members. He did leave fairly detailed notes to his family. It is a tragedy what happened. He committed suicide in December, basically, after his career was destroyed by many of his colleagues in the mainstream press, and he was basically sold out by his editor Jerry Ceppos. His career was wrecked. He did work for the state for a while. As I understand it, his marriage broke up. When he lost his job with the state, he could not find a job in journalism. He was running out of money, and as he was about to be evicted from his own house, he took his own life. There are real prices to pay. And I think that that's a factor. I think that this is an extreme case, but that's a factor that I think explains why some reporters don't do their job. They know if they cross certain lines, they pay very high prices, and we have seen that repeatedly now, especially during the 1980s and really through to the present.

KEVIN MICHAEL KEY:

Has there been any intimidation directed at you personally for some of the stories that you wrote?

Robert Parry:

Well, not physical. You don't get threatened physically in the U.S. as a journalist. But your career can be threatened and it can be very much damaged. I go into it in the book *Lost History*. I go into the history of how this drug case happened, but also of how the Iran-Contra scandal happened. I also spend time going through what the strategies were for the Bush and Reagan administrations in the '80s in trying to get control of the press. They had a very conscious plan, which we now know from their documents, of how they were going to do what they call "public diplomacy" domestically, and how they took aim at journalists. They also, by the way, went after the CIA's analytical division, in trying to get them to report events in ways that the White House wanted. But much of this was focused on the Washington press corps. And there were rumors spread about people's personal lives.

The most famous case is perhaps Ray Bonner, the Central American correspondent for *The New York Times* who wrote very heroically about the death-squad operations in El Salvador in particular, and effectively lost his job; he was sort of pushed out. He left *The New York Times* for quite a while. These kinds of examples were being made among those of us who did these sensitive issues across the board in Washington journalism. So reporters learned what not to go after. One thing that happened with Gary Webb, thinking about what Al said, is that it is also a case that by the time we get to the 1990s, the people who had succeeded in the '80s, they had survived by playing ball. They had not asked these questions. They had not tried to get to the truth on these stories, and they rose through the bureaucracy in the news organizations. And by the time that Gary Webb shows up reviving this story in 1996, which everyone thought had been buried, many of these former correspondents and reporters who missed it in the '80s were now bureau chiefs and deputy managing editors, and had a personal need and interest in making sure that this story was buried. It is also true, as Mary reported in her piece, that there was concern about the challenge of the Internet. And I should say that there was also a sense among some of the reporters in Washington that the African-American community was out of place in trying to assert itself as aggressively as it did. Some of the stories that appeared when they were attacking Gerry Webb, in places like *The Washington Post*—I'm not talking about *The Washington Times,* but about *The Washington Post*—are about how African-Americans tend to be conspiracy oriented.

KEVIN MICHAEL KEY:

Ha, I wonder why.

ROBERT PARRY:

So part of the way this was handled was to make fun of Gary Webb, to put him down personally, and also to put down African-Americans, who supposedly were just silly. As the case played out, and as the evidence became clearer that in fact there was a serious problem with the Contras and drug trafficking, many of those journalists could not face the fact that they had been wrong. At that point, it was easier to continue to destroy Gary Webb, continue not to report this story than it was to face up to it. Then Volume 2 came out, which was the major admission by the CIA, an historic set of admissions. There probably has never been a case where a U.S. government agency has admitted such crimes of state publicly. After Volume 2 came out, the *LA Times* did not write a story. *The Washington Post* waited about a month and did basically a "kiss off" story. *The New York Times* did do a piece a couple of days after the report came out. It was buried deep inside. It did have some of the facts right, but it was clearly underplaying some of the major admissions by the CIA.

KEVIN MICHAEL KEY:

I want to take questions now. It should be noted that the chairperson at this committee actually was a man named Porter Goss, who today is the director of the CIA. So there is a system of rewarding the good soldiers and consequences.

AUDIENCE MEMBER:

Do you think that Sy works in that position today?

ROBERT PARRY:

In terms of this covering Abu Graib and so forth? Well, Sy Hersh is a historic journalist. He was really a cutting-edge journalist in what might be called the golden age of investigative reporting in our era anyway, in the 1970s. He was with the Associated Press and then he left AP and worked for the Dispatch News Service, sort of an independent outfit, where he broke the My Lai story and some others. He was then hired by *The New York Times* and broke, in the 1975 period, some of the major CIA scandal stories. He was eventually kind of iced out of *The New York Times* as they went through certain changes at the top. He left and tried to make it as a freelancer, basically, and perhaps wrote some stuff that was less high quality than the stuff he had done earlier. And then with *The New Yorker,* more recently, he has done some very powerful stories, including the Abu Ghraib investigation.

FOLLOW-UP QUESTION:

But he has to talk to the people in the military.

ROBERT PARRY:

I think you'd be surprised that a lot of the people in the government are not dishonest. And I know that in these areas you suspect that, "Oh, they are all gonna lie to you." That has not been my experience. Now, some of these people might not want to talk, some have reasons to be careful. But a lot of the people, especially in the Pentagon, that I have dealt with, like all the police officers, they tend to be very straightforward in what they tell you. Obviously, some are professional liars. But it's true in the CIA too. Many people that I've met with within the agency are very interested in the truth. But, there are these policies. People in the CIA, like anywhere else, get a job to do. If you're Dewey Claridge, or one of these guys working on the Contra program, you had a job, and that is to get rid of the Sandinistas, to get the Contras into power in Nicaragua. How you did it was less important to the people who were your superiors that that you did it. And so there was a certain practical approach for those guys. And part of that practical approach was to ignore the fact that they were dealing with some very unsavory people in many cases. Not just drug traffickers, many of these people were torturers, they were assassins and murderers. These were not nice people. And I suppose you would expect that, so in some ways the drug trafficking was one of the lesser things they did. Obviously, it had more of an effect on the American population, but some of these guys were implicated in some of the worst human rights violations in Central America.

Follow-Up Question:

In terms of the press, who wrote these stories? Who were the anonymous sources?

Robert Parry:

Well, at different stages of the Contra drug story we had some anonymous sources. We had a number, though, that were on the record, and we had documents too, even from the beginning. One of the interesting cases prior to this was the Hugo Spadafora case. Hugo Spadafora Franco was a Panamanian who had been a government official who'd gone to fight with the Contras in Costa Rica. He became disgusted with the Contras involvement with drug trafficking and also worked with Noriega on the drug trafficking. He made the fatal mistake, however, of going to the U.S. embassy and talking to the head of the DEA at the U.S. embassy in Costa Rica, Bobby Nievas. He told Nievas that he was going to Panama to denounce the Contras and Noriega for drug trafficking. Now, Nievas put that into circulation at the embassy, and it got to a number of people, including people in the agency. When Spadafora reached the border of Panama, he was intercepted by Panamanian intelligence and he was decapitated. There was evidence from that case, that we already had access to in 1985, that pointed to serious drug-trafficking problems involving the Contras. So, even from the beginning there was a lot of evidence, but there was a lot of resistance to accept it. That was a hard story. And for various reasons *The New York Times* in particular chose to attack the story rather than seriously report it. Why that was is not entirely clear. But at the highest levels of *The New York Times,* like at *Newsweek* where I worked later, at AP where I worked, in a number of these organizations, the senior executive level was very sympathetic to the Reagan/Bush policies in Central America. Some of them were neoconservatives, some of them were just old hard-line cold warriors. At *The New York Times* Abe Rosenthal was executive editor. He was essentially a neoconservative. So we were dealing with people who really thought that the U.S. needed to do these hard, tough things. And I think that explains a lot of why people below them where inclined to try to spin these various stories in ways most favorable to U.S. foreign policy.

JOHN MALPEDE:

Can you explain about the present moment?

ROBERT PARRY:

This explains a lot. I think what happened with the Washington press corps in the 1980s was very effective in terms of breaking down any kind of independent source for information. And this applies also to the CIA's analytical division, which is also attacked during this period, and broken down as a source of independent information. The idea was to control the information flows. And this came through some of the neoconservatives who were coming to power at that time. They were very smart people. They understood the power of information. They felt that if they could control the information that got to the American people, they could control the American people.

And none of that was fixed during the 1990s. In fact it probably got worse during the 1990s. Clinton did not really care about the CIA; he just sort of let it be there. He had other priorities. The press never really realigned itself. It was even worse when it attacked Gary Webb in the Clinton years. And so you get to the period of this presidency, George W. Bush, and the idea of critical analysis, independent information, going against the grain. Those traditions were lost, at least in areas that I deal with — national security and those sorts of things. I'm not saying that there were not parts where the press was doing a fine job. But in these areas the independence of the American press had been broken. The reporters were now conveyer belts. And the American people have paid a very high price for that reality.

But it does go back to this Contra drug problem in some ways, and to other issues that you can see coming out of what this show was about. Even what was admitted to in Volume 1 of this report was quite damning. After it came out, I called Gary Webb. I said, "Gary, I guess you really screwed this up. It was much worse that you thought." And it was. And Volume 2 was far worse. And also, by the way, the Department of Justice report — if one actually read it, not just through the executive summary, but read the actual report — it's extremely damning of how the U.S. government protected these people from prosecution. But the fact that that could not be dealt with continues, with some of the same players and journalists becoming the people who basically gave a pass to the Bush administration's case on WMDs and other issues about Iraq. And, as you know, 1600 American soldiers are dead, along with tens of thousands of Iraqis, as a consequence.

Alfred McCoy:

On that same issue, one of the things that has been rather surprising is that since we got mired in the Iraq war the press has been almost engaged, if you will, in an act of independence since May of 2004. In the extraordinary aggressive reportage over the Abu Ghraib scandal, the Guantanamo scandal, the torture issue. And not just the national press; indeed, many of the regional papers are doing a superb job in covering the story. To know about the way this story is covered, I think, it's significant to look at who is being faulted in the stories, and look at who is being exempted from coverage.

One of the articles that Robert referred to earlier was *The New York Times* story by Tim Golden on the kind of black paranoia in response to the "Dark Alliance" case. It was the major report from *The New York Times* in response to the Gary Webb story. It basically talked about Tuskeegee and the historic propensity of the African-American community to be seized by almost collective panics. And indeed, now, in our present age, there was this fear, this paranoia, this belief that the CIA may have been protecting drug traffickers, and there is even a belief in the African American community that the flooding of cocaine into the African American community is willful. And this was the coverage of the story by Tim Golden in the *New York Times*. Not focusing on the CIA, not focusing on the issues, but in many ways attacking, or criticizing the community that was raising the issue.

The Congressional Black Caucus — in a certain sense, the leaders of the African-American community — had made, as their number one legislative agenda item, the resolution of the "Dark Alliance" case. That was a formal motion. And this is a community with many problems, and a leadership with a very full and long agenda. This was number one. So, in effect, was this a very sharp critique of the African-American leadership and the African-American community.

Now, if you juxtapose this, with what we just saw over the weekend, Tim Golden has now written a very detailed report in *The New York Times* about the Abu Ghraib scandal, and it's official, okay? And what is the source of the problem at Abu Ghraib and in this case, Baghram, which is the focus of the report? It's those hillbillies, it's those redneck sergeants all over again! We saw their work in the photos from Abu Ghraib, and now, in Tim Golden's report, we can see what they are up to again. It's just these rednecks, testosterone brutes! And there are two oblique references to the CIA in this massive, two-part story. The first part started on page one and it spilled out over two full pages of *The New York Times*. Tim Golden says that *The New York Times* was given 2,000 pages of documents. Unlike *The Washington Post,* they will not be posted on the web. *The Washington Post* does, most of the papers do; *The New York Times* does not. We are never going to see those documents independently, to make up our own judgment about what he did cover and what he did not cover. There are two oblique references to the CIA. One about a meeting in which the CIA was discussing interrogating parameters. And if you look at those two fragmentary reports, it is clear that the CIA is a principal in the interrogation. I'm not sure, but I think that there is almost an indication that the CIA is in fact the lead agency in Baghram.

So here we have, in fact, a report on these red-neck sergeants, this disastrous brigade, savages you know, out of their trailer parks are unleashed upon the world and, "Oh my God, get them inside the prison!" Now that's gonna solve that. Meanwhile, two fragmentary references to the CIA, and no examination in any of this tidal wave of coverage about the CIA's role in this scandal.

KEVIN MICHAEL KEY:

Well, you know, Al, I always say, "Just cause I'm paranoid, it don't mean they ain't out to get me."

AUDIENCE MEMBER:

I just wanted to add that it is disturbing in this kind of climate, a climate where the press lacks competition and becomes more and more complicit, more like the police reporters that Al described. Whatever you do as a member of the community is problematic. Let's say that we want to do our own independent reporting, investigating and have our own means of finding out, and don't have to go through a major newspaper to get it out there. You are fighting the battle on two fronts, which makes it much more difficult. Like Gary Webb, who was not only doing an exposé on the CIA, on the Contra connection with the CIA, but he was also doing an exposé on the mainstream press. And that was a major component of the sensation this story made, and a lot of the commentary that this story got: "How is it possible that the mainstream press is not covering it?" And Gary wrote on the Internet for all in the world to see: "They are chicken shit," was his actual phrase, and that went out all across the world. Everybody could see, on the web site, that he was calling the mainstream press chicken shit. And that put them on the defensive, and so they turned around and they attacked him. In the meantime the CIA was doing their damage control, so he really found himself in a battle on many fronts at once. And I think that anybody who tries to uncover something in the mainstream press, or in the press generally, and particularly newspapers, they will get challenged individually, they will get this "circle the wagons effect" from the press. And they will also get a reaction from whatever agency or outfit whose scandal they are exposing. So the challenge is, in the current climate, to figure out how not to make so many enemies at once that everybody is going to turn you into the story. And that is really difficult, because it is much easier to turn to the messenger of the story than to focus back onto the original story itself.

Susan Burton:

You're punished for life. You serve time, the judge says that you're sentenced to one year, two years, three years... whatever the sentence is. But upon release you have a mark, you have a mark that is never removed.

A mark that says that you cannot be a nurse; a mark that says you cannot sell real estate; a mark that says you cannot be a nurse's aide; a mark that says you cannot work for the county, the state or the government; a mark that says you cannot go in corporate America; a mark that says you cannot get your relative out of foster care.

So in other words you're punished for the rest of your life.

My question is: When does the punishment end? When will your rights be fully restored to participate wholly in life?

When will my salary not be compromised because I have a felony conviction? When will the barrier be removed for me to get into senior housing? People are denied senior housing based on a conviction that might've took place twenty years ago.

We have all these people coming into the community, some in their geriatric years that cannot access housing. I can buy a house, but I cannot rent an apartment.

So my question is: when does the punishment end?

Mark Perdue:

The media. The media portrays everything. When I turn on the six o'clock news, I see my people all over the place, doing ridiculous things... everything black is just portrayed horribly. And we do it to ourselves. Me being a rapper, I was signed to a developmental deal. They don't want to hear about a change or anything; the first thing the songs have got to talk about is girls, we've got to talk about Crips and cars, we've got to do it ourselves. I always say, if you stand for nothing, you'll fall for anything, it's not that deep, stand up, trust ourselves and stand up together.

DEBORAH SMALL:

I think that it's not an accident that the war on drugs started at the same time that we decided to end the war on poverty, and what we have done is criminalized two or three generations of those of color for engaging in the only types of economic activities that were available to them.

Public Conversation

Compton, 2005

Topic:
The War on Drugs
May, 2005

Panelists:
Dave Fratello: Political Campaign Manager, Manager of Proposition 36
Susan Burton: Founder and Director, A New Way of Life, Housing for Women Getting out of Prison
Kevin Michael Key: Moderator

Kevin Michael Key:

I'd like to welcome everybody. There are some familiar faces, some unfamiliar faces, but by the looks of it, these are community faces, which is what we're trying to do here with this showing of "Agents & Assets." First, before we get started here, let me introduce the panel members. To my right we have Susan Burton. She's the executive director of "A New Way of Life," which is a re-entry program for women and children. To my left is Mr. David Fratello. Dave was the manager of the Proposition 36 campaign that was passed. Proposition 36 had to do with the decriminalization of simple possession of narcotics, and people of California through the initiative process said that we would prefer to see people with substance-abuse problems, with the disease of alcohol and addiction treated as opposed to incarcerated. One of the things that Dave is going to talk about is the broader implications of that policy, and the fact that it is going to be revisited. It was funded for five years, and very soon we people of California have to decide whether or not we want to continue along the road of treatment and rehabilitation, or if we want to return to more punitive methods. Before we go on there's a lady here, Miss Donna Warren, who is a former candidate for lieutenant governor on the Green Party ticket, and who also, I believe, sued the CIA for the harm that was done in our communities as a result of their policies. [*Applause*]

So we'd like to welcome her and any comments that she would like to make. I believe the first thing that we are going to do is to turn the mic over to Dave.

DAVE FRATELLO:

Well, thank you very much. You asked me to lead into this, so that's what I'm going to do. I'm not wearing a tie today because I don't want to be confused with a politician. But, my name is Dave Fratello, and I've run a number of political campaigns around the country, starting with Proposition 215 in California, that legalized the medical use of marijuana. We put that out into several other states, Maine, Colorado, Oregon, Washington state, and passed it there, too. But we knew that when we began working on that, that the drug problem — and most specifically the problem with the laws regarding drugs — was much bigger than the use of marijuana by cancer patients. That the incarceration was really happening to average users and as a result of an overwhelming national policy, but also in California, where we had treated addiction as a crime.

Today's presentation takes us back to the 1980s. And, something was happening in the '80s, something was happening in the '90s which penetrated and permeated the entire political culture. And that is, that everybody just accepted the war on drugs, which fundamentally was a war on people. We just let people get away with orchestrating policy that was saying fundamentally that people who make some wrong choices, people who have the disease of addiction, who get caught up in this drug trade — clearly because of a lack of other opportunities — are not only treated as criminals, but we're going to start hitting them over the head harder and harder and harder. Incarcerate our way out of this problem.

Probably in this room we all know what a ridiculous choice that was in the first place, but it took a while for America to experiment with that before the revelation came again that this was the wrong course. All you have to do is look at some of the results that we got in California from trying to incarcerate our way out of the drug problem. The year 1988 was a good marking point because George Bush, the first one, launched his drug war in 1989. So in 1988, California had 52,000 people in prison, of which about a quarter were there for drug possession. Going up until 1999–2000, we tripled the prison population to about 155,000. And we quadrupled the number of people serving time for simple drug possession. Twenty thousand people, serving time in state prison, whose only crime was that they got busted for possession of illegal drugs. There are probably 35 states in America that don't even have 20,000 people in prison today.

But that's the way that this fever caught people up. There was a lack of questioning of this policy, and these choices that we were making, in that environment, the incarceration rate just exponentially rolled and rolled and rolled ahead. Well, we finally had to change that. And, in my business, in politics, if you're going to go to the ballot directly, you've got to have your education taken care of before you get there. So by the time we got to 1999–2000, we didn't actually have to do much education. The voters had seen the results of this policy. They were seeing their communities being destroyed by people going to jail, and that it wasn't helping anyone.

They had reached a conclusion, in a very broad sense, that the war on drugs was causing more harm than it was solving. And that treating it as a criminal problem was fundamentally a wrong choice. Well, when we saw that, in polling that we did, in 1998–99, we realized that this was an incredible opportunity to offer the voters a choice, by asking them: "Have we made the right choice, shall we treat this as a medical issue instead?" So we sat down and wrote Prop. 36, and basically made this as simple as we could. If you get busted for possession, and you haven't been committing another crime at the same time, and even if you've got violent priors, but they're pretty far back, you're going to get treated. It passed with a vote of "yes" of 61 percent, despite the opposition of the "thin blue line," which was fat on the other side.

All law enforcement, every elected leader, all the newspapers opposed this thing and the voters said, "I don't care, I don't care what you're saying." Whatever your fine point, whatever your objection is, there's something big and sweeping and important that we've got to change, and we're going to say "yes," so we got 61 percent of the vote. On July 1, 2006—our five-year anniversary is coming up on, July 1, 2011—this became the sentencing law of California.

Now we've got a few years to look back, as we come up on the fourth full year that the law has been in place. Thirty-six thousand people every year enter treatment under Prop. 36. Can you imagine what we were doing to these people before? Well, you probably don't need to imagine. Half of those people had never been offered treatment before. And I'll tell you something about the way we wrote the law; we knew what we were doing. It was very controversial during the campaign. And some of the people would say, "Well that's a good law for people who are really getting busted for the first time. But you've got to treat people with priors differently, because people who have been addicted for years, coming out of the system, well they've got serious problems, you can't just treat them like a first-time offender."

Well, we wrote the law to say, "You know what? It's a blank slate. Everyone after July 1, 2001 is going to get their first offense after July 1, and their second offense the next time, if they come back." It's a clean slate, because you know what? We have failed them, by not offering them a treatment opportunity before. So that means we are not treating just a bunch of teenagers smoking a joint on the weekend; we are treating the population that has a severe, extended drug history, and we're doing pretty well. We've got some statistics, but I'll just breeze over them. We've got charts and graphs, but I didn't bring them today.

KEVIN MICHAEL KEY:

Thank you!

DAVE FRATELLO:

You're welcome. Just imagine this: 36,000 people, 57 percent, have used drugs for 10 years or more before they come into the program, and 25 percent for 20 years or more. What kind of results are we getting from this diversion? Well, the first thing that we're getting is a big change in the prison system. There are 7,500 fewer people serving time in prison today for drug possession than there were when this was on the ballot. [*Applause*]

People are being kept out and they're staying out. We can't even count the number of people not in county jails now, but it's probably two or three times that. County jails are real hard to get numbers on, but we know that overwhelmingly people were facing jail time, so when you see the effect on the prison system, it's much bigger when you include the effect on the county jails. California stopped building prisons. [*Applause*]

When Prop. 36 was on the ballot, if you remember when you got your ballot, there was a line item at the end that said what the costs are going to be, and maybe the positive fiscal effects. That was written by an agency called Legislative Analyst. So they wrote that California would find it unnecessary to build one of the prisons that we were then planning to need. If you see the hysterical reports put out by the Department of Corrections in 1998: "We need four new prisons, or else!" But by the time this was on the ballot, we needed two new prisons, and I wish we could have stopped the one new one that they did build. We stopped the second one; plans for that are scrapped. And Roger Hickman is quoted as saying that the era of building prisons in California is over. [*Applause*]

You take 7,500 people out of the system and promise to take

more out, I think that has an effect. So those are some great momentum pieces.

But what are we doing within people's lives? Well, there have been some great studies—on both Prop. 36 now and on some other systems — and when you link criminal justice and treatment, and you've got a population that's this tough, and most of the people have never had treatment before, it ain't easy.

I mean I don't need to tell anybody here, you're not going to have 80 percent–90 percent success. But there's a general average out there when people have studied these things all over the country. If you get about a third of these people who come into these programs to complete it the first time through… boy, you're skating man, you're doing great. And that's exactly what we're doing here in California. We've got 34.4 percent completing the program, statewide, and in LA County they've been averaging 38 percent. We've got some tough populations in LA, and in Bakersfield . I just got this report last week, and it's blowing my mind—in Bakersfield, Kern County, 42 percent.

And they said it couldn't be done. And they said if you force this mandate on the courts, you force this mandate on the cops, on the judges, on probation officers, there's no way you're going to pull it off, because we haven't got the treatment. So how did we get the treatment? We put the money where the policy was. A lot of people who objected to this law while it was on the ballot said: "We agree with the idea of treatment, but you've got to be really careful about who you let in. We've got to supervise them, we've got to do all of these other things." We said, you know what, there's a mandate, you've got to give everybody an opportunity, and second of all, we've doubled the amount of money going into drug treatment in the state. We have seen the coincident rise, now twice as much treatment is now available.

We've got many more residential spots; programs that existed have been able to expand, and it's allowed new programs to come online. And that's how you do it. You put your money where your mouth is. You put $120 million extra into drug treatment. Every year, we're saving at least $180–$200 million a year as a result of all of these downwind effects. If we can ever get around to calculating this, if you take someone that has been cycling in and out of the system and now, they're home with their families, and their families aren't in crisis, the families aren't on the dole, people are earning money and taking care of themselves, well, how do you calculate all of those effects? So we're seeing a lot of great things.

Now, I also want to address the problems that we're facing.

KEVIN MICHAEL KEY:

Upcoming.

DAVE FRATELLO:

Upcoming. The good story that I just told you has not permeated our legislature. The people who have access to the legislature are the cops. And so they have basically never stopped fighting this law. And they've come in to the legislature, and there's a Senator in San Diego who sponsored the wish list from law enforcement. Some of the judges have bought into it, and I hate to say, some of the treatment people have bought into this. There are some trade-offs that they like. But it's the total wish list. They're going to find new ways of excluding people from Prop. 36. If you come in with certain kinds of priors, they want to be able to say, "You know what, not you, we'll save your slot for someone else." It's a slippery slope. We used to offer treatment to about 3,000–5,000 people a year in this state who were coming into the criminal justice system. We have multiplied that by about 10 times. If you start giving them the ability to say who does, and who doesn't get it, it won't be long before this is a tiny program.

They also want to be able to jail people during their treatment. And their argument, coming from the law enforcement perspective, is that: "Well, we've got criminals here, and they're on probation, if they screw up in the middle of their treatment, we should be able to put them in jail for a few days." And, the rhetoric quickly goes from, "We'll put them in jail for a few days and then we'll bring them back into treatment," to "Well, how about seven days, two weeks, 30 days… it's all disputable, up to thirty days in jail." Like that's not going to interrupt your community-based treatment, it's not going to interrupt your job. It's not going to interrupt your childcare? I mean, give me a break. But these folks have no love for this law and they're cutting deals in the legislature, and they are really starting to roll over us. I can't believe it. I can't believe how fast this stuff is moving, on the Senate side anyway. So we've got some hope that on the Assembly side we're going to have some friends. Karen Bass has sponsored a bill, and she's going to be taking some of these amendments as a trade-off. But we're trying to say: Don't take the worst of them. We've got an assembly public safety committee that is probably the only real backstop, with Mark Leno as the chair there, from San Francisco.

But, make no mistake, they're trying to rewrite this law; not because the results say there's some problem, but because they hate this thing in the first place. They want to go back to what it used to be. We'll talk more about what we can do about that. But we've got a great story to tell, and they just aren't hearing it, and it's funny because both Susan and I were watching the presentation earlier, and we said this is what we're already seeing in Sacramento, with all the things we care about, the evasion and the failure to deal with the real issues. It's really shocking, especially when we've got something so good to protect. Thank you very much.

KEVIN MICHAEL KEY:

The way the format goes, is that after Susan speaks, we will then open it up for questions from the audience — audience participation. But Dave, real quick, one of the things that I know was different about Prop. 36 was that the funding was written into the initiative, so hopefully when we open it up, you will address that, and that there are already funding issues coming up when it gets revisited.

DAVE FRATELLO:

I can do that now, very quickly. I wasn't clear about why this is happening now in theegislature. There are two reasons. It's because the cops are still fighting; but the other reason is that we put into the law this $120 million for five years, and the money sunsets after five years. And we thought this would be an ideal length of time, and that by then the legislature would be able to look at the program, assess the results, and arrive at a number that really works best. And frankly we thought that that would probably be higher than the $120 million per year that we have had. But we felt that we had to have some experience for that to be clear to everyone. We called for this independent evaluation, and the numbers that I started to give you were coming from that independent evaluation that UCLA is doing.

Anyway, the funding for the five years expires as of July 1 of next year, 2006. So in some ways this is a little bit early to be starting to have this legislative discussion; but people are trying to get worked up because next year, this budget has to be settled. And what the cops are saying is that: "No more money for this program unless you make some changes." That's what's generating a lot of this activity, and we'll see if it actually plays out this year, or if it gets pushed to the next year.

KEVIN MICHAEL KEY:

Thank you. Susan?

SUSAN BURTON:

I want to thank the people that did the play, thank you very much. [*Applause*]

As you were performing it, I went back a ways, right there with you, to some of the results of the CIA flooding our community with those substances. And still every day I work with the results, the ongoing results of our community being saturated with crack cocaine. "A Way of Life" specifically targets women who are coming out of the criminal justice system, tries to reunite them with their children, to begin to heal their harm, to begin to educate them about things like this play, to give them the bigger picture of what's going on in the community, and to keep them out of the criminal justice system.

I was incarcerated in 1981. I had a five-year-old son that was killed as a result of an accident, a car accident, and there was a detective that was driving the car that ran over my son. And my community, at that time, in 1981, it was full of crack. And that's what I did: I medicated my grief and my pain. By 1985 I was sentenced to two years in state prison for possession of a controlled substance, and I stayed on a turnstile, in and out of prison, in and out of prison for the next 10, 12 years. I was sentenced to prison a total of six times, and in 1997—October 4 of 1997—I went into a treatment facility. I emerged 102 days later, on my path to healing, going back to my community, reclaiming my life, reclaiming my life and helping others to have a better life. [*Applause*]

And then I reflect on the rise of incarceration for women, coming out of low-income communities, and knowing there was something different to do besides incarcerate me, punish me, demoralize me, and then eject me back into the community with $200, saying: "Pick up your bed and walk." It's a little bit more difficult than that. It was 1997 by the time I got back into the community. By 1998 I was able to get a small house, and in that house I began to invite women from the prison system, women from recovery, and to make it a safe haven and a healing place.

Since then, we have two more homes. One is for women with their children, because during those first few years, I watched women completely lose custody of their children; their children were adopted out simply because they did not have enough money to reunite as the Department of Children and Family Services ordered them to do. You know the house, the bedroom, separate bedrooms for the children, separate bedrooms for boys and girls, without any resources to do this with.

And this year we opened a third home for some of those women who had been through the house, who were working, but couldn't actually come up with $3,000 to move into their own place. Those women are working, so it just goes to show what the efforts of the community can do to begin to address its own needs. Because I've seen and I've experienced waiting on the system to address the problem. And it's just not gonna happen when the system is the problem. It's gonna take people like you and me to begin to make the changes that need to be made.

Last week there was a Peace and Justice Summit in Watts at WLCAC, put on by an organization or organized by an initiative called All of Us or None. And close to 400 people came together to talk to policy-makers about the conditions they face daily in the community, and to begin to build a dialogue with these policy-makers. And I believe that what's going to have to happen is that people like you and me build a strong alliance and a political movement, to tell the policy makers that they need to pay attention to us and our needs. We're low-income people, but nevertheless we're people, and we are the majority. And we need to understand that we are the majority, and we need to vote. We need to go to the polls and we need to vote, and we need to carry our friends to the polls and we need to get first-time voters registered, and encourage and be knowledgeable about what happens in the vote, and to build some political weight for ourselves. That is the process of this country, but it's not working for me. I don't know if it's been working for you, but it hasn't been working for me. Prop. 36 was voted in, and I simply come to say, why can't it work like we voted it in? Why do you have to put your twist on it? Look, that's how simple it is for me: We voted it in, why isn't it staying the way we voted it in? I run my mouth too much sometimes, but I got voice now. [*Applause*] And you do too. And you do too. So with that, I'm going to return it to the moderator and say thank you. Thank you for allowing me to visit there again. I feel that since that time, it's not quite as painful, but it's still amazing how the CIA inspector general can say, "They don't want to talk to me" and it plays.

KEVIN MICHAEL KEY:

Thank you! Now is this a question or a comment, Hylen? You've got voice, as they say. Come on with it.

"AGENTS & ASSETS" CAST MEMBER HYLEN BURT:

I want to make a comment, and then a sort of statement. Being in the play, I heard about the drug trafficking and CIA involvement, years ago, but look how long ago that was. And before this play came back again, it was just hushed under the rug, whether that be from media influences to leave the story alone, or this interest had died down. But why did it? When you think about the effect on the crack babies and separated families and the burden on the social-economic system as far as the welfare system is concerned, it would seem to far outweigh the amount of money they got for the Nicaraguans, because this affects generations, generations of families that have just been lost and so forth. But why did they do it? Why, because low-income people are notorious for not standing up for their rights. And they won't say nothing. And, well, we'll complain and moan to each other, but as far as becoming active in our propositions and our government, they look down and say, "Let's shoot some craps." They're going to get high and have some fun, and so forth and so forth, and then that'll be the end of it, and no one will be the wiser.

But drugs crosses every social and economic barrier, rich, poor, black, white, whatever, so what we really need to do is make sure that everybody is involved in making the solution. One more thing, there was a person working here at Compton College, that I was talking to before the show today, and he ran it down. I'm not from Compton. He really educated me. He's been at the school in Compton for 20 years, and he was here when crack was going crazy in Compton, and teenagers with $20 or $30,000, and mom's struggling on social welfare or whatever. But everybody gets involved in that socio-economic system, buying houses, cars, whatever, and the police need to bust somebody. But my comment for all of us is that we really, really need to get involved and stand up and say the holocaust that was initiated in South Central, we need to stand up and say, not only will we not let it happen again, we want somebody to atone for what was done.

Kevin Michael Key:

Reparations, I hear you buddy! [*Applause*]

Paula LaBrot:

Hello, my name is Paula, and I want to thank all the people in the cast for putting on such a beautiful play. And I want to say something about this. I feel scared, but I want to say something about it. Drugs cross all lines. It is in Thousand Oaks. It is in Montebello. It is in Santa Clarita. It is in San Pedro. There are families that suffer from this so terribly, not only families but our whole system. I'm so glad I came today. Although I never heard your name, I voted for your proposition. I'm in Topanga. It's a lot easier sometimes to preach this kind of gospel in a neighborhood where people are hurting and need to go down on their knees to God, than it is sometimes in wealthier neighborhoods, where people don't talk about these things, and don't get active about these things. And the fact of the matter is there are emergency rooms all over this city that are closing, there are things that we'd like to do in education for families on welfare, families that are really needy. And we can't do them because there's no money. Because all of the money is going to those people who work in the jails, and what do people in those jails need? They need prisoners to do their jobs, that's just the bottom line, it doesn't matter. There are kids from South Central, kids from Beverly Hills. I want to work really hard, I don't care where someone's from, I don't care what color they are, what socio-economic status they are, I don't want anybody polarizing us, rich and poor about this issue. It's a very, very important thing that people in California have to come together on, and I'm really kind of scared talking about it. But I'm proud of my husband, because my husband is a Santa Monica physician working at Saint John's who got up in front of the White House on a box and spoke for medical-marijuana laws several years ago, and we've been working very hard on this, and I never knew who you were, so we've got to get together, we really do.

DAVE FRATELLO:

I do need to comment on the prison guards, since you raised that. For those of you don't know, she was right. Just about the most powerful union in the state is the prison-guards union. The Indian gaming tribes, they have their own interests, I'm not too worried about their public policy issues. But about 80 percent of the money that was spent to oppose Prop. 36 in 2000 came from the prison guards. They put the money in, or got it together and funded it. This last ballot, we had Prop. 66 to change the Three Strikes law rather fundamentally. And the first million for that came from the prison-guards union. I would just let that hang there, except that Governor Wilson and Governor Schwarzenegger convinced a billionaire to drop in the next $4 million, so there's lots of other disturbing forces that we come across here. But those folks, the prison-guards union, have had a stranglehold on criminal-justice policy for years. It was only by going directly to the voters that we had a chance. And it's not easy. It was a strange moment in history that we had our own billionaires who were willing to fund the campaign in California. That's how we were able to put $5 million together to win that campaign. That's not going to happen every time either.

Paula LaBrot:

But it's very important to know that the prison guards were one of the biggest supporters of Gray Davis, and that's why it's so important that we don't allow ourselves to get polarized. And I use as my inspiration for this Nelson Mandela's work in South Africa where he said, "Let's all go in, and we'll start at zero, start over together." And I think that that's exactly what we need to do in California. We have a system in which prison guards are sucking us dry of every resource we have for treatment programs, and for emergency rooms and for social welfare. And, I think your organization should print a list of those candidates that the Prison Guard Association endorses. [*Applause*]

Susan Burton:

You mean a list of those candidates that the prison guards give contributions to, is that what you mean? [*Nods and smiles in agreement*]

Audience Member:

Can I just ask a really quick question? Can you elaborate on what constitutes more power to a movement? Is it money, or higher membership, or …

Dave Fratello:

In this case it's money and how it's used in Sacramento. I'm blanking a little bit about the relative amounts. But the prison guards, it's like 20,000 guys, but they take more money out of their checks proportionately than most other unions, to use for politics. And so it gives them something like $16 million, I believe, a year that they dole out to political campaigns and to lobby groups and to independent expenditures. So they play the Sacramento game almost better than anybody else. They get everybody to owe them something, and then they call in the favors when it's time. Sometimes they use these front groups, they've got these victims that will go out and speak publicly, because everybody understands the conflicts of interest, if they were the ones up front. They fund the victims groups who will go out and lobby, and they'll be the silent partner for law enforcement. So I'm fighting right now in the legislature, the district attorney's association, the police chiefs, the narcotics officers, but they're all bankrolled, and their access is all guaranteed by the prison guards.

KEVIN MICHAEL KEY:

This next question is coming from a young woman who is part of an organization whose main purpose is to counter-balance the power of the prison union.

NICOLE:

I want to add another piece of the puzzle to our conversation today. And in the play it's called the Iran-Contra scandal, and what we're leaving out here is Iran. And we have to remember that the reason that one critical piece of circulating arms and drugs to the world was the CIA's desire to support a regime change in Iran, which it already had a history of doing in Iran. And today, we are looking at the consequences of cold-war success for regimes that we now call terrorist. It's not only the prison guards and the prison-industrial complex that is sapping the political will and the foundation resources from alternatives, it's the prison-industrial complex's Big Brother, the military-industrial complex. And it's enormously powerful, globally, and right now it's manufacturing other kinds of alibis for punitive policy-making in the form of U.S. nationalism and to support the military.

We have to follow all the ducks, to see the full picture, and withhold our support from the war in Iraq. And not support U.S. military interventions, and not be nationalist ourselves, and not support policies that claim to be in the name of America, or not even perhaps in the state of California. We have to see the webs that connect us to people all over the globe, and the ways that our national identity is used and taken from us by people who like to incarcerate and oppress. It's up to us to make the connections, and to resist participating in all the oppressive structures worldwide. [*Applause*]

DAVE FRATELLO:

[T*o Rickey Mantley, who played Mr. Hitz.*] Do you have a follow-up on your report from earlier?

RICKEY MANTLEY:

Good afternoon. My name's Rick Mantley, and I work with a grassroots organization, in the heart of the downtown community called the Los Angeles Community Action Network. (LA CAN) We don't deal with the issue of drug use or drug policy directly, but we deal with women and children and homeless people, or people who are formerly homeless, issues of poverty. But still, the drug issue cannot be ignored and it truly is at the epicenter of homelessness, or the epicenter of a lot of the social ills that plague America.

My statement first is, as you said, Dave, that Prop. 36 is coming up for reauthorization in terms of funding. They're already trying to whittle away at the funding. They're going to take that figure that you were saying earlier of the 36-percent success rate and they're going to say, well that's way too low, that's not enough to continue to justify spending what we're spending on it now. The $120 million was what was authorized for what we were spending on the program for five years. Well, they're probably going to try to whittle down that amount, and also attach these very restrictive provisions and amendments, to further tighten the program, or to move it to what it was before the program.

But what I'm very concerned about is that we've taken "Agents & Assets" to Cleveland and Detroit where similar initiatives were placed on the ballot and they didn't go anywhere. In fact, in Ohio we learned that the governor himself, in league with political operatives from within the White House were very diligent to beat any kind of social reform in the state of Ohio. And they did. The same thing happened in Michigan where a similar drug-treatment initiative was disqualified on the basis of a technicality.

I'm very concerned, that again California has been known for years as a trendsetter in terms of social trends and social upheaval and the future of this country in terms of social justice. But Prop. 36 hasn't translated well into other states. In fact the conservative rightwingers have seen what has happened in other states, and they've learned their lesson. They're like the Borg. They learn to assimilate. They've learned how to defeat these types of initiatives when they come to their states.

So I'm really concerned that the drug-reform initiative which was started by you and others is stagnating because, first of all, we're in the era of Bush and the era of conservatives who reign supreme in Washington. I just hope somehow that the election with Villaraigosa, and the election of the senator from Illinois, Barack Obama, is sort of the harbinger of a brighter future, because again, the drug reform is being stymied, and that's what my real concern is at the moment.

Kevin Michael Key:

Is that a question, or is that a statement? Well, I think, going back to the rooms of recovery, is there somebody with a burning desire?

Donna Warren:

My name is Donna Warren. I'm the chapter coordinator for the California Committee to Amend California's Three Strikes and I work directly with Mr. Fratello. In 1999 I sued the CIA and the Department of Justice for infecting South Central LA, my home, for infecting us with crack cocaine. Fortunately, you were talking about what people can do. We also have to recognize that the government at every turn is trying to stop us. We saw a demonstration right here at Compton College, and what the production didn't say is that after these hearings Julian Dixon, a standing member of this judiciary committee, under Porter Goss, who is now the head of the CIA, announced... as a black man, announced to the world that the CIA was not complicit in the devastation of South Central by crack cocaine.

And if you remember, soon after Maxine Waters left the fight, she quit. She quit the fight after going to Nicaragua, after knowing everything that she knew. So it's obvious, and demonstrated in this play, that they knew that there was a lot more to be investigated. This young man mentioned several times a secret agreement... yes, a secret agreement between the director of the CIA, William Casey and William French Smith, attorney general of the U.S., that we will report all kinds of crimes, but we will not report narcotics violations.

That alone should have caused a lot of fear and that was the smoking gun to the class-action lawsuit. Because of the class action lawsuit here in California we have a thousand plaintiffs who filed court claims. It was also filed in Oakland at the same time. Because of it, cynicism just spread. They were filing class action lawsuits by the dozens. What the U.S. government did was file a suit that had some technical things wrong with it, sent it to a hostile judge in Florida. He dismissed it. Then they said —in the interest of, or the spirit of efficiency—they took every suit, including the one that I filed in Los Angeles, gathered them all up, sent them to Florida and dismissed all of the suits.

By the time all this happened, they decided we were small potatoes and we couldn't go forward. I must have asked every attorney in this city, I asked Connie Rice, the famed civil-rights attorney. I asked Johnny Cochran, I asked attorneys I don't even remember their names, and no one would take this case forward.

I'm going to leave you with this. I actually live in Gardena, California, and I got a chance to jam up the mayor yesterday because I went before the city council twice, and I asked Gardena to pass a resolution that says that the Three Strikes law needs to be amended. This is what he told me: "You live in Holly Park where there is primarily black folk. In other parts of the city where they also have homeowners associations, it's not black, and they are adamant that they want the Three Strikes."

And because the mayor knows that the area where I'm from does not vote in large numbers, they're comfortable telling me: "Ms. Warren, I am not comfortable amending the Three Strikes,

I am not going to pass a resolution. When I run for office, if I need the support, I am going to appeal to the fear and the hatred of those people who want to keep the Three Strikes enforced."

The politicians know that this is an easy way to gain re-election. All they've got to do is go out there and put the boogeyman out there, and they can scare people, and they can be grandmother Latinas, or black grandmothers who should know better, and they'll go right to the polls the issue of safety and vote No against their own self-interest. [*Applause*]

KEVIN MICHAEL KEY:

Folks, some of us ain't had no Memorial Day barbecue yet. And what I would like to do is, if someone's got a burning desire... Yes.

GEORGE LABROT:

I don't approve of prostitution, drugs and gambling. But I run a household budget, and I run an office budget. I believe that California is so wealthy that it can afford anything it wants. But, I don't believe it is so wealthy that it can afford everything it wants. And we need funding for health, education, streets and highways, parks and recreation. I believe if the public is actually educated, they may make a reasonable decision. If they feel strongly that people who are guilty of victimless crimes should be soaking up their tax money sitting in prison, if that's how they feel about it, fine. But most of this sentiment is the result of cynical manipulation.

If the voters understood only the economic value here, if they only understood that throwing people into prison for life for minor felonies is going to ruin their way of life, and that incarcerating people for being involved in drugs, prostitution and gambling is going be so expensive, that it's going to ruin their way of life in their nice suburb, then I don't think they would be able to be manipulated.

And the other thing is the concern about releasing violent felons. Legal industries solve their disputes with lawsuits and threats of lawsuits. Illegal businesses do not have that luxury. They have to settle their disputes with violence or threats of violence. There is no other way to settle contract dispute in an illegal industry. So a lot of the concern of the violent felons is that they have no other way to settle their disputes, other than violent dispute-resolution. The two biggest funders of the Democratic Party are the trial lawyers association, and the prison-guard union. So I believe that if the public of California were educated to that fact—because one doesn't usually think of that as the agenda of the Democratic Party—they could cause that party to change it's agenda. It's time for the people of the state of California to take their politics back. [*Applause*]

SUSAN BURTON:

I want to announce about the demonstration to keep King Hospital open. We are going to meet in front of the Martin Luther King Hospital Wednesday at 12 noon. There will be a ribbon-cutting, a reverse ribbon-cutting. They're closing down a hospital, and opening up prisons. And we're going to hold a demonstration. How crazy, how ludicrous and how bad that is for our community. So when you talk about getting involved, it starts with you. Bring a friend.

KEVIN MICHAEL KEY:

Monday at what time?

SUSAN BURTON:

I'm sorry, Wednesday at 12 noon, right at 120th and Wilmington. Come out for an hour, give an hour of your day. Come out to this demonstration, the reverse ribbon-cutting. They're closing down an emergency room, child care, a trauma center. It's the only hospital in South LA, and we're opening a prison in Delano to hold more of us. So please come out. [*Applause*]

KEVIN MICHAEL KEY:

Thank you. Heather, we saved the best for last.

HEATHER:

Wow, that's a hard thing to follow. Thank you, Michael, for inviting us. I'm really happy to be here because the discussion that we're having here contains topics affecting my life and my two children's lives directly. But our generation of our family is getting stronger every year, so I'm proud about that. The question that I have is: What is the purpose of this? What is the primary objective of the play? Here? And what happens after this? We could talk about this all day long, and just like we have these discussions, we have a town-hall meeting here, and there, but then things are easily forgotten until they're brought back, and sometimes they're brought back with the issues and the struggles at that very time. So we want to deal with these things. We want to deal with drugs, and we want to deal with Three Strikes. We want to deal with all of those things, but it's not until we're faced with those things that we're dealing with them. So while we're all here today, and we're having this discussion, what are we going to do about what we're talking about? We could all meet at the hospital and it's great, and we all have our passions. For one of us it may be a hospital, or it may be Three Strikes, or it may be drugs. But until we get ourselves together, like Ms. Warren said, and organize, and have one agenda, and we all organize behind that, what good is it? It's just a discussion.

SUSAN BURTON:

It's not just a discussion, it's a coming together, and it's the beginning of building alliances. I believe in abolishing Three Strikes, not amending it, abolishing it. So when I'm able to support the Three Strikes movement, that's what I do. But I think all of our hope here is for a healthier, safer community. And from wherever you're working on to get there, I think our alliances we build with one another, the support and encouragement, and the education that we get from coming to events like this, is just needed for us to continue a long struggle, to have safe, healthy, happy families and communities. And sometime along the way, I had to commit, I had to commit to continue in the face of the uphill climb. I had to commit to continue, and to pour my energies into it. And sometimes I have to go and I don't want to go, and sometimes I go when I do want to go.

But I have to stay on task, I have to stay in the march. It's not an easy march, but it must happen because of my great-grandchildren, my granddaughter. I don't want them to have to face all of these things that I face. I want to enable them to have a broader, stronger platform to work from, to make the distance just a little bit shorter. It is a long haul, and it's hard on us, but if we don't act and continue to be active, it's going to be harder for our generations.

HEATHER:

What is the purpose, what is the objective of the play?

Hylen Burt:

Can I answer that? Ooh, ooh, I've got a burning desire, and I say this unequivocally: I am very very proud to be an American. I'm a black American. America's what I know, America's what gave me everything I'll know, I'll be honest. Hundreds, hundreds of people who came before me, who shed blood so that I could be here, and I'm not just talking about black people. Hispanics, Indians, and when you look at things, we're really a village, a really large village, and everybody's got to do their part. Somebody's got to be out there gathering wheat, somebody's watching the children, somebody's building huts, but if you don't get involved they will blow bullshit right past you, if you're not aware.

And sometimes, you can't read the paper to find what the real implications of this are, or what's leading them over there. This hospital closing thing is another example and it's crazy, because somebody's going to get sick and can't get to a hospital. I say it's my responsibility, as a member of this village to take a part in this and see that when they came up with a bullshit report, and that ain't right, and it's my responsibility to say something. Each one of us got a responsibility. Especially when you're young and a little bit crazy.

I'm a little bit older. You've got to stand up, and you do have a responsibility, because the people before you did what they did so that you could have what you have. And we need to do for our grandkids and everybody that comes through after us, so there will be something that will be worth having.

Kevin Michael Key:

I'm not going to try to give the definitive answer to what you have to say, but let me ask John, the director of the play, to answer.

JOHN MALPEDE:

I think that as everybody who was here, pointed out, this play cuts in different directions. And, as Nicole said, this hearing was about Iran-Contra, and it was about circumstances where the president and his inner circle had figured out a way to go around the Congress of the United States in order to pursue their own foreign-policy objectives. And they didn't care what effect that had on the Constitution, the citizens of the United States of America, or the citizens of Nicaragua. So the harm is distributed into all of those areas. I notice the same CIA was coerced into giving false intelligence in order to support an invasion of Iraq. A lot of people, Americans and Iraqis, are dying right now, and at the same time, not only is the prison-industrial complex huge, it's like the baby of the military. $400 billion plus goes to the defense department of the United States.

Just like George said, people in the state of California get to choose whether or not they want to have decent education, decent healthcare, any education, any healthcare, any parks, any welfare. People of the United States generally also get to choose whether they have Social Security, Medicare, or whether they want to take all of the resources of the United States and send it after chasing the boogeyman, and creating more boogeymen and chasing them. We're the biggest debtor country in the world, and the country, in both it's domestic and foreign policy, is living on fear and bankrupting itself in the process.

So what happened with Iran-Contra is not "history," because we need a truth and reconciliation commission to see what really went down. Because in fact the second Hitz report came out—this hearing happened in March of 1998 after the first Hitz report came out. When the second one come out, it actually confirmed what had been alleged, not only by Gary Webb but by Al McCoy and others, involving the CIA and drug smuggling, going back to the Vietnam War. It wasn't covered in the press. It was dropped by the Black Caucus. It just disappeared.

So that's why when the President wants to go to war in Iraq, he can do it; because there's a history of not getting the truth out. So this is historical, but the reason we're presenting it is that all the problematic parts of it are still with us today. It's not history. It's happening today.

HEATHER:

So you're doing this to expose what happened?

JOHN MALPEDE:

What is happening.

HEATHER:

To expose it. And after you bring it to the level of awareness, then what?

JOHN MALPEDE:

Well, then I think people here are working on these different issues 24–7, and then it's a question of building bigger alliances.

HEATHER:

So what would you say that I should do as an individual? Because we work — that's what I was saying — because we work a lot as individuals, and I'm talking about working more collaboratively. So me being a single mom and working full-time and being active in a lot of areas, what can I do? Because there's a lot of issues out there pertinent to my life. How do I know which one to choose? This little girl wants to be an attorney. She's a junior in high school, and that is her goal, to be an attorney....

KEVIN MICHAEL KEY:

Defense attorney!

HEATHER:

I told her that once you know about something, you have to do something about it. That's your responsibility. So how do you go about doing that?

JOHN MALPEDE:

I think you've got it figured out. I think find one thing that you're passionately committed to, and work for that.

RICKEY MANTLEY:

I also want to answer your question directly. What's the purpose of this play? To let you know that the war on drugs continues. There's been no cease-fire. The war on drugs continues. It devastated whole communities, and it goes on today. That's why they passed the Three Strikes law. Because we continue to have casualties from the war on drugs. There are still casualties to this day. This play is about letting people know that this war still goes on, that there are still casualties to this day, that people are still damaged by this war, and again it's a war against communities of color, and low-income communities. The casualties are in our prisons. The casualties have been sentenced to Three Strikes.

HEATHER:

The casualties are also in our schools.

Rickey Mantley:

The casualties are a direct result of this so-called war on drugs, and what it boils down to actually, what we want people to recognize, is that it's not a criminal issue, it's a health issue. That's what we want to educate people to. Don't think in terms of addicts or drug users as criminals. Think in terms of the people who have a health problem.

Kevin Michael Key:

Hey people, we gotta go.

Interview with Susan Burton

Earlier in the day, before the Compton performance, I had time to talk at length with Susan Burton. — **John Malpede**

Susan Burton:

My name is Susan Burton, executive director of A New Way of Life re-entry project for women coming out of prison. I'm also an organizer with All of Us or None.

John Malpede:

What's the transition like now for women coming out of the prison system in California?

SUSAN BURTON:

Oh, my goodness, it's horrific. California is, I think, behind all other states in looking at the prison system and making the changes. People are released back to the community without housing, without jobs, without state IDs, without social security cards, really just kind of ejected. It's pick up your bed and walk. It's so many barriers, that it makes it real difficult to the point that the recidivism rate in California is above 60 percent.

When you get off a bus, when you're released from any prison in California and you're coming back to Los Angeles, you get off a bus in the heart of Skid Row downtown. A Greyhound bus station, and you get off a bus with a package in your hand that has the California Department of Corrections number on it. You're sticking out like a sore thumb, and there are people there just to bring you back into harm's way, into activities that landed you into prison. And women are especially subject and preyed upon at that downtown bus station. "Do you need a place to stay? I have a place for you to sleep." Or there's a drug seller and they know that you have $200 release money: "Do you want to get high?"

The night before you're released from prison you have all of these emotions going on. There's the fear of what will happen when I leave: Will I make it? There's excitement: I'm getting out of this place, this cement jungle. I'm returning to my family. How will my children act? How will my community receive me? I'm going to have $200 and on the other side of the wall $200 seems like a bit of money. But when you hit society $200 is just nothing.

So you have all these emotions: the fear, the anxiety, the excitement, once again resuming your life. And then there's this small, small reality. The odds are stacked against you and you really don't want to embrace that. You want to be able to say that you can make it, because that's your challenge. So you're really going on with all these emotions just jumping and bouncing around all through your head and your body.

Women in California are the fastest growing part of the prison population. I was one of those women. By grace, by mercy, by sheer determination, by luck, I now am able to use my abilities to be an asset to the community. To house a person in prison every year at that cost, and not be able to bring them back into the community, and not be able to spend $1,000 a year in a humane way to support their lives being reestablished, to support their health and their well being—it's kind of backwards to me, real, real backwards.

I have seen over 150 women come through A New Way of Life with the bare minimum of services. Actually, what we do most is to provide a safe and clean environment and an environment of support and love and encouragement. I guess you cannot buy those things. And it takes $6000 for a person to live there for a year. And when we turn those numbers around, I mean what are we doing!?

JOHN MALPEDE:

How long do people stay there?

SUSAN BURTON:

We have had people stay there for 30 days, 90 days, and we have had a person stay for two years. There is no set time for when a person is going to get it together. There is no set time for how they are going to navigate through all these systems that are mind-boggling to me. All of the systems to get them up and running, to get them a job that will sustain them. Or to get to a place where we can find a niche somewhere to get them into, that will allow them to be independent and go on with their lives. It's about sustaining yourself. What can we do for you, where you can get a to a place where you can sustain yourself? And what do you need personally to be able to continue on?

JOHN MALPEDE:

There are so many programs that make no sense because they put a time limit on it. That you can do it in 90 days is in itself a miracle. And that you don't have a limit, but work individually, is wise.

SUSAN BURTON:

Some people can get it together in 90 days, 30 days. They get their California ID card. It takes much longer for some people, because many people coming out of the criminal-justice system have mental-health needs. They need to get back with their children and that takes time… to get through the Department of Children and Family Services, the court system. Many people are tagged with these outrageous child-custody payments, where a woman comes out of prison and she may have to pay $36,000 in child support. And I have seen women come home, get a job, go to save money, and all of a sudden their bank account is frozen because they owe child support money.

And that can just blow you straight out of the water. That is like pulling a rug from under a person. All the progress they made has been just stifled. And we have to try to work with them to get the child-custody payments to a place that their bank account is not attached and they can make some payments. Or go through some real lengthy nine-month procedure where they can take the payments away for the time that they where in jail. But without a Ph.D., an M.S.W., you can't even get through those systems.

It is a devastating experience to try to make it out of that criminal-justice system. And when I began to provide services and help women to break free, I began to understand more of myself and of my own long history in the criminal-justice system. After seeing the larger picture, I went to a deeper level of forgiveness within myself for failing so many times to make that successful transition. And that was a really good thing for me, because we need to understand deep within ourselves, and really be close, deep within ourselves, with ourselves. And providing services really allowed me to get that deeper connection with myself and my purpose.

I work full time and I have a social worker that works part time, and I have another formerly incarcerated woman who works with me and who helps keep the house with the food and the groceries and helps the women, just encouraging them. So it's myself and two part-time staff. But the women who live in the houses take the leadership of what's happening and helping one another along.

We have had some training about systems in the home and taught them how to speak out and to understand what systems are for and who they are serving. They are supposed to be serving us. But if they are not serving us, then those systems are broken. Those systems are demoralizing. And do not let the system get to you; understand it. At this point we need to navigate through it until we can change it. That is empowering. When somebody comes and says, "No, you are not the wrong one. That system is broken. You are feeling what you are supposed to be feeling. But don't let that feeling be your downfall. Understand that that feeling is what you are supposed to be feeling right now."

Sending a woman to get General Relief (G.R.) benefits is one if my most worrisome times. For a woman coming home from prison, it is such a demoralizing and inconsistent system that I worry that she'll be so rattled there that she might not be able to make it back to the house. That happens. So we try to get somebody, a buddy, to go with her to get through that system, to apply for General Relief benefits, until she can get back to work.

JOHN MALPEDE:

I worked for Legal Aid, at the welfare offices, helping people get General Relief, and with their G.R. cases. I also worked on class-action lawsuits where we got the county to raise the welfare benefit. Now G.R. is down again. It is like pushing a rock uphill.

SUSAN BURTON:

Yeah, the way that people get treated and talked to, and the way that you just have to sit up in a building all day to apply. It's just not working. It's too long, too much time.

JOHN MALPEDE:

When did you get involved in All of Us or None?

SUSAN BURTON:

Two years ago we had a statewide meeting of formerly incarcerated people that came together in Oakland at the Center for Third World Organizing. It was a three-day meeting. And at that meeting we made a decision to organize around the issues of formerly incarcerated people in our own voices. We looked at the areas that needed to be organized around, and chose reentering services, youth imprisonment and welfare benefits, and to remove the box from employment applications. The starter campaign is removing the box. Our whole platform is to end the discrimination of formerly incarcerated people. But the employment box is just high on the radar for what we are organizing around.

JOHN MALPEDE:

How is that going forward?

SUSAN BURTON:

There is a resolution in Oakland, California to remove the box before city council, or before their board of supervisors, I'm not sure which one. Down here in LA at our All of Us or None Peace and Justice Summit, we got the county criminal custice planning department to begin to dialogue with us about what they would do in the area of hiring people. And we will begin to discuss with them about banning the box here in Los Angeles. All of Us or None is a national campaign. We are meeting in San Francisco in northern California, LA in southern California, Oklahoma, Tennessee, New York. All of these places have chapters that are beginning to build campaigns. What we are saying is that we need a movement of the formerly incarcerated people, the family members, and people committed to changing the discrimination of formerly incarcerated people.

JOHN MALPEDE:

I was talking to Kevin Michael Key about 12-step programs and making a movement.

SUSAN BURTON:

What happens is that many people whose lives have been negatively impacted by the drugs or the war on drugs, we make it through the 12-step rooms, and we are really grateful that we found a process to get our lives back.

But when you make it to that point, I myself found that there is so much more outside of that to be done in the community. While we have the 12-step fellowship and the 12-step movement, our communities are continually being damaged. And I have taken the principles that I have learned there and applied them outside, to help not only those who are in recovery, but my community at large.

The question is: How do we move from the 12-step rooms into activism and standing up outside in the communities against these systems of oppression? That is one of the questions that I pose. After we get our lives back, how to broaden and reach out more? How do we stand up and unite out of these rooms around policies that we know are unjust.

We get to build a relationship with a God of our own in the 12-step rooms. And it has empowered me to touch 150 women's lives. It has empowered me to go to my policy-makers and ask for some aggressive policies, and to not leave anybody behind in those policies. But still I see so many who are left behind by policy. So many who are making progress despite the policy, that I believe that the God of my own understanding has empowered me to go beyond that and say, "Let's unite, let's organize, let's stand." Let us stand in our own dignity, and our own principles to say what is right. What we know is right.

JOHN MALPEDE:

Dave Fratello of Prop. 36 was saying that the people are way ahead of the politicians. They are more willing to look at what is right. Politicians use fear to control the discussion.

SUSAN BURTON:

What is politically safe? It's not about that. It is about finding solutions. Whatever those solutions are. Making humane decisions and being inclusive of all the people and represent all the people—and that is the world, that is the nation! That is not just one group of people that is middle-class. How am I just going to understand only the middle-class? We need to understand that the formerly incarcerated vote too. We are not disenfranchised from the vote in California. After we discharge parole we can vote, and there hundreds of thousands of us. There are 30 million people across this nation who have felony convictions. So when we connect with the majority of those, I believe that we are going to have a powerful, powerful movement and a powerful voice. And it might just not be about middle-class America. It will be about all the people.

Bigger things can happen. We need a political movement around those that are impacted from the war on drugs and from the whole incarceration thing. I mean incarceration has limited so many lives across America. Has limited so many people in their ability to have full and thriving lives. If you are a husband that needs to provide for his wife and children, but you cannot get a job that gives access to health insurance, what happens there? That happens to many, many people who are formerly incarcerated. Maybe a few get through to access a job that will give them a minimum or above-minimum wage. But most of them don't. And we are just not going to continue to have it.

JOHN MALPEDE:

A huge number of the people who can vote do not have affordable health insurance.

SUSAN BURTON:

Yes. There are a significant number of people in this country who do not organize, who do not have middle-class wages, who do not have middle-class lives. But those people are able to cast a vote. Those people have been impacted by criminal justice. And our goal is to organize all of those people nationally under All of Us or None. And cast a vote.

Public Conversation

Utrecht, the Netherlands, 2005

"Amnesty International, in its campaign against torture, has effectively been following the footsteps of the CIA, picking up their pieces. In 1983, the manual we got was the so-called Human Resources Exploitation Manual of 1983, a CIA training session with the Honduran military. And, by the way, Honduras, was the forward base area for the Contras that this play is discussing. So in fighting the Contra war, we were allying with drug lords, and as another part of it, training the Honduran military in torture techniques for the pacification of the local population. So the two things are actually operating in the same space. These are the visible and invisible aspects of the play." —Alfred McCoy

At the end of November, 2005 LAPD traveled to Utrecht, the Netherlands, for a week of performances in the Vrede van Utrecht Festival. The festival organized by the city and provincial government of Utrecht is a program of cultural activities that will continue until 2013, the 300th anniversary of the signing of the Treaty of Utrecht which put an end to a century-and-a-half of war. In celebration and commemoration of the Peace of Utrecht, the Vrede van Utrecht Festival has invited a diverse group of Dutch and international participants for an artistic examination of civic themes, including war and peace, and conflict and dialog.

The performances took place at the same moment that the Dutch parliament was authorizing the deployment of 1,000 additional Dutch troops for duty in Afghanistan, and amidst revelations that CIA flights carrying prisoners to torture in secret jails had flown through European airspace and used European airports, including airports in the Netherlands.

LAPD performed three nights and held post-performance conversations. The first night's conversation focused on Dutch drug policy, particularly as it impacts "mules": poor people from the former Dutch Caribbean colonies who are arrested for entering the country with ingested cocaine balls in their bellies. The second conversation focused on homeless policy in the City of Utrecht. And the third evening's conversation focused on the situation in Afghanistan, including its economic dependence on poppy-growing, the military situation and the impact of these factors on the significant number of Afghan refugees living in Holland. — **John Malpede**

TOPIC:

MARIA FULL OF GRACE — ANTILLIAN BOLLITA SWALLOWERS IN THE NETHERLANDS

Utrecht, Netherlands

Wednesday, November 30, 2005

TIMELINE:

November, 2005 — *The Washington Post* Reveals "Extraordinary Rendition," CIA Flights Using Western European airports

January, 2006 — NATO Forces, Including Dutch, Prepare for Increased Military Role in Afghanistan

PANELISTS:

JOHN LEERDAM: Member of the second house of the Dutch Parliament, Spokesperson for Culture in the Labor Party (PvdA), one of the major parties in the Netherlands, and a member party of the current coalition government

BART SWIERT: Criminal Defense Lawyer with extensive experience in representing people from the former Dutch colonies who have been charged with drug crimes

JAN LANGENDIJK: Moderator, Director, Department of Social Development, City of Utrecht

JOHN LEERDAM:

I'm a member of Dutch parliament. I'm a Congressman. I lived in the States for almost six years, studied at Columbia University, did my masters in fine arts, did a postgraduate degree in international and public affairs. I used to run a multicultural theater here in the Netherlands called Cosmic Theater, where I worked with youngsters that lived in poor neighborhoods and also youngsters that were in jail. I've made nine films and seven documentaries. Since 2003 I am a congressman. I'm the spokesperson for my party, the Labor Party, regarding arts, culture and media affairs, and also for kingdom affairs—issues concerning the former Dutch colonies. In the later capacity, I have much to do with the trafficking of "bollitas." In the interview I just did I told the journalist that tonight's production made me think of the issues that I am dealing with in parliament, this whole drug-trafficking issue in the Netherlands and Suriname. And it gets very dirty at certain moments.

BART SWIERT:

Thank you very much, Mr. Chairperson. I'm a criminal defense lawyer. Some 10 years ago I started here in Utrecht. I got my masters and my Ph.D. here. After that I became a criminal defense lawyer in Amsterdam. I'm here because I'm assisting a lot of people who are accused of trafficking drugs. I helped a lot of "mulas," or "pack donkeys," as they are called by the prosecutor.

I see the trouble they find themselves in when they are arrested here, in a strange country where they don't know the rules etc. I see that the system is becoming worse here in the Netherlands, in it's way of dealing with drug traffickers. I see the problems which caused the mulas' decision to traffic drugs. That is the reason why I'm here. So I'm looking forward to having a discussion about that.

MODERATOR:

We would like to organize the discussion along the following lines: Does what we have seen and what we have heard have anything to do with the situation in Europe and the Netherlands? Is there a similarity between what we have heard and discussed in the play and the relationship that the Netherlands has with the Antilles?

So, my first question is to my two guests. Do you have a comment about what we have seen tonight? Is there anything that you would like to say about it, or ask John and his crew a question? He is not here every day. So this is an invitation to you but also to the others here, the public, to comment on what we have seen tonight.

JOHN LEERDAM:

First of all I would like to make a compliment to the crew and also to the director. I think that the material is quite complex and I understand that some of the crew is professional and some is not. To understand this kind of material and to perform it for more than one hour the way you guys did, I thought it was well done, my compliments to you for that.

Secondly, I am from the Labor Party in Holland, and I am the spokesperson for arts and culture. I always say that arts and culture is not something only for the elite, it is something that you can actually bring to the people. The people can be much more in involved than is the case now. I think that this is one of the ways that arts and culture can involve people to think about issues like this, and also other issues, like the bollitas, the mulas, like my colleague here at the table was explaining. I think that if you want to address these issues you can make it more accessible and make it much more reflective of their experiences. I think it is very important that you put it in an art form. You have to address the issues and break it down, so people understand what you want to say. You have to keep it simple and address it in all kinds of ways, in community centers, wherever you can.

In schools you can introduce it in a very simple way. You cannot start young enough. And even those who are elderly will enjoy this form of art, what you guys are bringing. That is the first thing I would like to say, because it is very important.

Drug issues concern everybody, not just a certain group of people who are only doing it to make money. I'm a politician, and I met a lot of people because I wanted to get behind the stories. Why are they doing this? I went into the prisons like Zeist, which is not so far from Utrecht. First of all I was shocked to see people there that I know from school. People that I knew from working for the government, people who I knew had good jobs, who had homes and kids in the Antilles. And I was shocked to see them there and I did not understand. And so I asked them: what is going on? And for a while I was thinking about making a documentary on this, until I went to the States, two years ago, and I saw the movie *Maria Full of Grace* and read about it in *The New York Times*. And I said to my wife: "We have to go see this, because this is exactly what I was talking to you about." This is the story, which we don't hear most of the time. We hear about the 100 controls and the so-called drug epidemic, and the people who are the swallowers of the bollitas who are making a mess out of their lives. And the Dutch who are saying: "Sell the Antilles, sell Aruba, let's get rid of the islands. We don't want nothing to do with them. These people are trash."

That is the other side of the story. And when you get into the jails, and you hear their stories, you understand that the policies that are made in The Hague affect the lives, not only of the people who swallow these bollitas, but also their kids and sometimes three generations of their families. And it is actually sad. And I'm in politics to actually do something about it. But you cannot do it all by yourself.

MODERATOR:

Would anyone in the audience like something to say about John's statement?

KEVIN MICHAEL KEY:

I would like to say that it is interesting to hear that the same type of terminology and characterization of the people who are victims of these drugs is used here in the Netherlands. Some of us in the U.S. seem to think that Holland is "enlightened" with respect to drug policy. But now I come over here to this so-called enlightened place and it's the same issue. I suspect it is the same class of people who are being impacted and who are being demonized and who are being trashed. They are society's throwaways. You know: "It's not my problem." I thought before coming here that here in the Netherlands they have an enlightened policy. They recognize that this is not a criminal-justice issue, but that this is a medical-social issue. And then I come here and find out that somehow the same draconian perspective is also in this country.

JOHN LEERDAM:

That is absolutely right. I am the only Antillean in Congress. You said it right: They are victimized. When I see the policy that has been set out in order to help the islands, the decisions that have been made 10 years ago, and that the poverty level has risen more than 60 percent since then; then you have to ask the question: What are we doing? Is this policy helping them to go forward, or are we going backwards? And you see that mothers or even fathers are swallowing drugs to seek money, to provide for their kids or for their families some kind of dignity or decency. Because sometimes the wives and the children don't even know that the husband is doing it. The husbands don't know that the wives are doing it. It is a form of survival, an attempt to find means, to take care of the people you love.

You know the islands are very small. They are very fragile. Colombia is right on the border. Venezuela is right there. They are infiltrating the Antilles from Colombia and Venezuela. They are using the islands as a stepping-stone to sell the drugs in Europe, because they are making much more money in Europe. They are using the people there as cows, as animals, to bring in the drugs. And if you hear what they are being paid! It's hardly anything. Do you know how many milligrams they are swallowing? They are risking their lives in order to come here with the drugs.

BART SWIERT:

Up to one-and-a-half kilos, which is a lot.

JOHN LEERDAM:

Sometimes they swallow 39 or 40 bollitas, depending on how big they are. It is serious stuff. And then you say: "Let's get the education. Let's deal with poverty. Let's deal with arts and culture. Let's stop criminalizing all these people in the islands and let's address the real issues in order to go forward."

And sometimes you wonder: What is behind all of this? What are they hiding? There is a congressman who actually died in a car crash. His name is Van Traa. He was doing something similar to what you guys are doing here, a hearing about drugs: the IRT affair here in Holland, where policemen where accused of selling drugs with the approval of the government. And through that we got to know a lot about the "bouwfraude," which is fraud in construction projects. At a certain point in the building-fraud investigation, the names of politicians in the Antilles were being mentioned. They were involved. They were top people in politics. They were top business people. They were picked up and put in jail. Most of those people who went to jail were set free later, because they had the right lawyers, I think. I don't know what the reason is. But the small people, who were actually doing the dirty work, they remained in jail, because they did not have the means, the knowledge, the lawyers who could fight for them. That says a lot about the system.

AUDIENCE MEMBER:

Here we see a relationship between economic interests, drug trafficking and poverty. The drug problem and people dying of drugs will go on until you have solved the poverty problem.

JOHN LEERDAM:

No. What I don't understand is that we invest 77 million in enlarging a jail and invest five million into poverty. It does not make any sense to me.

BART SWIERT:

But you are a member of parliament.

JOHN LEERDAM:

That's why I am addressing it in parliament. I have been there two-and-a-half years.

BART SWIERT:

I work in the prison that is called "Camp Zeist" and that is where a lot of the "mulas" are incarcerated. It is the same prison that you have visited. And you must have seen too, that the circumstances in that prison are much worse that in other prisons in Holland. All in all, circumstances here in Holland are not very bad, but they are not very good either. There is a big difference in the circumstances. For example, in Camp Zeist there are six or eight people staying together in one cell, whereas in other prisons it is only one or two people. I don't see the justification for that difference. The only justification that the government gives, and your Labor Party as well, is that we don't want to spend any money on trashy people like that. It is not being said in those words, but it is thought of like that. I'm glad to hear of you going to Camp Zeist, but I'm not hearing of your party doing anything about that.

JOHN LEERDAM:

We did address it.

BART SWIERT:

It was during the Labor Party's administration that that same prison was built.

JOHN LEERDAM:

The prison is supposed to be for transients. The people in Camp Zeist are supposed to stay there only for a short while. They say they are only going there for a while and then they will be transferred to another jail. But what I have seen is that this is not happening.

BART SWIERT:

Even if they would stay there only for a short while, would you find it acceptable under the circumstances that I've described?

JOHN LEERDAM:

No, it is not acceptable. We have had heavy discussions about this with Aleid Swiers who is from the justice department. We cannot justify this. This is not human.

LORRAINE DILLARD:

I want to echo the sentiments of my colleague from the LAPD about some of the similarities here in the Netherlands that, seem to emulate the policies around the war on drugs in the U.S. The question that I want to ask is about economics. What I see in the U.S. is that the war on drugs is based on fueling the prison-industrial complex, which is based on building more prisons as opposed to universities or schools, because it is a money-making business, and that is why there are more strategies and more energy and think-tanking devoted to it. That is why we continue to enlarge this population.

Do you see that? I'm not sure how the economics work here in the prison-industrial system. Is it seen as a business venture that contributes to the economic infrastructure?

BART SWIERT:

Well, rumors have it—correct me if I'm wrong—that a lot of the prisons in the U.S. have been privatized. Thank God that has not happened in Holland up until now. Although a particular thing is that in Camp Ziest, where all the drug traffickers go, all the prison guards there are from a private company. And that situation is obviously a money thing, because they are not trained like regular prison guards, they are less trained. It is chaos there because they didn't know what to do exactly. It is a specific aspect of how the economy is part of it there. It is a remarkable equivalent of what you are saying. But, thank God, no, the prison is not privatized, and it won't be.

EMMANUEL DELEAGE:

In Holland they think that by making hashish and marijuana legal they can deal with the "demand aspect" of drugs. And the thinking behind it is that if people are allowed to use soft drugs that they won't use hard drugs. They have very lenient policies for heroin users; they get methadone for free. The U.S. and France see that differently and they have this enormous drug problem. How is that in the Netherlands?

BART SWIERT:

There are two reasons to legalize soft drugs. One is that if you don't hunt down the traffickers who deal in soft drugs you can concentrate on the hard drugs. The other reason is that soft drugs are considered less harmful than hard drugs.

AUDIENCE MEMBER:

At this moment we have programs where people are being treated for heroin on a medical basis. This means those people get a lot more quality in their lives. Also the politicians and people who are concerned about law and order are satisfied because people get heroin for free, so they don't steal.

AUDIENCE MEMBER:

We have now forbidden soft drugs worldwide. These drugs are not the most dangerous. Nicotine is very dangerous. Hard drugs are relatively harmless. Of course you need to know what the risks are. But it does not justify the consequences of criminalizing these activities. It destroys our society. Camp Zeist is not what we would call the perfect prison. And if you want to go to visit, you have to phone and that line is very busy. You cannot visit. We have at least one prison that does not qualify for the fire regulations, and they actually had a fire there.

Worldwide, we all have the same problems and it is destroying societies. What I want to say is: Let us please do the things we can do. We have some 300 methadone centers in the Netherlands. Utrecht has 50. But people who don't use methadone — because it does not work very well — don't qualify for heroin as a medication. And that is a very big problem.

AUDIENCE MEMBER:

You just said that there is really no difference between the drugs that are prohibited and not prohibited. I would like to ask our guests: Do you agree with that?

BART SWIERT:

I definitely see the destructive effects of cocaine and heroin. Especially in large amounts, these drugs are very dangerous for one's health. On the other side you could ask the question: Are drugs destroying our society, or is penalizing and criminalizing drugs destroying our society? I am inclined to choose the latter.

The biggest problem is that the profits the drug traffickers can make are very high. That is why there are so many people from the Antilles going to Holland, swallowing so many bollitas, and endangering their own bodies, their own lives. There is only one reason to do that, and that is to get money. So decriminalizing drugs would be the only way to really fight that.

SASHAE:

I, too, like my LAPD colleagues, was enlightened by the similarities in the problems related to drugs here in the Netherlands and the U.S. I just want to say that I do think that the arts is a strong way of educating, and as the congressman said, we can use art to reach people across the spectrum of ages. And I really want to talk about recovery, and the effects and the dangers of drugs. I don't know how we get rid of this poverty problem. But I am a woman who faced homelessness and was on drugs, and is now in recovery. People looked at me at the time as a harlot, and as someone who could never be something. You know, it is awful. So, this is something that we have to work on, and work on immediately. Drugs will ravage people. They have no respect for social economics, gender or color. Addiction knows no barriers. And this is an intergenerational problem. Now I may face my own son doing drugs, maybe marijuana, maybe prescription drugs. It goes on.

AUDIENCE MEMBER:

Bart, what he is saying is we should fight poverty, but we should also legalize most of the drugs. What is your opinion about this?

SASHAE:

We should fight poverty in a real way, but legalizing? People need to be educated on the effects and the devastation of drugs. We just take it because we cannot have it. Because all of us are kind of like a child; if you cannot have it you want it. But advocates should say: "If you choose to do this, just like you choose to drink alcohol, you will break down every major organ in your body, even your brain." So maybe people will make a conscious decision: "No, I'm not gonna touch that." People need to be educated and see that this has ravaged people. It has broken people down to the lowest.

BART SWIERT:

You didn't answer the question. Should it be legalized or not?

SASHAE:

I think no. No.

KEVIN MICHAEL KEY:

I'd like to respond to that. I'm in recovery. I'm a former criminal-defense attorney. I'm a member of an organization called Critical Resistance. We're abolitionists of the prison-industrial complex. We believe that it is the modern-day equivalent of slavery. Because if you look at who it impacts on, it's primarily the offspring, the great-grandchildren of slaves. And you see that it is a continuation of that same system under a new guideline. As a criminal-defense attorney I can say unequivocally that over 90 percent of the clients that I defended were brought before me as a result of the use and abuse of drugs, including alcohol. As a person in recovery, I know that I cannot use the so-called legal drugs, because if I had a drink with somebody in that fine Netherlands mindset, I would be back out on the streets sooner rather than later.

In the U.S. we have over 2 million people who are incarcerated. That's an enormous number. If you were to decriminalize this medical problem—because I have come to find out that it is a medical difference, most of the time, for people who are alcoholics and addicts—then you would have vast amounts of resources which you could then pour into the social issues, the social concerns: the lack of education, the lack of housing, the lack of job training. Then you would be able to bring the bottom of society — these sons and daughters and offspring of the slaves — up to a point where they would not have to swallow life-threatening things in order to pay the rent. So I am clearly in favor of the decriminalization of these drugs, and if you were to do that there would be enormous benefits that would cut across the width and breath of the society.

JOHN LEERDAM:

Your point is very clear. The discussion within the Labor Party is: Shall we legalize the soft drugs? The majority of the parliament, I think, is now in favor of legalizing it in certain cities. We have problems now with people coming in from other countries, like Germany and France, who come here to use drugs. So it is an ongoing discussion.

But I want to stress that I have my own way of thinking. When I go into prisons like Camp Zeist and other prisons, I see the sons and daughters of good families, who are now being criminalized because they were doing it. They were doing it because they had to pay the rent. And those who are giving them the drugs to swallow are not being criminalized. They are walking around, driving in their Lexuses, and you know actually who they are.

BART SWIERT:

Driving their Lexuses? Is there still press here? Hearing him say this?

JOHN LEERDAM:

I said it freely. I don't have to be afraid. I'm a person by myself. I just said that.

Melina Bielefelt:

Can you say what the hard drugs are that are criminalized in this country? And also is it true that the "mules" are just sent back to their country?

Bart Swiert:

Heroin can be given by the government to drug addicts who have serious health problems. It is only meant for a really small amount of drug addicts under very severe conditions. So it is definitely not legal.

Second answer: Yes, it is partially right what you are saying. If a drug trafficker has less than three kilos of cocaine, he is sent back to the Antilles or Suriname. But nevertheless, he has been indicted and punished by the criminal court here. The condition is that if he returns to Holland he will be sent to jail. So he is only escaping punishment if he doesn't come back to Holland. At this moment the prisons are not as full as they used to be. Or better said, we have more prisons. We have more capacity to incarcerate them. So now we are incarcerating drug traffickers if they have more than one-and-a-half kilos.

Annzella Victoria:

I wanted to say that even if you legalize drugs, the problem that you have is that you are not dealing with the fact that certain people have a propensity to become addicted. I have a friend that I met when she was 21, and she had an addictive personality. She happened to be addicted to putting a facial mask on her face. You know, anything! And you don't deal with the root of the problem. Education is a key that has saved people from ever being involved in this. I had a neighbor who as a teenager got involved in drugs, had a job, got high working as a barmaid. She stood on top of the bar, took a gun, put it to her head, but she survived. She came home, got out of the hospital. I went in to see her, because you know that's what good old Christian girls do: You go visit the sick. She took the scarf off and said: "Would you like to feel the bullet?" because it was still in her head. Yikes! No! That moment was the best thing—because right there, I went through 12-steps. Done. I was through with drugs that day. And I had not even seen drugs. So that when I became of age and a friend of mine who was dealing drugs—as a way to make money to pay the rent! —offered me free cocaine, I was like: "Thank you, goodbye," because I understood where the road led. Legalizing is not the answer quite frankly.

BART SWIERT:

Education won't solve it. Education would not prevent every person in the Netherlands or the U.S. from using drugs.

AUDIENCE MEMBER:

Perhaps the combination of both things would be most powerful.

ANNZELLA VICTORIA:

Yes, and there is something that both countries could benefit from, as the congressman mentioned. We should split the amount of money that is spent for jails and put it into the causes of poverty, why these people have to live in poverty. Some people are just not going to make it. But the point is, give them a fair chance. Give them education. Give them programs and make available job opportunities. If you don't think they should, just ask Villepan in France.

Public Conversation

Utrecht, 2005

When we arrived in Utrecht, the city had just been honored for its progressive homeless policy which it turns was a combination of carrot-and-stick provisions, which created homeless services dispersed throughout the city, and punitive measures for people who remained in the city center. The conversation revealed both the limitations of this policy and its connection to homeless policies in Los Angeles.

Topic:
Homelessness in Utrecht
December 1, 2005, Utrecht, The Netherlands

Panelists:

Riet van Denderen: Staff of G.O.U.D.: Organization of Independent Utrecht (hard) Drug Users
Han: Formerly homeless and a member of G.O.U.D.
Marry Mos: Groen Links/Green Left party, Utrecht
Rien Sprenger: Moderator, Coordinator, Community Arts Lab, Vrede van Utrecht, and past Director, Utrecht High School for the Arts

RIEN SPRENGER:

Here are some headlines of the newspapers in the Netherlands: "Two-thirds of the Visitors Feel Safe in Utrecht"; "Homeless Person Tells His Own Story About High School"; "Utrecht's Program for Shelter Is Successful"; "Hoog Catherijne [shopping mall] Has Become Much Safer"; "Utrecht Wins the Hein Roethof Prize"; "Parliament Wants to Forbid Blowing Hashish." These came out yesterday: "No More Blowing in Public Spaces"; "Ecstasy Use Is Diminishing." Maastricht was in the news today; they shut down a big coffee shop there, and moved it to the border, where the Belgians and the Germans can profit from it. And the last big article: "I Don't Hurt Anybody with My Joint?"

Behind the table is Mrs. Riet van Dekkeren. She represents the foundation G.O.U.D. G.O.U.D. stands for "Gebruikersorganisatie Onafhankelijke Utrechtse (hard) Druggebruikers," which means: "Organization of Independent Utrecht (hard) Drug Users." She has brought somebody with her who will assist and give reactions. Next to her, someone whom many of you who are interested in these matters will know: She is a city council member from the Green Left Party, Marry Mos.

First of all I would like to ask each of you to say something about what you have seen.

MARRY MOS:

Yes, what I liked about it is that you see how a committee like this is trying to find out the truth, and that it is covered up at the same time. These are processes that we also encounter in our city council meetings.

Riet van Denderen:

I saw that the bottom layer of society has to take in the blows again and that the upper part pulls back and does not say: "We influenced or contributed to the situation." And I also saw very clearly that millions were earned with it. We have had the parliamentary investigation here of police corruption in drug importation and everything reminds me of that. People are making a lot of money on drugs and at the same time the people who it affects get poorer and poorer all over the world.

Rien Sprenger:

Some six years ago a complete new homeless policy was put into place in Utrecht. They cleaned up the central-station area and implemented a lot of new policies. Marry, could you say something about what is so remarkable about the new policies Utrecht has worked with concerning the homeless and drug addicts? We won three or four prizes in the past few weeks. Why is that?

Marry Mos:

Part of it was that Utrecht was far behind in her accommodations for the homeless. In the train-station area we had a tunnel with some 250 drug addicts who lived there permanently. So we said we should close the tunnel. We should find new places for the homeless in other neighborhoods in Utrecht. We decided to find one facility in each neighborhood, and the residents of those neighborhoods had their say in where this facility should be.

What you see is that by giving these people care and a place to live, you stabilize their lives. We also created day-and-night care centers for 250 people and we made the agreement: "Now that we have those facilities you cannot sleep in HC (Hoog

Catherijne), anymore." Having created these alternatives, people were no longer allowed to sleep in the tunnel connecting the train station to the shopping center.

Additionally, now there are many "blue zones" that you cannot use anymore. I am not a big supporter of that, but...

HENRIETTE BROUWERS:

What is a "blue zone"?

MARRY MOS:

A "blue zone" means that you are not allowed to stand still with more than one person at the time. Yes, at Jans Veld it is forbidden to get together, and also at de Stek and the Sleepin. There are cameras there.

HAN:

You cannot stop there anymore. But it only counts for known users.

MARRY MOS:

So they choose a mix of social services on the one hand and hard measures and repression on the other. With that you can serve the whole political spectrum, because the very right parties say: "We find repression important," and the parties of the left say: "We want the services." So everybody agrees with it.

HENRIETTE BROUWERS;

But are the homeless people happy?

HAN:

No. We are not happy with it. We get the most ridiculous

fines from the police. I got a fine for "forming a group" while I was only with my bicycle.

AUDIENCE MEMBER:

You can stand together with three people for instance. But when they know that you are homeless they give you a ticket. You cannot stand together and you cannot sit together for five minutes.... If you sleep outside it is 95 errors.

HAN:

And every 45 errors result in a fine.

LORAINNE DILLARD:

How do they know that you are homeless when you are grouping? Because it sounds like the equivalent of what they do in the States and we know it as profiling: racial profiling. So I guess this would be class profiling. How do they distinguish "grouping"? How do they know if it's homeless people and that it is more than three people grouping? How do they distinguish what grouping is from a couple of friends meeting in the mall to chit-chat, as opposed to...

HAN:

There is a special team of police officers, and they know us. They have pictures, movie fragments of us.

LORAINNE DILLARD:

So, okay, my understanding is the volume of homelessness for the city is large enough, but not as big as with us in Los Angeles. Because in Los Angeles, where we come, from being homeless is criminalized. And people are locked up for being homeless, instead of being helped. What they try to do is take people out of the area and dump them into other areas. You are seen as unwanted, you are seen as a leper or something. And I'm sure the analogy is similar as to why people here are profiled.

HAN:

They give you as many tickets as they can so they can put you away for a certain time.

LORAINNE DILLARD:

That is similar with us.

AUDIENCE MEMBER:

How many homeless people are there in Utrecht?

RIET VAN DENDEREN:

Four hundred to 800. It is hard to say. It varies from day to day because homeless people travel. So one day it can be 1,000 and another it can be 600. It varies. The estimate is 800.

IBRAHIM SABA:

Is the drug problem automatically connected to the homeless problem?

RIET VAN DENDEREN:

Yes. You have to connect them because every homeless person has a habit that does not fit in with normal life. It is alcohol, drugs, gambling…

HAN:

…women.

MARRY MOS:

But almost one-third of the homeless do not have such a habit. They are complaining a lot. They say: "There are all these facilities for addicts, so apparently I have to start using drugs to get some place to go."

IBRAHIM SABA:

What is the reason for becoming homeless?

RIET VAN DENDEREN:

That can happen to you at any time. There are so many facts in life why all of a sudden some people don't see a solution. And in the Netherlands we of course got the Euro. That has had a big impact. There is a new law that when the people cannot pay the rent anymore they can be thrown out of their houses.

This is a problem that Marry is referring to: some people are not addicted. Often there are people with double jobs who lose their job. But they are used to spending according to a double income, and then soon the scale is tipping over and then it is finished. At this moment we see this with a lot of men who are just above or under 65 years old, and young families.

MARRY MOS:

Also the numbers of young people are increasing. That is quite alarming.

RIEN SPRENGER:

I want to go back to the policies in Utrecht.

MARRY MOS:

What I still find a shortcoming is that now in each neighborhood you get a group house. This is, if you say it in an ugly way, a real mini-institution. Now we say: "If you go to live there you can calm down. Your day-and-night rhythm will improve." But I believe that you have to give people more opportunities, something to do in the field of work, or theater, or learning, so that you can learn how to develop yourself.

HAN:

But if you lock addicts up in hostels they are not going to look for development. They are still busy making their dope every day.

GARA:

We have about 1,500 homeless. That's all the types of homeless people in Utrecht, together. And we have about 250 beds. So that's how the government is doing for us; not too good, I would think.

JIMMY SLOTHOUWER:

To what degree is the situation in Utrecht representative of the rest of Holland?

MARRY MOS:

Utrecht has taken a frontrunners role. It is doing a little bit better than other parts of the country. This is because other cities are breaking down their facilities, and Utrecht on the contrary is building them. And if you ask us what are we doing for this group that Gara was talking about, those 1,000 people who have no place to go, well, the answer is, very gradually: housing, accompanied/guided living, psychological help and making sure that people get help when they need it. Some people will never get any further than group living. But there are also people that get further. They will move on to living on their own and pick up a normal life from there.

AUDIENCE MEMBER:

I am from Holland, from Utrecht. I did not belong to any particular group, like a group that you have been hit by your husband or something. So at a certain point I asked; "Do I have to go out and get attacked first before I get some help?" They don't do enough. I work with the homeless people, too, like Riet and Marry, and I believe in them. But not enough is done. And it is worse in the U.S.A. My son lives in Los Angeles. It is worse there.

They are not conscious enough of the problem and of how big the problems are becoming, because here in Utrecht, too, the number of homeless is growing. It is growing really fast, and they cannot just throw them out of town. If we don't keep communicating with each other, and asking each other what we need, it is not going to be solved. And that counts for all over the world, I think.

RIEN SPRENGER:

Well, Utrecht is taking a leading position. But if you hear this, then you would say that the situation actually looks really bad. Jan Jaap, can you say something about that?

JAN JAAP:

Utrecht is really doing a lot, and if you do what you're supposed to do, then you do get your money. But it does not fit with the lifestyle of homeless people, which is a life-long lifestyle. The people who earn the money in the care sector have their own interests. That makes it very difficult.

The real problem is that we have social security that is maximized now, and you can't really live off of it. It is 70 percent of the minimum wage. If you have two incomes and lose one part of it, you have to survive from the one income that is left. But because that is the minimum wage, it is not enough to keep your house. We have homeless people who can afford a house, but they cannot afford the electric bills, gas etc. In this province we have a group of 5,000 people who are homeless and who need care. But you cannot find them, because they have no facilities. One of the most important things to do is to create continuous day care where people can sit, drink a cup of coffee and take a shower. Hans Speckman, the big boss here in city hall, has been so clever to get Internet into the night care and users centers. But it is not working well enough yet. It has to be perfect. You cannot build on your own existence. You have to make a connection between care and education. Because people need an atmosphere where they are invited to develop themselves. And now they are just fighting to get back their orientation.

GREET:

This goes back to what you said: it does not fit their lifestyle. And Han said: "I don't like it that they try to put us together in those hostels." If you put addicted or homeless people together, it does not work.

HAN:

Those hostels are big user facilities with separate rooms. They don't take it a step further.

Sashae:

I think it is just a worldwide thing, and we need to wake up and be aware of that. We are being criminalized for not having a home. In the U.S. I am considered homeless because my name is not on a lease. I have been homeless for four years, and because of the degradation I felt while homeless, I started using drugs. I am now in recovery. But this is something that we all have to wake up to. What is the lifestyle of a homeless person? Degradation and dehumanization — that is the lifestyle of a homeless person. And it is unfair! I am a well-educated woman and very informed, but who is going to give me a place to stay? You have to go out there and advocate for yourself.

Kevin Michael Key:

While we were doing the performance of all the people in the audience, Han was the guy that somehow I was attracted to. And at first I thought that it was the N.Y. insignia on his cap,, cause I grew up in New York. But it turns out that he is the European equivalent of me. I just got stabilized from being homeless, and I know his struggle. This is supposedly a left-leaning enlightened community that you have here in Utrecht.

In Los Angeles we have just elected a Latino, Chicano, Mexican-American mayor. But the problem remains. Just like you got the CIA guy over here saying: "Oh, we did the best we can." All they're really doing is whitewashing it and covering it up. It is the same thing with homelessness. They are not doing anything to impact the fundamental reasons why. Where we live at downtown, that was a place where there were services and housing for homeless people. Now all of a sudden the bulk of you, even middle-class people, could not live there. They gentrified it, and turned it into a place for the rich and the near-rich and the want-to-be-rich who can manipulate the credit system. So the people who have lived and died and bled there, even under this new mayor who promises that he is going to take care of the people. It's not happening.

So what is most enlightening to me is that here we are 5,000 miles away, and we get to talk with you folks, and find out that it is still the same issue. It is our struggle against the power structure: the people who have the money. The people who can characterize us as less than, right? You can be criminalized for your class, your life style, your skin color, your sexual orientation, whatever it is that pushes you out of the mainstream and allows them the privilege of throwing you a few crumbs. There is more of us then there is of them and we need to make our demands met.

JAN JAAP:

The money is there. People can be diagnosed. That is what is going to happen in Utrecht. You can say it is the elite who makes all the trouble. That is not true. It is also the people themselves, they have to do something. I am very disappointed with the homeless people in Utrecht, with exception of some of the addicts, because they did not even take one step to improve their own situation. But that is also an indication of how damaged and hurt these people are. Homelessness is very destructive. Maybe they cannot.... They cannot understand.

MARRY MOS:

I think there are possibilities to address homelessness and improve the situation. But you have to start with giving people more personal attention. That is also what people were saying eight years ago: "I have never had a private conversation with anyone." When no one ever asks you, "How are you doing?" it makes the chance to improve your situation very small. So it starts with personal attention.

The second step is that when someone asks for help, applying for social security or getting into the homeless circuit for the first time, you have to give them the helping hand. You have to see what you can do for this person. At the moment the people have to fit into all kinds of rules, and they fall outside the boat because of it.

RIET VAN DENDEREN:

G.O.U.D. is only a very small foundation. We do a lot, and we work very broadly. We do everything ourselves. We solve all the problems that occur, ourselves, on the spot. It is my experience that when people get into a "service-giver circuit," they work with an agenda. We work with two people in our office and we finish everything that occurs. So, for example, last week we got a family with a child seven-years-old, who were homeless. If you go to government assistance for help the whole family will be split up: the man and the woman and the child all go to different places.

What have we done in three weeks? We found housing for this family; they get the key tomorrow. This is not the only one, because we have housed a lot of people in the mean time, but this family is a recent example. We make sure that the welfare office [*sociale dienst*] will pay the rent. People who live on the street never have money in their pockets because it is much more expensive to live that way. Then we take a look at what is needed in the house and we go to churches and private persons to get the stuff that is needed to make them a happy family again.

A very nice example is this: I have the family crib for a baby and that crib has now already had three babies—from pregnant women who were homeless—in it. And I like very much that the crib has been used in this manner.

RIEN SPRENGER:

During these last few months we've heard of Utrecht winning prizes for its homeless policies, for doing a good job. But when we listen to the stories, you must also conclude that there is still a lot wrong and that we have a long way to go. We have cleaned up the problem areas in the city and to most people the burden seems to have gone. But still there are problems for the homeless and addicted.

Topic:
Afghanistan
December 2, 2005, Utrecht, The Netherlands

Panelists:

Martin Jeltsma: International drug policy advocate from the Trans National Institute (TNI), Amsterdam

Fawat: Afghani filmmaker and law student, seeking asylum in The Netherlands

Jan Langendijk: Moderator, Director of the Office of Social Development, City of Utrecht

Martin Jeltsma:

I want to commend the team here for the play. It has been a marvelous attempt to the get the whole case on the table again. I think it is also a nice homage to Gary Webb, who has since committed suicide.

The pattern that is visible over the decades in the various conflicts where the U.S. has intervened — be it Nicaragua, or before that in Vietnam, and after in the case of Afghanistan: We see a constant pattern where the CIA is playing a role on the darker side of the conflict. There has also always been a dark side of financing their main allies in the dirty part of the war. In the case of Afghanistan it was during the Russian occupation of the country. The Mujahideen forces where financed substantially with heroin trafficking. The CIA was directly involved in that as well, primarily through working closely with the Pakistani intelligence: the ISI. It is well documented. So I think a jump from this play about Nicaragua to the situation in Afghanistan is quite possible.

FAWAT:

First of all, I want to add that politicians need good reasons to legitimize their acts, and one of their reasons in drugs. They play a two-sided game: on the one hand, they stimulate people to sell drugs, in order to have money to fight their enemies. And on the other side, they use drugs as a reason to legitimize their deeds and wars. For example, they can attack countries, claiming to fight a war on drugs, in order to control those areas.

KEVIN MICHAEL KEY:

My question is: In the States there has been a rise in the use of crack cocaine, and heroin had become a lesser drug. More recently we begin to see a greater influx of heroin: more of the white type, as opposed to the one that is produced in Mexico, which is black-tar heroin. In your opinion is that related to the increased production in Afghanistan?

MARTIN JELTSMA:

Frankly, I don't think there is a strong connection, for several reasons. Drug epidemics have certain characteristics. They don't follow the users, or supply or demand reasons. Instead, they have the character of an epidemic. The crack epidemic was a clear example. It followed certain patterns — that you can also see in other countries with other drugs — that go up and then down again. In other countries crack is on the rise, for example. There are constantly shifting patterns in the drugs of choice for certain groups in the population. The DEA has a heroin-signature program; they can determine where the heroin comes from on the basis of random samples. And the big majority of the white heroin now on the U.S. market comes from Colombia. There is new production there, and they do produce the white type of heroin. Afghan heroin, in spite of the boom in production there, has in the past years not risen above 10 percent of the U.S. market. So it has not really influenced that market.

KEVIN MICHAEL KEY:

Given the connection between the various government agencies, the CIA and DEA, is there an independent group that checks the signature or the DNA of the country of origin of the drugs? Otherwise we have a situation again, like the one we just showed, where the government just says: "Well, we know that there is no correlation between our involvement in Afghanistan and the rise of heroin in the U.S. because we're checking to make sure that it comes from Colombia. Because of course we are not involved in the drug trade and the targeting of our own people." Is there an independent group, such as your group, that is actually doing the testing: testing the tests of the DEA/CIA?

MARTIN JELTSMA:

We don't have the technical equipment to do that. So there is not, in that sense, an independent verification of that DEA signature program. However there are other types of evidence and analyses of the international heroin market that do corroborate these reports. It is relatively clear where the Afghan heroin is going. More then half of it is directly consumed in the region, in Iran and Pakistan, which are the two main heroin markets of the world in terms of consumption. There is the growing market in Eastern Europe, in the former Soviet Union, and of course Europe. Those markets account for almost 100 percent of the Afghani supply. Another signal of the patterns in the market are the kind of seizures that are made in international trafficking. That is a not a very reliable figure, but there are very few shipments intercepted of Afghan heroin on the road to the U.S. So there are several data that support more or less the findings of the DEA.

AUDIENCE MEMBER, MICHAEL VAN DER PUTTEN:

Just from the economic point of view, how much money is involved? What will happen to the people, the farmers and so on, who produce it, when they have to stop producing? And then, of course, it is a gigantic health problem.

FAWAT:

As far as the economic aspect is concerned, the profit of drugs in Afghanistan is almost $3 billion per year.

AUDIENCE MEMBER:

How much is this compared to the national income?

FAWAT:

More than one third. I cannot say exactly how much.

MARTIN JELTSMA:

Of the export, that is maybe 80 percent. It is almost 60 percent of the gross national product. And of those $3 billion, according to the U.N. numbers, between $100 million and $150 million remains with the farmers. So that is a very small part. $700 million is circulated in the smaller opium trade. Then there are people who work in a small army, but also people who have to finance the bridal money (dowry) and trade because of that. And the rest of it is for the big exporters.

AUDIENCE MEMBER:

When the economic interests are that high, how can you solve the problem?

FAWAT:

It is almost a lost battle. Afghanistan has become almost a narcotic country. What else can you expect when a big part of the economy is depending on the income from drugs?

AUDIENCE MEMBER:

How big is the problem of addicted people amongst the Afghan population?

FAWAT:

It is very alarming, and it is also increasing rapidly. Living conditions are bad and the unemployment rate is high, as a result of the war in Afghanistan, and also because of the influence of foreign abusers. The Afghan lords want to use the situation to their own advantage.

AUDIENCE MEMBER:

What kind of economic base was there before the war? How long has this drug trade been going on?

FAWAT:

Afghanistan used to have a small economy. We were exporting dried fruit, tapestries and carpets. We had a small industry. But all this has been ruined by the war.

JAN LANGENDIJK:

There was a U.N. report that came out just before I arrived here. It says that in the year 2000 there where 80,000 hectares of land that were used for the cultivation of opium poppies. And then the war came. And now there are 110,000 to 120,000 hectares. That is an enormous increase in the production of opium. So the problem is growing.

SASHAE:

How do you determine what is an epidemic in drug use? Right now there are Dutch soldiers in Afghanistan, fighting in less dangerous areas, that have to go to more dangerous areas. With the growing opium trade there, are the Dutch people concerned that they will get addicted to heroin? Because when our soldiers came back from Vietnam they where addicted to heroin, and they are still displaced right now.

MARTIN JELTSMA:

The first question demands a lengthy answer, but in short: The use of the word "epidemic" means that it has a pattern, that it spreads in a way similar to what a virus does. Not because it is a disease, but because it is tightly connected to subcultures. It is difficult to explain how a culture changes in certain groups of the population. If you compare the crack epidemic in the U.S. with the one here in Europe, it did not require a "mad scientist" to develop crack. The fact that someone figured out that it could be smoked instead of snorted, I think that triggered the crack epidemic in the U.S. The crack epidemic in Europe is not a marketing technique of dealers, because most of the users make it themselves. They cook the cocaine with some ammonia and they convert it themselves to a smokeable form of cocaine.

AUDIENCE MEMBER:

Are there any facts about drug addiction in Afghanistan?

FAWAT:

In Afghanistan there are almost 1 million people who are addicted, according to a recent report of the United Nations and the Afghan health department. Eight percent are men, 13 percent are women, and seven percent are children.

MARTIN JELTSMA:

There is still the second question. What about the Dutch soldiers in Afghanistan?

I have visited the camp north of Kabul, where most of the foreign soldiers are. And I have to say that if I would be a soldier who had to spend months there, I would start using something. It is an extremely boring situation. They are not allowed to get out of the camp. They are there with thousands and thousands of soldiers in a very small compound, and there is definitely a risk that one would start using under those circumstances. Now, of course, with the new mission, the Dutch soldiers are getting into a much riskier environment. For the first time there will be a risk that they will be directly part of a conflict. They can be drawn into far dirtier operations. So far, in the North, they had really nothing to worry about. I am sure Fawat can tell you more about Uruzgan where the Dutch soldiers will be stationed. So that could be another reason they start to use drugs: out of stress, as was the case with the U.S. soldiers in Vietnam.

SASHAE:

Is there support here in Holland? When they come back to Holland is there help?

MARTIN JELTSMA:

I would assume so. It is not comparable with the U.S. soldiers in Vietnam, because we only have a small number of troops there; at this time there are about 1,000 soldiers there. And there will be about 1,000 more. So it won't be, as was the case in the U.S., that hundreds of thousands are coming back. That had a real impact on the population in the U.S.

IBRAHIM SABA:

Are the soldiers influencing the production of the drugs? Are the soldiers attacking people who are producing the drugs? Or are the drugs there because the soldiers are there?

FAWAT:

The soldiers are busy fighting terrorism, more than the battle against drugs. They don't realize that drugs are more dangerous in Afghanistan at this moment than terrorism. The areas where the drugs are grown are areas where the U.N. and U.S. are fighting the war on terror.

In these areas the people are very strictly religious. And they are involved with drugs. They are practical religious, not theoretical. They are bribable. These are people that are very vulnerable. In this way the U.N. and U.S. are fighting the war on drugs and the war on terror at the same time.

JAN LANGENDIJK:

I heard that the area where the soldiers are going to has significant active Taliban support and also active drug lords. And I heard that there is a tendency now to work together with the drug lords in order to fight the Taliban. If that is true, you get into a similar situation as the situation we saw tonight. Just like with

Osama bin Laden, who once was a friend of the U.S. because he was fighting the Russians.

Audience Member:

How is the Afghan government involved?

Fawat:

The Afghan government is very involved. The conflict between president Karzai and the ex-minister of foreign affairs has made it public that Karzai's own brother was involved in the drug trade. The minister wanted to make his name public in publications, but Karzai protected his brother. As long as the minister held that position he could not publicize the name. It was only after he was fired that he gave the name to *The New York Times*. There are many warlords who were involved in earlier wars that are still functioning in the government at this moment. They are still active, and they know how to use this opportunity to increase the drug trade and do what they want. They are very influential people in their own regions. This means that the president, who is supported by the CIA and the U.S., is involved in the drug trade.

Audience Member:

I hear a lot about mapping out the problems that are there. Do you two also think that there are solutions or answers? What could be the influence of legalizing drugs, like we are lobbying for here in Holland? What would be the influence of that in Afghanistan?

Martin Jeltsma:

Of course it would make a difference for the situation in Afghanistan if the whole world would legalize. It won't be a solution, because it will not happen in the near future. So we will have to look for other solutions as well. But for Afghanistan it would not be a logical solution at this moment. Because of the corruption of the politicians and the warlords we just talked about. At the same time we should not forget that it is this illegal economy that allows this country to survive at this moment.

We have to work on real, long-term solutions, including reconstruction and peace building, and forget about quick solutions. But we should give up the urgent need to suppress this opium economy. It is too important in this stage of the reconstruction. We have to let it go for the moment. And only through this kind of transition to development, towards peace-building, can we establish a path that can slowly reverse the dependence of Afghanistan on the illicit drug economy.

AUDIENCE MEMBER:

I was wondering if the US soldiers are burning the poppy fields at this moment?

MARTIN JELTSMA:

No. This year, for the first time there was a serious tendency to destroy fields. That is not done by burning, but by using tractors. This year for the first time the Americans wanted very much to be involved in this. They created a special eradication force, a bit like they are doing in Colombia. They trained the whole thing and they wanted to deploy it to the different provinces. But in total the US force managed to destroy only 200 out of the 130,000 hectares. It has been a useless exercise.

AUDIENCE MEMBER:

Are the Taliban more successful in stopping the drug trade than the Americans?

MARTIN JELTSMA:

In the last year of the Taliban regime there was almost no opium in the areas that they controlled. But there is a downside to it, because it was like many other things the Taliban did. They were very repressive to the farmers. It was one of the reasons why hundreds of thousands of farmers fled the country. Because of the Taliban opium ban there was simply no means to survive anymore. We don't know what would have happened the next year. It is possible that it could even have contributed to a revolt against the Taliban. Because the eradication, the downsizing of the poppies, was so quick, many were left in total disaster.

JOHN MALPEDE:

What about the news articles of the last few days here in the Netherlands that there are secret CIA operations that bring terrorists to Eastern European countries to torture and interrogate them? Is this part of the discussion why the Dutch don't want to send their soldiers to Afghanistan?

FAWAT:

According to me, the discussion is not specifically about this problem, but about getting guarantees from America regarding the safety of the Dutch soldiers. They said very clearly that the mission is too risky. They feel there is a great danger.

Jan Langendijk:

We are typically Dutch. We are sending soldiers, but they are not allowed to fight.

Audience Member:

How reliable are the guarantees that are being given?

Jan Langendijk:

The discussion is about the fact that they cannot give any guarantees.

Jan Jaap:

Of course they can do that. It is the same situation that we had in Srebrenica. It is just a matter of regulations and changing the legislation. If we are going there to fight, then we have to have the means to fight. Otherwise the question remains: What is our purpose there? What are we there for?

Jan Langendijk:

Last question, to Fawat. He is a refugee. The Dutch government is saying to him, "Well, it is quite safe there right now, you can go back." Could you explain why you say, "Well, that is very kind of you, but I'm not really planning to go?"

Fawat:

Well, it is very clear. The government says that it is too risky when it concerns their own soldiers' safety, but when it concerns asylum-seekers' safety, then they say the country is totally safe! What is the army there for? To fight or to feast? Maybe they go because they can get heroin for free there.

Thank you very much!

EPILOGUE

"One of the great things that the United States likes to do from time to time, is just announce something will be eradicated, you know, just as a solution. And so we have zero tolerance, and the idea that you can will it out of existence. And a sufficient amount of force, violence and intolerance will solve the problem."
— PETER SELLARS

The following is from an interview I conducted with Al McCoy when we were in Cleveland. I think it's a fitting conclusion to this narrative. I'd identify the theme of this part of the interview as "The Theology of the Drug War."

—**JOHN MALPEDE**

AL MCCOY:

The drug war is really one of the most bizarre aspects of U.S. domestic and foreign policy. A century from now, when historians look back upon the U.S. drug war, they will write about our generation like we now write about the crusades. You know: "irrational, violent, impassioned, destructive, crazed beyond all imagining." They will look at us like we were theological primitives, rather like we look at the 12th-century crusaders. I mean it is truly one of the most bizarre policies that any modern government has ever framed. And we are now about to begin the second century of this bizarre crusade against drugs, and nobody has begun to examine it really rationally. Let's just take a look at one of the most fundamental absurdities at the international level, the idea is that we can somehow suppress supply internationally. The idea is that we can go out and defoliate or uproot, that we can seize, that we can disrupt the supply, that we can ultimately eradicate this plague. It is the stated policy of the U.S. government to reduce U.S. domestic consumption by eradicating the supply abroad. That is the logic of the drug war. But here is a very simple fact. I started saying it 20 years ago and the World Bank has now begun writing it in its latest report on Afghanistan. And that fact is that suppression of narcotics stimulates the traffic.

This invisible agricultural economy operates very subtly, very sensitively, along the same laws of supply and demand as does any other legal, economic/agricultural economy. So what happens when demand for a commodity is constant, as it is with heroin, and there is a shortfall of supply? Price goes up. What happens to farmers around the globe, whether it is wheat or sugarcane or whatever? When price goes up farmers plant more. We move in to Turkey, we wipe it out. That raises the price the next year axiomatically. Farmers in Southeast Asia plant more. The Golden Triangle — boom. So we go around the world attacking drugs in one place. We attack coca in Bolivia, so it pops up in

Peru. We attack in Peru and it pops up in Colombia. We attack Colombia. It is now rising back up in Bolivia and Peru. So it is self-defeating. How did we get from 1,000 tons of opium in 1970 to 6,000 tons of opium today? Much of the drive, much of the pressure that has raised production has been generated in these failed attempts in suppression. So the drug war at the international level is a travesty. It is an absurdity.

The other absurdity is the domestic policy. From 1930 till 1980 — for 50 years, through depression, WWII, the Eisenhower years, the cold war — there was one statistic that remained constant in the U.S. We had 100 prisoners per 100,000 population. Reagan started the drug war and it started rising. By the time that Bush became president, we were up to 400 per 100,000. Today we are over 700 per 100,000. We have at least 2 million people behind bars. We have at least one-third of the African-American male population between the ages of 18 and 32 in the criminal justice system. We are reaching new points right now — in states like California, Michigan and Wisconsin — where the social-welfare dollar, which is paying for the prisons, is eating up the education budget. All right, we put 2 million people behind bars. We have more drugs, more drug users, more drug addicts, and more drug traffickers than when we had 100 prisoners per 100,000. It has done nothing.

These are the twin irrationalities of the amplification of coercion applied to this complex global economy. One: the idea that coercion can end supply; and, two: the idea that coercion, — you know, book them, put them through the criminal justice system, put them behind bars — the idea that this solves anything is just crazy. It compounds the problem.

In the beginning of the 1870s we had a populist movement among the partisan churches of the United Kingdom and the

U.S. for the idea of getting the state to prohibit alcohol and narcotics. And this was a genuine populist movement. This whole global prohibition regime that we are living in right now, with all its treaties, federal laws and state laws, is a part of a genuine populist movement. In the realm of alcohol, of course, that era ended with the repeal of prohibition in 1933. But the drug part of the prohibition regime is persistent at a national level.

But now what we have got is really very interesting. Now, after a century of this attempt, we have another populist movement that is trying to end this prohibition, that is persistent in states all over the country. People are signing petitions and there are plebiscites. Proposition 36 in California said that for nonviolent first-time drug offenders, it is mandatory treatment. That is really a brilliant solution. I think that half a century from now, ideally, we will take down, demolish this whole edifice of prohibition. But in the meantime a state cannot decide that it is going to opt out of the drug laws. Because we have the federal laws and treaties that require us to specifically criminalize the use and possession of these drugs.

The only thing we can do right now, as citizens and in the movements, is to change the penalties. It is amazing what that does. First of all, you remove people from the criminal-justice system, so that you are not spending $20,000 to $30,000 in most states to incarcerate people. Treatment is far less expensive. Moreover, when you think about what happens to some people: You take some young person, 18 to 30 years old, and you put him in that criminal-justice system. You put them through the living hell that is the American prison system, where they are brutalized, traumatized. When they emerge they cannot get a decent job. They are stigmatized socially. In 17 states, by my last count, they cannot even vote. They are stripped of a lot of their civil rights. They get no training. They've got no skills. They've got no capital, no money in the bank. They come out and what are they gonna do? They are going to go back out on the street. They are going to go back and start dealing. The prison system truly criminalizes a person. They live for another 30 or 40 years out there in the streets, dealing. We turn ordinary users into hardened criminals and career drug dealers. It is an enormously stupid and contradictory policy. And they are just beginning to realize it. The whole drug war thing, one of the dominant areas of U.S. policy, is not based in any way on a rational discussion of cost and benefits. It is theological. It started as a religious movement. It remains a fundamentally religious policy.

In essence, for theological reasons, for religious reasons, 100 years ago, we launched a prohibition campaign against narcotics and alcohol. In 1933 it became clear that the alcohol prohibition was completely irrational. We persisted for another 40 years. And then in the drug war under Nixon and Reagan we began to expand the penalties with mandatory minimums. In the 1980s, under Reagan, we took the Rockefeller laws in New York and we made them federal laws, and the states imitated that across the county. And now we are hitting the brick wall of rationality. We are discovering that when you apply coercion to extirpate a vice—to regulate personal behavior by the most extreme coercive measure possible: incarceration—you get to a point where you go from 100 per 100, 000, you get to 400 prisoners per 100,000, you go to 700 prisoners per 100,000. The doomsday machine is ticking away. We are up to 700 prisoners per 100,000 today. Two or three years from now, it will be 800 or 850. And suddenly you cannot afford it anymore, you just can't afford it. Then the policy begins to break down. What we are witnessing today is that this irrationality—this theologically driven policy, this religiously driven policy which has been masquerading as rational and social policy—suddenly hits the brick wall of rationality, and it begins to collapse. But there is nobody, there is no political leader in this country who has had the courage to stand up and just say clearly that this is not working, that it is stupidity, that this needs to be radically changed.

What is going to happen is that, eventually, those same popular forces that put the repeal of probation in play will arise. That was a popular movement, the movement to repeal prohibition. At the moment, you've got this prison-industrial society that is standing on one side, and then you've got the ephemeral social reformers, George Soros, who comes in through Open Society and funds a ballot initiative. You have a popular movement that builds up, and then it goes away. It loses. And at any time that one of these initiatives comes in, the enormous countervailing forces mobilize and counterattack. The drug enforcement administration, the drug czars, the administration in power. All the conservatives come in and stomp it. And it gets broken, because in the balance of forces the anti-drug forces are much stronger than this very weak, very ephemeral movement.

But ultimately it has to change, because it is irrational, and we push it to a point where as a society we can no longer sustain it. We are getting to a point right now where we really have to choose between funding schools and training the next few generations to keep our society up to standard in a very competitive world. Or, we are going to put everybody in prison?

JOHN MALPEDE:

Last question. The war against gay marriage was again a real populist theological issue that had nothing to do with the real problems facing the electorate. Even though you laid out a perfectly good case, with the doomsday machine, for why this cannot go on, nevertheless there might be some religious counter-machine that might allow us to destroy ourselves, or go much further in the direction of hysteria or irrationality?

Al McCoy:

If we look at the package of issues, gay marriage is attached to two other issues that I think are very relevant. The key one is abortion. In this campaign that got launched in the late-19th century globally, but particular in the Anglo world — in England, the U.S. and Australia — there were three types of drugs that were of concern: alcohol, narcotic drugs and abortions. This was part of an idea of using the state and the state apparatus, not only to cover the globe with this regulatory regime, but also to envelop the body in a regulatory regime. Adult males could not drink. At that point the main opiate users in the U.S. were middle-class women. Mary Tyrone and *Long Day's Journey Into Night* is actually an accurate portrait of a typical golden-age drug user: a middle-class woman. Women didn't go into the saloons. That was a male environment. Retail sale of alcohol was not well-developed. So basically saloons were male and opiates were for women.

The other idea was to regulate abortions. This was actually a regulatory regime to impose control of the state over the human body, to envelop the human body in regulations. We have seen a kind of reaction to this. The prohibition against alcohol was the first to go. The irrationality was extreme. It led to the rise of organized crime, massive bootlegging and the total corruption of state and city governments in key trafficking zones. We shut that one first. I think the Prohibition Party still exists, there are still advocates of prohibition, but is has gotten weaker. The next one we have on our agenda, which I think will fall next, is the prohibition of drugs. But the third one, abortion, is still a zone of contention. In my view they are all part of the same bold experiment at the start of the 20th century: the idea of using the power of the law to regulate the individual's control over his or her body.

AUDIENCE MEMBER:

I'd like to add on to that, that the language politicians use to talk to us has changed over the last 30 years. Now we are usually called "taxpayers"— in other words, "consumers" in political language. We're only called "citizens" when we're asked to volunteer to pick up the pieces of government programs that didn't last or have been cut. When you're called a "citizen" it means that you are asked to do something. When you are called a taxpayer, your question is: "What's in it for me?" And for the last 30 years, that's what we've been called: taxpayers and consumers. So we're all stuck in this role, living on the outskirts of activity in our own country, our own government.

Endnotes

January, 2007

"Agents & Assets" links domestic-policy and foreign-policy concerns of the United States. It links the resulting experience of poor people in this country to the consequences of these same policies as experienced by poor people in other parts of the world. And we've seen how major media coverage helps keep this dynamic in place.

In the past year, we've seen these elements play out in Skid Row Los Angeles in an ever-more-confrontational and violent atmosphere fueled by the real-estate bubble and those scrambling to make billions from it before it pops. In September, 2006 the 9th Circuit Court of Appeals reversed the opinion of the lower court and upheld the ACLU case regarding the constitutional rights of homeless people to sleep on the street. This is the lawsuit that ACLU director Ramona Ripston spoke of at one of our May, 2005 "Agents & Assets" events. The judge ruling on the case stated that arresting people for being homeless was in violation of the constitutional safeguard against cruel and unusual punishment. The judge ordered the city to sit down with the ACLU and negotiate a compromise solution. The mayor and the police chief expected the LA city council to approve the court's recommendation for negotiation. But, just before the vote Jan Perry produced a legal opinion generated by her own lawyers arguing against the settlement. Jan Perry is the African-American councilperson who represents the Skid Row district. She has been an aggressive representative of the business and development interests in Skid Row. In an unanticipated reversal, the council rejected the court's recommendation and accepted Perry's assessment. The result was an aggressive police-harassment campaign: 50 additional officers on the streets of Skid Row, with numerous arrests daily. The police assess the number of available shelter beds and arrest that number of people daily.

The *LA Times* contributed article after article in support of the cleansing of Skid Row. One such article claimed that 600 drug dealers had been arrested in the first week of the clean-up. Could the poorest community in Los Angeles support a whopping 600 drug dealers? To me, that story suggests 550 drug dealers in need of a better business plan. The only way to generate such numbers is to charge every user as a dealer. It's a massive criminalization of two social issues: housing the homeless and healthcare treatment for users. The *Times'* inability to critically assess such ridiculous claims should have led to their embarrassment. But, instead, their complete alignment with the development interests has been an important element in rationalizing police tactics and winning over public opinion for the "revitalization" of the area. In the process, people on the streets have been demonized. They now provide an excuse for the displacement of the housed population and support-services infrastructure that has been developed in Skid Row. $100 million dollars had been appropriated by the county government for the proposed dismantling of Skid Row, with people and services to be distributed throughout the county (which is a vast area of hundreds of square miles). This money is a pittance compared to the amount that has been invested in establishing effective programs in Skid Row.

In the course of "Agents & Assets" we've learned many things. We've learned from Al McCoy that the world drug trade is bigger than the world textile trade — and clothing is one of the three basics of life, as in food, shelter, and clothing. The drug issue reaches around the world and into cities and "hollers," and into families wherever they might be.

We've learned from Chris Parks that an addiction is any rigid behavior pattern that is impervious to change. We've learned from the U.S. Congress—through close reading of the hearing, the edited version of which is the script for "Agents & Assets" — that an addicted government produces policies that generate despair, including addiction.

In the course of "Agents & Assets" we've witnessed successes and defeats on the road to achieving a more rational, equitable and humane drug policy. We've learned from Dave Fratello that "the people are out front of the politicians." And we've seen — in Ohio, for example — the relentless nature of the drug warriors who are all-too-willing to do whatever is necessary to manipulate the public.

In this context it's important not to lose sight of what has been achieved, through the process arising from Gary Webb's "Dark Alliance" series of newspaper articles. Largely at the insistence of the African-American community to get to the bottom of these charges, a remarkable outcome has been achieved. Namely, the eventual admission (in Volume 2 of Inspector General Hitz' report) of numerous instances of Contra drug-smuggling intertwined with CIA support of Contra operations. These admissions are an important achievement, not only for the African-American community, but also for the entire nation.

This sense of achievement had been derailed, as we've seen, by burying these revelations deep in the reports, as well as by the failure of the media — including the country's most prestigious newspapers — to give them appropriate coverage. This has meant that these admissions of CIA and executive-branch wrongdoing have not registered with the American people. As Robert Parry has said, a truth commission is needed to prevent our leaders from continuing to build the future based on a false reading of our past.

Furthermore, the sense of achievement has been derailed because of the overwhelming, egregious conditions that continue to exist in poor communities, in communities of color, and in the criminal-justice system. We know that justice is a long way from being here, now. That's exactly the reason why we must recognize our achievements along this road. They are sustaining.

"Agents & Assets" has been an effective, exhilarating project because it links to the hard-earned, lived expertise of community members. Iit provides a platform where the voices of these citizens seeking change are joined with those of policy-reformers, public officials, and professionals. As I said at the top of this Endnote, "Agents & Assets" links U.S. domestic and foreign policy. It links the resulting experience of poor people in this country to the consequences of these same policies as experienced by poor people in other parts of the world.

JANUARY, 2014

This book was constructed in 2007 covering the first five years of "Agents & Assets" (2001–2005). We've continued to do the project as the U.S. war on drugs has morphed and continued to lose credibility.

At the very first performances in 2001, Sandra Alvarez of Global Exchange planted the idea in our heads that we should travel to Latin America to hear peoples' perspectives there on the effects of the war on drugs. In 2009, we were able to tour Bolivia with the Spanish-language version, "Agentes y Activos," with a combined cast of LAPDers and Bolivianos organized by Willar Vidaurre and Zulma Galván of Cochabamba's Esquela de Arté y Talento. There, as always, we rehearsed the project with a combined cast of LAPDers and local people, in this case residents of Cochabamba. Then we traveled together for shows in La Paz, El Alto, Oruro, Sucre and Santa Santa Cruz and Plan Tres Mil.

Now, in 2014, as part of our Queens Museum retrospective and residency in New York, we are able to perform "Agentes y Activos" in the U.S. and to hear of the consequences of the war on drugs from the perspective of Latinos living in the U.S.

John Malpede
Los Angeles, CA, January 2014

"Agentes & Activos"

Texto fechado el 18 de marzo de 1998 de la Audiencia del Comité Selecto del Congreso sobre Inteligencia

**Guión editado por "Agentes y Activos"
Director del performance John Malpede**

El Presidente (Sr. Goss):

Muy buenas tardes honorabeles miembros presentes. Este comité de inteligencia dará inicio a la audiencia del día de hoy con para revisar el informe del Inspector General de la CIA referente a alegaciones formuladas en una serie de artículos publicados en un periódico del año 1996. Estos artículos indicaban que la CIA estaba involucrada en el tráfico de crack cocaína a California en el año 1980.

Antes de comenzar, deseo informar a los honorabeles miembros y al público presente el modo en que abremos de proceder. El Comité de la Cámara Nacional de Seguridad gentilmente nos ha concedido el uso de esta sala, por lo que estamos agradecidos. Como podran constatar son las 3:00 en punto. Sin embargo, se nos ha informado que el arrendamiento de este espacio expira a las 5:00 en punto, y hemos hecho un cronograma, de tal manera que esta audiencia concluya oportunamente.

Al concluir mis palabras iniciales, daré cabida a mis colegas del comité para sus comentarios preliminares, y después oiremos a los otros miembros de Congreso. Seguidamente prestaremos atención al testimonio del Sr. Frederick P. Hitz, Inspector General de la CIA, quien iniciará su presentación no más tarde de las 4 p.m. Agradezco ya a todos los que hoy están presentes por colaborar para que se cumpla este cronograma.

La audiencia de hoy marca un paso importante dentro del proceso de investigación en curso emprendido por el Comité de Inteligencia para evaluar la validez de estas alegaciones extremadamente serias, formuladas en una serie de artículos publicados en el diario *Noticias de San José Mercury* en 1996.

Estos artículos detallaron alegaciones de que la CIA estaba involucrada o de alguna manera implicada en el tráfico de la droga de crack cocaína a California en el año 1980. Los artículos además afirman que las ganancias de dichas transacciones fueron usadas para ayudar el financiamiento de las actividades del movimiento de resistencia en Nicaragua, para la mayoría de nosotros conocidos simplemente como los Contra.

Este comité emprendió una investigación de los mencionados cargos en otoño del año 1996. Durante este tiempo, dos investigaciones separadas fueron realizadas por el Inspector General. Primero el análisis del Inspector General de la CIA, que es tema de la audiencia del día de hoy, y secundo el análisis del Departamento de Justicia, que todavía no ha sido emitido. Me parece que el Inspector General de la CIA ha presentado a nuestro comité un trabajo sólido y es nuestra intención considerar sus conclusiones cuidadosamente.

Desde luego, seguiremos conduciendo nuestra propia e independiente investigación de este asunto como parte de la responsabilidad de supervisión que nos incumbe. Estamos claramente conscientes de que este episodio ha avivado las sospechas albergadas por algunas personas en cuanto al advenimiento del azote de la droga de crack cocaína en los Estados Unidos. Cualquier insinuación de complicidad por parte del gobierno en ese terrible desenlace deberá ser seriamente considerada y contestada.

Será extremadamente difícil presentar una respuesta absoluta que pueda disipar toda duda. Esa es la naturaleza de estos casos. Habiendo dicho esto, yo creo que el pueblo Norteamericano tiene derecho a confiar en que nosotros realizaremos un trabajo a consciencia para esclaracer los hechos y ofrecer conclusiones sobre los cargos que han sido formulados.

Así pues, permítanme nuevamente dar la bienvenida al testigo de hoy, y a mis colegas congresistas. Ahora cedo la palabra a los miembros para algún comentario preliminar. Damos la bienvenida a la Sra. Harmon y al Sr. Gibbons quienes ingresaron después del golpe de martillo.

Honorable Sr. Dicks.

SR. DICKS:

Señor Presidente, he visto la investigación del Sr. Hitz que se caracteriza como la más extensa emprendida por un Inspector General. La mejor defensa contra una injustificable crítica de una investigación de este tipo es garantizar que sea lo más exhaustiva posible.

En el resumen de dos páginas presentada por la CIA el 29 de Enero de 1998, la frase "ninguna información ha sido encontrada" fue utilizada 9 veces. Quiero que me garanticen que ninguna información fue encontrada porque ninguna existía, y no que la información no fue encontrada porque el empeño puesto para encontrarla no fue lo suficientemente minucioso.

Críticas han sido publicadas, por parte de al menos uno de los que fueron contactados por el personal del Sr. Hitz, indicando que la entrevista parecía estar diseñada solamente para cumplir formalidades. Quiero que el Sr. Hitz, quien conozco personalmente y por quien tengo mucho respeto, nos garantice que él ha quedado satisfecho con la investigación por haberse llevado a cabo tan exhaustivamente como fuere necesario poniendo todos los hechos al descubierto.

Entiendo que varias personas, la mayoría de ellos ex empleados importantes de la CIA, rehusaron ser entrevistados o procuraron limitar las entrevistas. Al menos uno de los individuos que rehusó ser entrevistado por el Inspector General no demostró la misma renuencia al ser entrevistado por la prensa. Considero que el incumplimiento de estas personas de colaborar al Inspector General en esta investigación es inexcusable.

Señor Presidente, estoy con expectativa de escuchar los comentarios que nuestros colegas congresistas tendrán respecto al trabajo del Sr. Hitz. Les doy la bienvenida y doy la bienvenida al Sr. Hitz y su presentación.

Gracias, Señor Presidente.

EL PRESIDENTE (SR. GOSS):

Muchas gracias Honorable Sr. Dicks. En este momento, doy cabida al distinguido caballero de California, el Sr. Julian Dixon.

SR. DIXON:

Muchas gracias, Señor Presidente. Me uno a usted y al Miembro Superior de la Minoría dando la bienvenida a los Miembros del Congreso y al Sr. Fred Hitz, Inspector General de la CIA.

He leído el informe del Inspector General titulado “Alegaciones de Conexiones Entre la CIA y los Contra en el Tráfico de Cocaína dentro de los Estados Unidos, Volumen 1, 'El Relato de California'."

Con la gran velocidad de la edad digital en la tecnología informática, la serie "Alianza Oscura" se propagó rápidamente más allá de los lectores del diario *San José Mercury News*. La serie fue puesta en el sitio web del periódico donde, de acuerdo al diario *Mercury News,* recibió más de mil visitas por semana. Ademas, estaciones con programas de entrevistas lo convirtió en su historia principal por semanas y las redes de televisión dieron extensa cobertura al reportaje de la historia en los noticieros de la noche.

No debería sorprender que esta historia haya tenido tan impactante repercusión fuera de las comunidades minoritarias. La propagación de la droga de cocaína en comunidades predominantemente mayoritarias ha sido bien documentada y ya no es un secreto. El punto no es si es que el uso de drogas ocurre en comunidades minoritarias o mayoritarias. Las drogas rasgan la misma fibra de nuestra Nación, la estructura de las familias. Familias caucásicas, asiáticas, afro-americanas e hispanas han sido desestabilizadas teniendo como resultado la pérdida de nuestras generaciones jóvenes y el aumento de crímenes relacionados con las drogas.

En la secuela de la serie del diario *San José Mercury News,* varios periódicos iniciaron sus propias investigaciones de dichas alegaciones. El *Los Ángeles Times* fue un periódico que llegó a una conclusión, y cito a seguir, "La epidemia de drogas en Los Ángeles no siguió un anteproyecto o plan maestro. No fue organizada por los Contra o por la CIA o alguna red de traficantes de droga en particular. Ni un solo traficante, ni aun los cabecillas que vendían miles de kilos y se embolsillaban millones de dólares, pudieron jamás acercarse a un monopolio del negocio."

Domingo, 11 de mayo, Jerry Ceppos, el editor general de *Noticias Mercury de San Jose,* escribió un artículo titulado: "A los Lectores de Nuestra Serie Alianza Oscura" en el artículo reconoce ciertas fallas de la serie "Alianza Oscura." El Sr. Ceppos afirmó específicamente que; "En algunos casos, presentamos interpretaciones unilaterales de complejos y a veces contradictorios fragmentos de pruebas. En una ocasión, no incluimos información que contradecía una afirmación fundamental en la serie. Formulamos nuestra propia apreciación y la reportamos como un hecho. Simplificamos excesivamente el complejo tema respecto a la manera en que la epidemia de la droga ha crecido en Norteamérica. Y por medio de lenguaje y gráficos poco precisos, creamos impresiones que daban lugar a interpretaciones erróneas."

Señor Presidente, a pesar de que la serie del diario *San José Mercury News* gira entorno a la comunidad afro-americana en el área sur-central de Los Ángeles, este tema tiene un impacto sobre todo ciudadano norteamericano. La posibilidad de que el gobierno pudiera haber estado involucrado en actividades de tráfico de drogas amenaza la credibilidad de todas las agencias y entidades gubernamentales. No se puede permitir que un gobierno del pueblo y por el pueblo esté involucrado en actividades de esta índole. Cuando alegaciones de abuso gubernamental llega a nuestra atención, tenemos la obligación de usar los recursos que fueren necesarios para investigar dichos cargos detallada y profesionalmente.

Señor Presidente, queda mucho trabajo por hacer.

EL PRESIDENTE (SR. GOSS):

Gracias Sr. Dixon. Deseo indicar a los miembros que llegaron con retraso que estamos asiendo lo posibile para que el Sr. Hitz comience a las cuatro en punto. Si miran el reloj en la pared, comprenderán mi amonestación de que las declaraciones preliminares sean lo más breve posible. Por favor, Honorable Sr. Skelton.

Sr. Skelton:

Gracias Señor Presidente. Me uno a mi colega dando la bienvenida a nuestros testigos congresistas y al Inspector General de la Agencia Central de Inteligencia, Sr. Fred Hitz.

Como miembro Democrático superior del Comité Nacional de Seguridad, estoy especialmente consciente del compromiso hecho por el establecimiento de nuestra Nación para combatir la importación de droga a nuestro país. La alegación de que una agencia del Gobierno Federal esté involucrada en el tráfico de cocaína a los Estados Unidos mientras que otras agencias Federales, incluyendo el Departamento de Defensa, estén dedicando funcionarios y recursos para luchar en la guerra contra las drogas, Señor Presidente, es una cosa horrenda.

La posición del Inspector General es a menudo una de mucha soledad. Con frecuencia, Inspectores Generales son criticados por el público cuando sus informes no confirman alegaciones de mala conducta y entonces se cuestiona su imparcialidad. Dentro de una agencia, muchas veces el inspector general es considerado como el villano cuyo fin es dañar la imagen y reputación de la agencia.

Sr. Hitz, usted ha hecho frente a todo tipo de crítica y siempre ha conservado una actitud profesional. Le deseo todo lo mejor en lo que el futuro le depara y le doy gracias por su servicio.

Señor Presidente, gracias.

El Presidente (Sr. Goss):

Gracias, Honorable Sr. Skelton. Honorable Sra. Harmon de California.

SRA. HARMON:

Gracias, Señor Presidente. Deseo hacer notar al Auditorio que la mayoría de los miembros del comité están presentes, y considero que esto demuestra la importancia que le damos a este tema.

Señor Presidente, sólo quiero decir que a la raíz de todo esto es una palabra: confianza. Una sociedad democrática simplemente no puede funcionar si la ciudadanía cree que las agencias y oficiales gubernamentales participaron en, o toleran actividades ilegales. No será fácil recuperar la confianza, sin embargo es una tarea indispensable para este comité.

Hablando como uno de los miembros de este comité, no podemos eludir esa responsabilidad ni pienso que lo haremos. Le agradezco, y cedo la palabra.

EL PRESIDENTE (SR. GOSS):

Gracias Honorable Sra. Harmon. Honorable Sra. Pelosi.

SRA. PELOSI:

Quiero elogiarle a usted y a nuestros miembros superiores por llevar a cabo esta audiencia pública. Yo todavía tengo preguntas, y tengo mucha expectativa por la presentación del Inspector General.

Este es un tema de gran preocupación en San Francisco, ciudad que represento en el Congreso. Desde la llegada de la epidemia de drogas al principio de los ochenta, ha habido una sospecha en nuestra comunidad de que la comunidad afro-americana fue un blanco, en especial las mujeres de la comunidad afro-americana fueron el blanco de una campaña para proveerles de drogas. Las sospechas fueron que esto llevaría a debilitar la comunidad afro-americana al debilitar a la familia. Esto es un pensamiento muy, muy terrible.

Más o menos en ese mismo tiempo el debate referente a los Contra estaba en pleno vigor en el Congreso de los Estados Unidos. El Congreso procuraba determinar si las ganancias del armamento vendido a Irán estaban siendo desviadas para los Contra, evadiendo así la prohibición hecha por el Congreso de financiar el movimiento de los Contra.

Por consiguiente, cuando esta historia salió a la luz, ya hacía tiempo que el terreno se hacía propicio para dar credibilidad a esta historia.

Yo no creo que la supuesta retractación del periódico *San José Mercury News* fuera de mucho peso. 1. Hubieron algunos casos, 2. no incluimos una afirmación que contradecía, 3. nos equivocamos respecto al dinero y 4. simplificamos excesivamente. Eso no es exactamente una importante retractación. Por tanto yo tengo, y más importante aun es que, mis electores todavía tienen algunas importantes preguntas en cuanto a todo esto. Tenemos especial interés en el caso Frogman – Hombres Rana. Durante el proceso de este caso, el Fiscal de los Estados Unidos para el Distrito Norte de California estuvo de acuerdo con devolver aproximadamente $36.000 en efectivo confiscados a uno de los demandados, después de que dos exiliados partidarios de los Contra escribieron cartas que fueron presentadas al tribunal indicando que el dinero era para el "restablecimiento de la Democracia en Nicaragua." Tengo mucha expectativa de escuchar al Inspector General concerniente a su fallo de que no hay información que la CIA tuvo conexión alguna con los demandados en el caso Frogman – Hombres Rana, y que no hay indicación alguna de que los Contra se beneficiaron del tráfico de drogas en el caso Frogman.

Una vez más, Señor Presidente, gracias por permitirnos presentar estos cuestionamientos abiertamente.

EL PRESIDENTE (SR. GOSS):

Gracias a usted Honorable Sra. Pelosi. Honorable Sr. Skaggs.

SR. SKAGGS:

Seré muy breve. Me adhiero en el agradecimiento al Presidente por convocar estas audiencias. Y, quiero de manera especial reconocer el servicio público de Fred Hitz al país y a la Agencia Central de Inteligencia.

Le conozco por algún tiempo, independientemente de su cargo actual. Lo que tengo que decir recojo de los comentarios hechos por la Srta. Harmon sobre la confianza. Este comité, autorizado para investigar las actividades de las agencias de inteligencia, debe por último contar con la confianza en sí misma para separar los hechos de la ficción de la insinuación. El individuo que es clave para establecer y fomentar una conciencia de fiabilidad es el Inspector General.

Yo creo que la conducta del Sr. Hitz en su cargo y en la ejecución de sus responsabilidades ha sido absolutamente crucial durante mi servicio en el comité para establecer la clase de fiabilidad en ambas direcciones que nos permita realizar nuestro trabajo a favor del pueblo norteamericano.

Y Fred, yo sólo quiero decirte muchas gracias y que Dios esté con tigo!

EL PRESIDENTE (SR. GOSS):

Gracias a usted Honorable Sr. Skaggs.

¿Honorable Sr. Gibbons?

SR. GIBBONS:

Gracias Señor Presidente. Y me adhiero a mis colegas al elogiarle por realizar esta audiencia el día de hoy, y por presentarla delante del público.

Agencias que proporcionan fuentes valiosas de información sobre antinarcóticos, así como también de índole económica o militar deben, ellas mismas, no ser manchadas por actos ilegales o peor aun la insinuación de una ilegalidad.

La importancia de la audiencia de hoy esperamos sea para disipar dudas respecto a estos temas, reafirmar la confianza entre los ciudadanos de este país y nuestras agencias de inteligencia; y finalmente de igual importancia: reafirmar nuestra confianza en la información que recibimos por parte de estas agencias. Los hombres y mujeres en nuestras agencias de recopilación de inteligencia no merecen menos que nuestra total confianza en su trabajo de promover una América mejor.

Gracias a usted Señor Presidente.

EL PRESIDENTE (SR. GOSS):

Gracias, Honorable Sr. Gibbons.

Se ha concluido con las declaraciones preliminares. En este momento damos la bienvenida a colegas congresistas que no forman parte del comité. Era mi intención llamar a los miembros en orden de antigüedad, el miembro de mayor antigüedad que debía hablar ha cedido respetuosamente su turno a la Honorable Juanita Millender-McDonald, ya que usted ha estado al frente de este asunto y ha realizado audiencias en su distrito.

Le damos la bienvenida a usted y a su comentario sobre el informe.

Sra. Millender-McDonald:

Gracias, Señor Presidente y miembros del comité.

Señor Presidente, elogio al Presidente por cumplir con su compromiso de llevar a cabo esta audiencia. Como el Presidente, yo también estaba profundamente perturbada por las alegaciones.

Como es de conocimiento de muchos de ustedes, yo convoqué a dos reuniones de ayuntamiento en el otoño de 1996 ante los sucesos en las noticias y en respuesta al sentimiento general de ansiedad, indignación pública y preocupación en todo mi distrito.

La primera reunión de Ayuntamiento, en la Casa Superior de Estudios de la Comunidad Compton el 19 de octubre, 1996, contó con la asistencia de cientos de residentes de mi comunidad devastada por las drogas. Procuré averiguar cómo respondía la comunidad local al extenso daño causado por el azote del abuso de sustancias peligrosas y les permití buscar respuestas a estas alegaciones.

Después, el 15 de noviembre, el Director de la Central de Inteligencia John Deutch hizo una visita sin presedentes a la Escuela de Secundaria Alan Locke en la sección Watts de mi distrito para responder directamente a las preocupaciones expresadas por mis electores.

Hoy estoy aquí para expresar claramente algunas de las preocupaciones que tienen mis electores en cuanto al informe y a la controversia en curso.

¿Es que el personal o recursos humanos de la CIA estuvieron de alguna manera involucrados en proveer o asistir a traficantes de droga en el área sud central de Los Ángeles o en cualquier otro lugar?

Cuando recibió información sobre una posible implicación de los Contra, ¿será que la CIA ejerció su rol de manera dinámica, para; cito "recolectar, producir, y diseminar inteligencia sobre aspectos extranjeros de narcóticos y tráfico de drogas"?

Los datos en este informe sugiere que la CIA se hizo de la vista gorda, en el mejor de los casos, ante información que sugería tráfico de drogas por parte de operativos de los Contra.

Y la pregunta fundamental es: ¿será que la CIA puede investigarse a sí misma de forma imparcial? El público permanece escéptico.

Yo espero que la Comisión Investigadora aplique el merecido escrutinio al contenido, métodos y hallazgos de este informe. Pienso que esto es crucial para restaurar la confianza del público y esta confianza es necesaria para permitir que las actividades de recopilación de información coexistan con la democracia.

Gracias, Señor Presidente y miembros.

El Presidente (Sr. Goss):

Muchas gracias, Honorable Sra. Millender-McDonald. Esa fue una muy buena declaración. Usted ha planteado unas preguntas específicas para que sean consideradas en el comité. Y así se hará.

Una de las razones por las que consideramos importante realizar la presente audiencia en este momento es por que el Sr. Hitz está en camino hacia mayores éxitos con un nuevo empleo. Queríamos asegurarnos de darle la oportunidad de explicar su informe, y por esa razón decidimos llevar a cabo lo de hoy.

En este momento, entonces, llamo a la honorable Sra. Maxine Waters del Distrito 35 de California. Maxine, estamos complacidos de tenerte hoy ante nosotros.

SRA. WATERS:

Muchas gracias, Señor Presidente, honorables Miembros y público presente. Primeramente quiero darles las gracias por realizar esta audiencia. La verdad no es algo que uno espera del Comité de Inteligencia.

Señor Presidente y miembros del comité, estoy aquí para testificar sobre el fracaso que tuvo la Agencia Central de Inteligencia al conducir una investigación seria y exhaustiva. Desafortunadamente, mi temor de que la CIA sería incapaz de investigarse a sí misma ha sido confirmado en este informe. Le falta credibilidad al Informe del Inspector General. Está lleno de contradicciones y conclusiones ilógicas. En un memorando del 3 de septiembre de 1996, el entonces Director de la CIA John Deutch diseñó un esquema para esta investigación. El memorando del Director Deutch declaraba, "No tengo razón para creer que haya algún fundamento en las alegaciones publicadas por el diario *San José Mercury News*." Si esta prematura conclusión del Director de la CIA estaba destinada a dirigir los resultados, él lo ha logrado. La contundente negación del informe que la CIA tenía conocimiento del tráfico de drogas relacionado con los Contra desafía la evidencia concerniente a lo que la CIA debería saber.

Muchos escépticos presumen que la CIA nunca podría producir un análisis verosímil o veraz de las actividades ilícitas de su propia agencia. Dichos escépticos podrían apuntar a *Los Ángeles Times* de este domingo para confirmar sus temores. Este mismo medio *Los Ángeles Times* reportó otro caso, que después de 37 años, la CIA finalmente admitió públicamente la más profunda decepción imaginable para una familia americana. El caso del señor Thomas Pete Ray y su escuadrón confidencial de bombarderos de la Guardia Nacional quienes fueron derribados durante una misión de bombardeo de la CIA en el fiasco de la Bahía de Cochinos en Cuba. Por 37 años la CIA negó que el Sr. Pete Ray y su escuadrón jamás hayan existido, y mucho menos que hayan sido derribados por tropas cubanas en el año 1961. Sólo este mes, confrontados por un documento adquirido por una solicitud del Acta de Libertad de Información es que la CIA finalmente admitió la verdad, treinta y siete años más tarde.

Yo después de leer la serie "Alianza Oscura," entrevisté a Gary Webb, escritor de esta serie y dicho sea de paso, Señor Presidente y Miembros, el Sr. Gary Webb esta aquí presente el día de hoy. Él está aquí sentado. Yo le invité a que viniera a mi distrito en el área sur central de Los Ángeles para responder a preguntas por parte de residentes locales. Mi comunidad alentó mis esfuerzos de indagar y profundizar en estas alegaciones.

SR. DIXON:

Un problema fundamental con el informe, Señor Presidente y Miembros, es que este informe astutamente se refiere a agentes. Pero, deberíamos estar hablando de agentes y/o activos.

Le diré hoy concretamente, el Sr. Adolpho Calero era un activo de la CIA. Muchos de los fondos de ayuda fueron canalizados por medio suyo. El Sr. Enrique Bermudez era un activo de la CIA; El Sr. Francisco Aviles, un oficial de la Contra en Costa Rica en el caso Frogman; El Sr. Iván Gómez, agente de la CIA, quien aceptó dinero de las drogas del Sr. Meneses; el Sr. Dagoberto Núñez, quien operaba una compañía de camarones para Oliver North en Costa Rica; el Sr. Edmundo Meneses, General nicaragüense entrenado por los Estados Unidos y hermano de Norwin Meneses, y el Sr. Sebastián González, líder de los Contra en Costa Rica y cómplice en las drogas con Meneses.

Sr. Bishop:

Hoy y aquí afirmo que todos estos son activos de la CIA. Desafío a este comité a que pida al Inspector General y a otros en la CIA, que puedan documentar si es que mis alegaciones son veraces o no. Ellos deben dar testimonio bajo juramento en cuanto a su conocimiento acerca de las personas que he citado como recursos humanos de la CIA.

Sr. Dixon:

Hoy, estoy pidiendo que este comité consiga por parte de la CIA respuestas escritas que confirmen o nieguen categóricamente que los mencionados son o fueron activos o agentes de la CIA.

Sr. Gibbons:

Otro problema fundamental con la investigación subyacente al informe fue la falta de poder de la CIA para llamar a comparecer. Esto implicaba que algunos de los oficiales más importantes de la CIA nunca fueron entrevistados. Tres ex-representantes de alto rango de la CIA sólo respondieron por escrito.

Sra. Millender-McDonald:

Otros seis funcionarios importantes de la CIA rehusaron ser entrevistados. Los agentes de la CIA incluyeron a Duane Claridge, Joseph Fernandez y Claire George. Todos estos oficiales superiores de la CIA tuvieron importantes responsabilidades en la operación Contra de la CIA. No puede haber una exhaustiva investigación sin testimonio bajo juramento de parte de cada uno de estos individuos. Los mismos debieran ser citados.

SR. DIXON:

Duane Claridge fue el oficial de la CIA quien ayudó a crear los Contra en un momento cuando el círculo de Meneses recién comenzó a traficar con cocaína para la FDN; la "Fuerza Democrática Nicaragüense" el brazo político de los Contra.

SR. DICKS:

El nombre de Duane Claridge también apareció en el cuaderno de Oliver North como el que hacía transacciones de compensación con conocidos cabecillas de la droga como Manuel Noriega.

SR. SKAGGS:

Claridge resumió cuán importante él consideraba que era esta investigación cuando dijo a los reporteros en diciembre de 1997 que la CIA "me envió preguntas que eran basura, y yo respondí que estas preguntas eran una basura."

SRA. PELOSI:

Alegaciones de tráfico de droga y conexiones entre los Contra y la CIA no es algo nuevo. El Subcomité del Senado para Terrorismo, Narcóticos y Operaciones Internacionales, presidido por el Senador John Kerry, condujo a una investigación de duración de dos años sobre alegaciones de la participación de los Contra en drogas y tráfico de armas.

SRA. HARMON:

El informe del Inspector General de la CIA resume algunos de los devastadores descubrimientos de la comisión de Kerry. Traficantes de droga proporcionaron apoyo para los Contra y utilizaron la red de provisión de los Contra.

SR. DICKS:

Los Contra a sabiendas recibieron tanto la ayuda material como financiera de los traficantes de droga.

SR. LEWIS:

El grupo FDN/Contra movilizaron los fondos de los Contra por medio de una operación de tráfico de droga y lavado de dinero.

SRA. MILLENDER-MCDONALD:

Fondos del Departamento de Estado de los EE.UU. liberados por el Congreso para ayuda humanitaria fueron pagados a traficantes de drogas. En algunos casos, estos traficantes de droga recibieron los fondos del Departamento de Estado después de haber sido acusados por agencias Federales del orden público.

SR. SKELTON:

En todos los casos, una u otra agencia gubernamental de los EE.UU. poseía información referente a estos asuntos.

SR. BISHOP:

Otros descubrimientos importantes del comité Kerry no están incluidos en el informe del Inspector General de la CIA. A pesar de estar traficando extensamente en las zonas de guerra en el norte de Costa Rica, el comité Kerry no pudo encontrar un solo caso que se haya levantado en base a un dato o informe de un oficial de una agencia de inteligencia de EE.UU.

SR. SKAGGS:

Y esto es, a pesar de testimonio directo de que informaron a oficiales de la CIA del tráfico de drogas en el frente del sur.

Sr. Lewis:

¿Cómo puede este informe incluir estas pruebas incriminatorias encontradas por los representantes electos, incluyendo a los Senadores Kerry, Brock, y Moynihan, y otros, y a la vez descartar con ligereza cualquier conocimiento o implicación de la CIA respecto al tráfico de drogas por los Contra en los EE.UU.?

Aide:

Esta es una escandalosa contradicción.

Sr. Gibbons:

Más aun, el informe está esparcido por confesiones perjudiciales. Este informe admite que Norwin Meneses fue uno de los más grandes traficantes de droga en América y que él le proveía a Danilo Blandon. Blandon, a su vez, era la fuente que le proveía a Ricky Ross.

Sr. Bishop:

Meneses traficó con drogas en los Estados Unidos por más de diez años, desde el año 1974. El negoció con las drogas sin interferencia, sin ninguna intervención. Él tenía bienes y negocios en San Francisco. La Congresista Pelosi hizo referencia al caso Frogman. Cuando localizaron a algunos de los hombres de Meneses, estos fueron rastreados hasta la misma casa que estaba conectada con el caso Frogman, lugar donde se hallaban involucradas muchas de esas mismas personas.

Sr. Dixon:

Meneses era muy bien conocido por la CIA, la DEA y DIA, y por todos en los Estados Unidos como un traficante de droga que proveía a Danilo Blandon, quien a su vez proveía a Ricky Ross.

Sra. Millender-McDonald:

Cómo es que él permaneció en los Estados Unidos todos esos años vendiendo drogas que acabaron apoyando a los Contra, y nadie, pero nadie, sabía de ello, es totalmente sorprendente.

Sr. Dixon:

Los registros de la CIA y de la DEA están llenos de información acerca de la operación de tráfico de droga de Meneses.

Sra. Millender-McDonald:

Esta información estaba corroborada en este informe, ¡aun en este informe!

Sr. Dixon:

Para el año 1984, la CIA conocía de sus actividades de tráfico de droga y la DEA estaba informada de sus actividades de tráfico de droga desde el año 1974.

Sra. Harmon:

Hay muchos otros datos cruciales que fueron confirmados por este informe. En las páginas 76–77, el traficante de drogas Norwin Meneses admitió haber entregado dinero a la división FDN/Contras de California y haber estado involucrado en el intento de 1988 para obtener "apoyo material, médico y provisiones en general" para el movimiento de los Contra.

Sra. Pelosi:

He sostenido que no importa cuanto haya sido el dinero, no importa si fue, como testificó Edén Pastora, sólo unos cuantos miles de dólares y unos cuantos camiones, o como Meneses mismo declaró, que él contribuyó con más de $40.000 en provisiones médicas y otras cosas.

Sra. Waters:

Como representante electa del pueblo, me siento indignada con esto. A todos nos debiera preocupar que nuestro gobierno pudiera haber estado involucrado de alguna manera en el tráfico de drogas. Tráfico de drogas. Esta es una ofensa muy, muy seria contra las personas de esta nación. No podemos darnos el lujo de que nuestro gobierno, no me importa cual sea el pretexto, esté involucrado en el tráfico de drogas.

La página 71 del informe del Sr.Hitz registra una conexión entre activos de la CIA y el líder militar de los Contra Enrique Bermudez junto a Meneses y Blandon. Sabemos que Blandon y Meneses viajaron a Bolivia en 1982 para hacer una transacción de droga y en su camino hicieron escala en Honduras. Estando en Honduras Bermudez pidió ayuda a Blandon y Meneses para recaudar dinero y provisiones para la FDN. Bermudez hizo saber a los traficantes de drogas que su apoyo sería bienvenido porque, cito y todos citan, aun su informe cita, que él dijo: "Los fines justifican los medios."

Blandon luego describe cómo él y Meneses fueron escoltados al aeropuerto por Contras armados, después de la reunión con Bermudez. Después de esta reunión Blandon salió con $100.000 en una bolsa para comprar drogas. Las ganancias de la venta de estas drogas debían ser usadas para comprar provisiones y financiar a los Contra. Blandon cuenta también como tuvo problemas en el aeropuerto de Honduras cuando le encontraron los $100.000. Pero ¿adivinen qué? Así como sucedió en el caso Frogman cuando fueron detenidos con la droga y el dinero y después se les devolvió los $36.000 al ser informados que era dinero de los Contra. De la misma manera, este hombre con $100.000 en dinero de droga destinado a la compra de más droga para más provisiones, fue asistido por los Contra en el aeropuerto. Aun cuando el había sido detenido y habían sacado los $100.000 de su maletín, con la intervención de los Contra, se lo devolvieron, y él siguió su feliz y contento su camino. ¿De donde salieron los $100.000?

EL PRESIDENTE (SR. GOSS):

¿Puedo pedir a la dama a que concluya sus comentarios? Hemos sido sobremanera generosos. Estamos restando tiempo a la presentación.

SRA. WATERS:

¿De donde salió los $100.000? ¿Se lo devolvieron a Blandon para la conexión Contra CIA? Quince minutos no es suficiente tiempo para educar o refutar.

Bien, Señor Presidente y Miembros, voy a concluir con lo siguiente: este informe no satisface la tarea, Señor Presidente.

¿Por qué hago todo esto? Porque ¿quiero encontrar algunos funcionarios de la CIA, activos o agentes y de alguna manera condenarlos y llevarlos a prisión? Eso no será posible. Y no es eso lo que estoy intentando hacer. Hago esto porque, como políticos de orden público, no podemos seguir escondiendo la cabeza en la arena. Al mismo tiempo ¿estamos gastando millones de dólares hablando acerca de una guerra contra las drogas?

Válgame una oportunidad, Señor Presidente y Miembros. Podemos hacer mucho mas que esto. Yo no me iré. Yo no me puedo ir. Mi comunidad ha sido devastada, así como muchas otras comunidades a lo largo de la Nación. Las personas están indignadas y preocupadas por el hecho de que este problema de las drogas no termina y con la idea además de que nuestro gobierno pudiera estar involucrado.

Desafío a que este comité elabore una regulación pública que no permita a nuestro gobierno involucrarse jamás en tráfico de drogas de ninguna manera.

Les doy las gracias.

EL PRESIDENTE (SR. GOSS):

Ahora quiero tomarle el juramento al Sr. Hitz.

Sr. Hitz, ¿puedo pedirle que levante su mano derecha?

[Testigo juramentado]

Jura usted decir la verdad, solo la verdad y nada más que la verdad, si asi lo hiciese. ¿Que dios le ayude?

Informo a los Miembros que el Sr. Hitz se tomó la molestia de acomodarse a nuestro horario. Entiendo que ha estado sin dormir por al menos unos cuantos días para poder hacer el viaje de retorno a esta, y estamos muy agradecidos por su deferencia. Le cedo la palabra a usted.

SR. HITZ:

Gracias Señor Presidente. Puedo garantizar al comité que estoy contento de estar aquí el día de hoy y espero poder responder a sus preguntas a pesar de la distancia que he viajado. Sin embargo, siento un poco como si nos hubiéramos servido el postre primero... Ha sido una discusión muy seria y minuciosa por parte de los dos Congresistas, respecto a sus opiniones de mi informe; así que estoy complacido de ahora tener la oportunidad de resumirla para ustedes.

Por solicitud del Director de la Central de Inteligencia John Deutch, el 3 de Septiembre de 1996, inicié una investigación de las alegaciones que provinieron de una serie de tres partes llamada "Alianza Oscura." Prometí al Congreso y al pueblo norteamericano que mi oficina "conduciría un examen de toda la información disponible tan minuciosamente como fuere posible y de informar sobre los hallazgos de manera abierta y completa."

Entonces, me complace presentarme ante este comité el día de hoy y decir que hemos hecho eso mismo.

Nuestro informe representa una recolección exhaustiva de hechos. Examinamos un estimado de 250.000 páginas de documentos y llevamos a cabo más de 365 entrevistas de personas en cuatro continentes. Revisamos informes de otras agencias de la comunidad de inteligencia incluyendo La Agencia de Seguridad Nacional (NSA) y la Agencia de Inteligencia de Defensa (DIA). Examinamos registros disponibles del congreso incluyendo información recopilada por el Comité Kerry y hablamos con individuos asociados con el Comité Conjunto de Investigaciones Irán-Contra.

Nuestro equipo de 17 personas trabajó unos 18 meses para identificar, y por favor, permítanme aclararles:

Número 1, cualquier información en posesión de la CIA relacionada a Danilo Blandon, Norwin Meneses o Ricky Ross.

Número 2, cualquier información en posesión de la CIA relacionada a posibles actividades de tráfico de drogas por parte de los Contra en California y en otras partes de los Estados Unidos y qué medida, si alguna, la CIA hubiera tomado al recibir dicha información.

Y número 3, cualquier contacto referente a dicha información entre la CIA y autoridades del orden público.

Ahora, Señoras y señores del Comité y público presente... permítarme ir a los hallazgos. Quiero aclarar que no encontramos ninguna evidencia en absoluto que indique que la CIA como organización o sus funcionarios, estaban involucrados en cualquier conspiración de hacer ingresar drogas a los Estados Unidos.

La primera mitad del informe, habla del conocimiento que tenía la CIA respecto a las actividades de Ross, Blandon y Meneses. Ross, Blandon y Meneses son traficantes de droga convictos. Nuestra investigación, no encontró información alguna que indique que algún funcionario de la CIA en el pasado a al presente o cualquier otra persona actuando de parte de la CIA tuvo tratados con Ross, Blandon o Meneses o que tuvo algún conocimiento de sus actividades en el tráfico de drogas.

Ross era un importante traficante de droga y cocaína quien dice haber hecho millones en el negocio de la droga. Y naturalmente, sus actividades ayudaron a fomentar la epidemia de la droga que brotó en la zona sur central de Los Ángeles. Sin embargo, Ross nos dijo que él nunca vendió drogas a los Contra ni donó dinero a los Contra. Permítanme aclarar nuevamente que la CIA nunca tuvo ninguna relación con Ross.

Blandon y Meneses, también traficaban drogas para obtener ganancias financieras de tipo personal. En este caso, tampoco la CIA tenía relación con Blandon y Meneses. Nuestra investigación, encontró evidentemente que ellos estaban afiliados a organizaciones que apoyaban a los Contra en California, y cada uno de ellos hacían contribuciones financieras a esos grupos.

Blandon dice que él se encontró con el líder de los Contra Enrique Bermúdez en cuatro ocasiones desde el año 1981 a 1983. Uno de sus encuentros fue en Honduras el año 1982 cuando él y Meneses estaban viajando a Bolivia para realizar una transacción de droga. Blandon dice que Bermúdez les dijo que los Contra estaban teniendo dificultades en recaudar fondos y pidió que él y Meneses ayudaran, afirmando que; "el fin justifica los medios."

Blandon cree que Bermúdez no sabía que él y Meneses estaban involucrados con tráfico de drogas, pero estaba consciente de las supuestas conexiones de Meneses con el crimen organizado en Nicaragua. Desafortunadamente, no pudimos obtener información por parte de Bermúdez ya que fue asesinado en Managua el año 1991.

Ninguna información ha sido encontrada que indique que la CIA estorbó o intervino en la investigación, arresto, proceso, condena o sentencia de Ross, Blandon o Meneses.

La segunda mitad de nuestro informe: "El Relato de California del Norte" concierne un caso en San Francisco que con frecuencia es referido como el caso Frogman, más conocido como los "Hombres Ranas." El caso obtuvo su nombre cuando autoridades del orden público en San Francisco arrestaron varios nadadores que habían desembarcado de un carguero colombiano el 17 de enero de 1983. Los que venían nadando tenían con ellos aproximadamente 215 kilos de cocaína. En total, alrededor de 12 arrestos fueron hechos el 17 de enero y muchos más tiempo después, incluyendo el arresto de dos nicaragüenses; Julio Zavala y Carlos Cabezas.

A diferencia de los eventos relacionados a Ross, Blandon y Meneses, este fue un caso en que la CIA se involucró, pero de manera equívoca porque pensó que tenía un interés a proteger.

La CIA, recién tuvo conocimiento del caso Frogman, hombres ranas, por primera vez a fines de julio de 1984, alrededor de un año y medio después del arresto de Zavala. En ese tiempo, la CIA fue informada de que los dos representantes de la Oficina de la Fiscalía de los Estados Unidos en San Francisco, quienes estaban enjuiciando a Zavala, planeaban asistir a declaraciones en Costa Rica de dos miembros de las organizaciones de los Contra, quienes le habían proporcionado a Zavala cartas que alegaban que los $36.000, que las autoridades habían confiscado de Zavala en el momento de su captura, pertenecía a los Contra. Oficiales de la CIA equivocadamente identificaron uno de los miembros de los Contra como un ex- Activo de la CIA. Había preocupación de que las declaraciones podrían exponer a un grupo que apoyaba a los Contra y del que la CIA tenía un interés operacional.

No se encontró información que indicara que los dos oficiales de la Contra, quienes escribieron las cartas en apoyo a Zavala, estarían involucrados en tráfico de drogas.

Un abogado de la oficina del Consejo General de la CIA se reunió con el fiscal encargado y posiblemente con otros representantes de la Oficina de la Procuraduría Federal de los Estados Unidos.

Los relatos difieren en cuanto al por qué el dinero fue retornado a Zavala.

El Sub-Fiscal Federal de los Estados Unidos, Joseph Russoniello, quien enjuició a Zavala, y otros involucrados en el juicio declaran que la decisión de devolver el dinero a Zavala no fue por alguna representación de la CIA, sino únicamente por decisión suya respecto a si es que merecía el tiempo y los gastos ir a Costa Rica para las declaraciones.

Sin embargo, encontramos un cable de la CIA que fue escrito después de que el abogado de la CIA se había reunido con el fiscal encargado. Russoniello. Este cable indicaba que el dinero había sido devuelto a Zavala por solicitud de la CIA. Pero desafortunadamente, el abogado de la CIA no recuerda los hechos del caso o de la mencionada reunión.

En resumen, yo enfatizaría que cualquier impacto que el abogado de la CIA en último caso hubiera tenido sobre la decisión de la Oficina de la Procuraduría Federal de los Estados Unidos para devolver el dinero a Zavala, no tenemos evidencia que indique que la devolución del dinero haya debilitado el caso del juicio contra Zavala. Tiempo después, Zavala fue condenado y enviado a la prisión.

Como dije anteriormente, no hemos hallado evidencia alguna de conspiración por parte de la CIA o sus funcionarios para hacer ingresar drogas a los Estados Unidos. Por lo demás, durante la era de los Contra, la CIA sí trabajó con diversas personas para apoyar el programa de los Contra. Estos incluían Activos de la CIA, pilotos que transportaban provisiones para los Contra, como también oficiales de los Contra y otros.

Permítanme ser franco en cuanto a nuestros hallazgos. Hubo instancias cuando la CIA no cortó relaciones de manera expedita o consistente con individuos que apoyaban el programa de los Contra de quienes se dice estaban involucrados en actividades de tráfico de drogas o no tomó acciones para resolver las acusaciones. Quiero subrayar el hecho de que aquí estamos hablando de alegaciones.

Para concluir, Señor Presidente, yo animaría al público norteamericano que lea el informe que está disponible en el Internet en www.odci.gov/cia.

Gracias Señor Presidente. Tendré gusto en responder a sus preguntas.

EL PRESIDENTE (SR. GOSS):

Sr. Hitz, muchas gracias.

Como dije al principio, colegas, tenemos la sala hasta las 5:00. Por lo que veo hemos podido negociar una extensión del alquiler hasta las 5:15, y si el Sr. Hitz está de acuerdo quedarse hasta esa hora, yo le estaría agradecido.

SR. HITZ:

Yo puedo.

El Presidente (Sr. Goss):

Quisiera comenzar preguntando, ¿hubieron advertencias en el sentido de que oficiales de la CIA tenían que mantenerse alejados de individuos que traficaban drogas y de hecho debían reportarlos?

Sr. Hitz:

Por lo general se mantiene ese tono presente en los cables, pero, se debe entender que la naturaleza de las alegaciones variaba. En algunos casos, era algo como rumores descabellados que circulaban mientras que algunas de las acusaciones estaban más profundamente arraigadas.

El Presidente (Sr. Goss):

Con respecto al individuo que se negó a ser entrevistado por su oficina ¿le presentó alguna razón por su falta de disposición a participar en esto? Suponga que usted no tiene el poder de llamar a comparecer.

¿Es eso correcto?

Sr. Hitz:

No, no tenemos el poder de llamar a comparecer.

La actitud que encontré habiendo en esa época pasado por la investigación Irán-Contra, muchos sentían que ya fue suficiente. Ellos no creían que había algún fundamento en las acusaciones del diario *San José Mercury News* y simplemente decidieron no participar.

El Presidente (Sr. Goss):

Finalmente por parte mía, Sr. Hitz, ¿ustedes entrevistaron a Gary Webb?

SR. HITZ:

No, no lo hicimos.

EL PRESIDENTE (SR. GOSS):

¿Sandra Smith?

SR. HITZ:

Disculpe Señor Presidente ¿quien fue ella? ¿Sandra Smith?

EL PRESIDENTE (SR. GOSS):

Sandra Smith es la agente de la DEA, el Departemento Anti Droga, en la primera historia de "Alianza Oscura," la supuesta fuente que dio principio a todo esto.

SR. HITZ:

No, no lo hice.

EL PRESIDENTE (SR. GOSS):

Gracias, señor. Honorable Sr. Lewis.

SR. LEWIS:

Gracias Señor Presidente y colegas. Quiero elogiar a ambas mis colegas de Los Ángeles, Sra. Millender-McDonald y Maxine Waters por sus esfuerzos.

Sr. Hitz, yo también aprecio el esfuerzo que hizo para venir y estar con nosotros el día de hoy y quiero expresar mi agradecimiento por su largo servicio al país.

¿Cuáles fueron las responsabilidades legales y reguladoras de la CIA desde 1979 al 96 referente al informar sobre potenciales crímenes y la conservación de relaciones con personas que se sospechaba estaban involucradas en el tráfico de drogas?

Sr. Hitz:

Bien, era variante, por así decirlo, los requisitos cambiaban a menudo. Desde 1976 a 1982, fue un asunto que realmente no se abordó. Desde 1982 a 1995, en un acuerdo finalmente negociado entre el Procurador General Smith y la administración Reagan, no había el requisito de informar sobre alegaciones de tráfico de droga de quienes no eran empleados de las agencias de inteligencia. Y en el periodo que no incluía agentes de la CIA, no incluía los Activos.

Sin embargo, eso ha sido modificado. El acuerdo de 1995 que sustituye al periodo de 1982 a 1995, incluye específicamente los crímenes de narcóticos como asunto a ser informado, independientemente de que la agencia obtenga información de que se esté llevando a cabo por otros que no son parte de los empleados, específicamente los Activos.

Sr. Lewis:

Muchas gracias, Sr. Hitz. Señor Presidente, cedo lo que queda de mi tiempo.

El Presidente (Sr. Goss):

Honorable Sr. Dixon.

Sr. Dixon:

Muchas gracias, Señor Presidente. Sr. Hitz, yo me uno a aquellos que lamentan su partida. Entiendo que esta rumbo a la Universidad de Princeton.

Referente al caso Frogman—hombres rana—usted dice que la CIA se involucró por equivocación. Si bien recuerdo, su informe indica que el abogado de la CIA viajó al norte de California y tuvo una conversación con el fiscal. Creo que su testimonio el día de hoy refleja que no pudieron encontrar el material escrito por el abogado quien, de hecho, tuvo esa reunión con el fiscal.

SR. HITZ:

Lo que si encontramos, por supuesto, y me parece que están familiarizados con esto, Sr. Dixon, es un detallado relato que fue elaborado por la Oficina de Consejo General de la CIA, comentando sobre ese intercambio en particular, es decir esa intervención con el Sub-Fiscal Federal Russoniello. El individuo que pensamos estaba involucrado en las negociaciones mismas, de hecho, no recuerda el incidente.

SR. DIXON:

¿Y acaso el informe no fue elaborado por la persona que estaba involucrada?

SR. HITZ:

Bien, no sabemos eso.

SR. DIXON:

¿No saben quién lo elaboró? ¿Verdad?

SR. HITZ:

Correcto. Él no lo recuerda.

SR. DIXON:

Ahora, usted llega a la conclusión de que ellos intercedieron debido a una equivocación. Y yo creo que el informe indica que es una identidad equivocada de alguien con quien la CIA tenía relaciones.

Sr. Hitz:

Eso es correcto, Sr. Dixon. Nosotros no. La CIA no se involucró en el caso Frogman hasta que pasaron varios años después del arresto de Zabala. Se dio como consecuencia de un cable, un cable del Departamento de Estado de Costa Rica indicando que un abogado particular y abogados de la Oficina de la Procuraduría Federal de los Estados Unidos estaban a punto de ir a Costa Rica para tomar las declaraciones de dos firmantes de una carta que había sido dirigida a la Oficina de la Procuraduría de los EE.UU, reclamando los $36.000 que habían sido confiscados en el arresto de Zavala.

Aparentemente, la carta procedía de grupos que apoyaban a los Contra, y la agencia identificó erróneamente a uno de los firmantes como un Activo de la CIA.

Era un nombre hispano, notablemente semejante al nombre de un agente que había trabajado para nosotros. De todas formas fue, un caso de identidad equivocada.

Sin poder ubicar al abogado que estaba de hecho involucrado en esto, y por tanto sin poder conocer la posición de él o ella, lo que parece es que ellos intentaban proteger la identidad de esta conexión con el grupo que apoya a los Contra y evitar que sea revelado.

Sr. Dixon:

¿Hizo una evaluación independiente en su investigación para determinar si esto fue una equivocación o es esto algo que la CIA le dijo?

Sr. Hitz:

La CIA no nos dijo, y a decir verdad, fuimos nosotros los que descubrimos que la identidad del agente era equivocada.

SR. DIXON:

Gracias Sr. Hitz.

EL PRESIDENTE (SR. GOSS):

Honorable Sr. Gibbons.

SR. GIBBONS:

Muchas gracias Señor Presidente. Sr. Hitz, permítame hacer una pregunta amplia y general. ¿Será que su oficina descubrió alguna información que pudiera haber dado indicio de que había alguna actividad autorizada o no del Gobierno de los EE. UU. y que a su ves hubiera facilitado el tráfico de narcóticos en los Estados Unidos o en el extranjero?

SR. HITZ:

No, no hubo nada. No encontramos información alguna que hubiera sugerido que había sido autorizada... o no autorizada; por supuesto, ese es el detonante. Obviamente, si no era autorizada en el sentido más puro no habría registro alguno de ello. Nosotros estábamos usando el registro escrito para poder formular preguntas inteligentes. No encontramos evidencia alguna de una maniobra por empleados de la CIA para promover el esfuerzo de los Contra con la venta de drogas.

SR. GIBBONS:

Gracias, Sr. Hitz. Gracias, Señor Presidente. Cedo el resto de mi tiempo.

EL PRESIDENTE (SR. GOSS):

Gracias Sr. Gibbons. Honorable Sra. Pelosi.

Sra. Pelosi:

Gracias, Señor Presidente. Nuevamente, quiero elogiarle por realizar esta audiencia abierta, pero solicito que tengamos otra oportunidad para interrogar al Inspector General, porque no tendrá suficiente tiempo disponible para nosotros el día de hoy para que podamos preguntar por lo menos los puntos más importantes de nuestro cuestionamiento.

El Presidente (Sr. Goss):

Concuerdo con su observación. Yo mismo tengo varias preguntas y sé que otros también las tienen.

Sra. Pelosi:

A su juicio, ¿era apropiado el contacto entre la CIA y la Oficina de la Procuraduría Federal en este caso, en el caso de Frogman?

Sr. Hitz:

Parece que el abogado que estuvo involucrado tiene una diferente interpretación en cuanto a lo apropiado del contacto. Él declaró en su relato detallado que sintió que estaba ingresando en un área que pudiera causar una situación embarazosa para la actividad de acción encubierta del Presidente en el tema de los Contra y las drogas.

Sra. Pelosi:

Mi preocupación es que la Oficina de la Procuraduría Federal talvez no proceda en nigun asunto por la misma razón que acaba de indicar; para no perjudicar las actividades de la CIA.

SR. HITZ:

Bien, Honorable Sra. Pelosi, mi experiencia con la Oficina de la Procuraduría Federal de los EE.UU. ha sido que si el Procurador Federal considera que él o ella tiene un caso en este asunto; le aseguro que ninguna intervención por parte de la CIA los hubiera tenido al margen. Ellos hubieran ido tras el caso y con toda propiedad.

SRA. PELOSI:

Señor Presidente, se que no tendremos mucho más tiempo. Por tanto ya no haré más preguntas pero quisiera hacer algunas observaciones.

Sr. Hitz, al escuchar sus palabras, le agradezco haya establecido sus limitaciones: usted no tiene el poder de citación la capacidad de llamar a comparecer, los lineamientos no eran claros, ciertos asuntos no podían ser informados en ese momento. Por ejemplo si un activo con el que estábamos comprometidos estaba involucrado en tráfico de drogas. Y eso me lleva a concluir que talvez de forma no intencional, y uso ese término generosamente, nosotros hayamos estado subvencionando a activos que estaban involucrados en tráfico de drogas.

Me complace que la ley haya cambiado, y ahora por lo menos se puede informar. Pero, yo, por mucho que intento, no puedo entender por qué, cómo usted indica en su declaración, la CIA no sabía si estas personas estaban o no involucradas en el tráfico de drogas. Deberían por lo menos saber, por más que sea algo que se deba reportar o no, nosotros por lo menos debiéramos saber. Nosotros somos la CIA. ¿Acaso no tenemos que saber? ¿Acaso no dice el lapicero (aquí): "el saber es nuestro negocio (trabajo)"?

Sr. Hitz:

Nosotros somos bastante categóricos en cuanto al tema de Blandon y Meneses y el hecho de que no sostenían una relación con la CIA. Tampoco Ricky Ross.

Sra. Pelosi:

Considero que en nuestra investigación debemos hablar con las personas que no se pudo citar. Podremos así entender por qué los $36.000 no valieron la pena para ir a Costa Rica por una declaración, y podremos averiguar si es que la CIA identificó o no a alguna persona equivocadamente.

Esto no quiere decir que usted no haya realizado un buen esfuerzo dentro de las limitaciones que tiene en la oficina de Inspección General, pero temo que aun algunas preguntas permanecen sin respuesta, las que tengo la esperanza sean respondidas. Pero, sin embargo, gracias.

El Presidente (Sr. Goss):

Honorable Sr. Bishop. Buenas tardes.

Sr. Bishop:

Buenas tardes y muchas gracias Señor Presidente. Permítanme disculparme por mi demora en llegar. Tuve una demora mecánica de dos horas con mi vuelo y no quería apurar la situación. Pero estoy encantado de estar aquí.

He leído el informe y tengo unas cuantas observaciones. El primero es que quiero unirme a mis colegas en elogiarle, Sr. Hitz, ahora que se retira de la CIA. Quiero tomar esta oportunidad para unirme a ellos para agradecerle por sus servicios a la agencia y a nuestro país.

También quisiera observar que las acusaciones de que la CIA este involucrada en la introducción y distribución de crack cocaína son muy, muy serias, y eso verdaderamente produjo una tormenta de fuego. En comunidades de minorías esto inmediatamente generó comparaciones con el estudio de la sífilis Tuskegee donde los afro-americanos eran inyectados con gérmenes de sífilis y non fueron tratados con el motivo de hacer un estudio.

Ciertamente quiero hacerle unas cuantas preguntas. ¿Cooperaron los actuales funcionarios proporcionando información y hubo algún funcionario de una agencia gubernamental o agencia estatal o individuo que intentó influenciar su investigación de alguna manera?

SR. HITZ:

No, recibimos buena cooperación y nadie intentó intimidarnos.

SR. DICKS:

¿Por el caballero ceder un momento en ese punto? ¿Y qué hay de ese compañero, el abogado de la CIA que no podía recordar los hechos del caso o la reunión en cuestión? Eso no me parece a mi completa cooperación.

SR. HITZ:

Nuevamente, Sr. Dicks, es lamentable, nos hubiera gustado tener su... si es que él era la persona quien fue autor del documento, y es él quien realizó la intervención con la Oficina de la Procuraduría Federal de los EE.UU... hubiera sido una ayuda si él hubiera recordado, pero nosotros teníamos un registro escrito bastante bueno y a decir verdad, eso es todo con lo que contábamos.

SR. DICKS:

Gracias por ceder.

SR. BISHOP:

No hay de que. Pudiera solamente decirme ¿cuáles eran las responsabilidades legales y reguladoras desde el '79 al '96 referente al requerimiento de informar crímenes potenciales y en cuanto a conservar relación con personas de quienes se sospechaba estaban involucradas con el tráfico de droga?

SR. HITZ:

Pienso que justo antes que usted llegara, hablé respecto a esa historia un tanto singular. A decir verdad, el periodo desde el '82 al '95 fue uno en el que no había un requerimiento oficial para informar sobre alegaciones de tráfico de droga referente a los que no eran empleados de la agencia, y estos eran definidos como Activos, empleados que no eran parte del personal de la CIA. Ese era el acuerdo que fue tratado entre el entonces Procurador General Smith y la agencia. Eso ha sido modificado, desde el '95.

SR. BISHOP:

Aprecio el consejo de la Presidencia de que continuaremos con esto a la voluntad del comité en una fecha posterior, y con eso, concluyo mis preguntas y le estoy muy agradecido, Sr. Hitz.

SR. HITZ:

Gracias, Sr. Bishop.

EL PRESIDENTE (SR. GOSS):

Honorable Sr. Bishop, gracias.

Hemos pasado la hora señalada, y estoy consciente de que

hemos añadido aun más tiempo a su día ya prolongado, Sr. Hitz, pero le quedamos agradecidos. Como puede ver hay bastante interés. Seguramente, habrá varias preguntas de seguimiento sobre este tema a medida que procigamos con nuestra investigación en el comité investigador.

Quiero indicar a los Miembros del comité, que he prometido continuar con el proceso. Y así se hará. Miembros, reconozco que existe mucha preocupación respecto a los siete individuos que rehusaron hacer comentarios. Hemos contactado a los siete y tenemos una variedad de respuestas. Les ofrezco esto como señal de la firme disposición que tenemos para proceder en el avance del presente asunto.

Quisiera hacer una última pregunta Sr. Hitz, si me permite. He leído este informe muy detenidamente. Hace un enfoque, como usted mismo dice, sobre una serie de alegaciones específicas. El informe, pienso, es muy claro en lo que plantea. ¿Es firmado por usted?

SR. HITZ:

Si.

EL PRESIDENTE (SR. GOSS):

¿Usted firmó este informe sin reservas, y usted respalda este informe y lo que en el esta escrito?

SR. HITZ:

Firmé y respaldo.

EL PRESIDENTE (SR. GOSS):

Le quedo muy agradecido. Se levanta la sesión.